365 Days of Devotion, Development, & Discipline with Jesus

Also by Dr. Roy Elton Brackins

A Marvelous Model of Ministry, A Message from the Man in the Middle

Making a Difference in the Kingdom of God

365 Days of Devotion, Development, & Discipline with Jesus

Dr. Roy Elton Brackins

ISBN-13: 978-1503100909
ISBN-10: 1503100901

Editorial assistance provided by:
Stephanie J. Beavers Communications
www.stephaniejbeavers.com / 888-823-2283

Dedication

This book is dedicated to the memory of my dear parents, Mr. and Mrs. Leroy and Lucy Brackins. The principles they taught me as a child will last for the balance of my days here on earth.

They are now resting in the presence of Jesus Christ, and I look forward to His return when we shall be caught up and raised together to reign with the Lord.

Contents

Acknowledgements

I thank the Lord for the encouragement of my wife Pam, my "Sweetie" and my "Grace Gift" from God. Your prayers for me, your passion for me, and your partnering with me, has helped tremendously in the completion of this project.

I thank God for our children Ayonna, ArRhonda, John, LaRoya, and Montel. Their support and inspiration has been beyond description.

I thank the Lord for those who partner with me in ministry, the full-time staff of the Grace Tabernacle Church: Jerry, John Jr., Lafayette and Tara. You all make coming to work and doing ministry such a pleasant experience each and every day.

I thank God for some of His most "Precious People," the members of the Grace Tabernacle Missionary Bapticostal Church. I love you with my whole heart. Your love and support has been the wind beneath my wings.

To my siblings Charles, Eleanor, Jerri, Regina, I thank God for your love, support, and encouragement.

To God be the glory for the great things He has done, is doing, and that He has yet to reveal.

I love all of you with my *whole heart.*

Introduction

If my memory serves me correctly, the year was 2008. I had such a realization, that it led to the establishment of a discipline in my personal life that I continue to practice today. Prior to that point, I had the habit, as most Christian people do, of getting up from bed, saying a brief prayer in gratitude to God for a good night's sleep, and then grabbing the remote control to turn on the television to catch up on all the activities that had taken place while I was asleep. I would then prepare myself to take my son to school and, after dropping him off, head to the gym. After my workout, I would run a few errands before finally arriving at my office to start my day as a pastor at Grace Tabernacle Missionary Baptist Church. I would pray again upon entrance into the church campus and in the sanctuary. Once in my office, I checked my messages and returned a few phone calls. After that, I would get my Bible and read from God's Word.

Then it hit me like a ton of bricks. I realized I was making the terrible mistake of doing all these things each morning and allowing my mind to become filled with a variety of worldly influences and responsibilities before even taking time to pick up my Bible to hear what God had to say to me.

Now, all of that has changed. I refuse to turn on the television, read a newspaper, or even start my day until I have spent some time with the Lord in prayer and in the reading of His Word. What I did not realize was that, by turning on the television before hearing from the Lord, I was allowing my mind to become polluted with nothing but negativity and worldliness. My mind was being bombarded with murder, rape, robbery, and molestations. It was being filled with scandals, arrests, drug abuse cases, and all kinds of demonic activities–all this *before* allowing the Lord to speak to me.

When the Lord called this sin to my attention, I immediately corrected my habits, and have not once forsaken this spiritual disciple, even until this very day. This is the main reason you are able to hold this book in your hand right now.

I wanted to share with you how my days have been made so much brighter and my outlook on life changed since learning the importance of starting every day in prayer and in the reading of God's Word.

I believe this is going to be one of the best years of your life. Even if you were not able to purchase this book by January 1st, don't let that hinder you. God is not a God of chronology; He is a God of purpose, structure, and development. These next 365 days are going to both strengthen your relationship with Him and stabilize your representation of Him.

Each chapter represents a month of the year. The chapter title contains the name of one month as well as the name of a breakfast food item or fruit. This is my way of helping us embrace the disciple of feeding our souls spiritually, *before* feeding our bodies physically. As people of God, we must learn the importance of starting our days not with hyped up newscasts and drama, but with the King of kings, the Lord of lords–Jesus Christ.

So, here we go as we prepare to spend 365 days with Jesus and make positive change in our lives daily–for the rest of our lives. When you're ready, just turn the page.

The Cardinal, Brother Roy

Notes to Reader:

Please begin your journey through this daily devotional on the day you purchase it or on the day it was given to you. To maximize its impact, each day contains information relative to the season of the year.

As a sign of my personal respect to God and His Word, throughout this work the terms *Godly* and *Biblical* will always be capitalized, given their close connection to, and representation of, God and the Bible. Likewise, the terms *satan, unbiblical,* and *ungodly* will never be capitalized.

God bless you.

Jam with Jesus in January

January 1st
Hebrews 12:1

Therefore we also, since we are surrounded by so great a cloud of witnesses, let us lay aside every weight, and the sin which so easily ensnares us, and let us run with endurance the race that is set before us.

Today marks the beginning of a new year, and affords new opportunities for us to experience the grace of God and new chances for us to make ourselves available to grow accustomed to the glory of God. Our verse for today reminds us that there were many people before us who experienced difficulties even greater than ours, and yet God's grace saw them through every situation. If this day, this week, this month, and this year are going to be what God desires for them to be through us, we need to do at least three things according to this verse: *eliminate* those things that hinder us; *embrace* the challenges before us; and *expect* God's grace to protect us.

Make a determination that this year will be about His will for your life and not about your personal goals and desires.

January 2nd

Hebrews 12:2

Looking unto Jesus, the author and finisher of our faith, who for the joy that was set before Him endured the cross, despising the shame, and has sat down at the right hand of the throne of God.

What are you focusing on right now? Is it possible that life seems cloudy and distorted because you are focusing on things that are negative and meaningless, on things over which you have absolutely no control? Why not purposefully turn away from harmful things and, instead, look at Jesus? Consider His unconditional love for you and His willingness to walk with you through not some, but every single one of your difficult days. He is the author and finisher of our faith. Jesus is the one who started before us, the One who walks with us, and the One who will remain when everyone and everything else has faded and passed away.

Jesus was able to look past the pain and the shame of Calvary, because He knew a glorious resurrection awaited Him. Release that pain and embrace His presence—and go out and have a great, God-filled day.

January 3rd
Hebrews 12:11

Now no chastening seems to be joyful for the present, but painful; nevertheless, afterward it yields the peaceable fruit of righteousness to those who have been trained by it.

One lesson we all need from God, but very few of us welcome from Him, is the lesson of correction. Our Heavenly Father uses this process to shape us, mold us, and develop us into the quality kingdom saints and the Christ-like children He desires us to be. This verse makes us aware of the fact that God's Discipline is never pleasant, it is never painless, but it is always productive. If the fruit is going to produce juice, there must be a squeezing process. Our Heavenly Father's love for us includes teaching and training, and it leads to spiritual maturity.

We love to embrace God's undeserved blessings. We must also learn to accept His well-deserved discipline. They all work together for our good.

January 4th

2 Corinthians 4:16

Therefore we do not lose heart. Even though our outward man is perishing, yet the inward man is being renewed day by day.

I believe I stand on solid ground when I say there have been, and for some of us there still are, times when we feel like quitting and throwing in the towel. Often, we try to keep these feelings to ourselves for several reasons. We sometimes think we are the only ones experiencing, or, in actuality, *are* the only ones experiencing this sentiment. Other times, pride causes us to attempt to maintain our public image when we are literally hurting beyond description on the inside. And still other times we think there is no one who can help us through what we are dealing with. I want to share with you from personal experience. I have faced and overcome my greatest challenges in life when I became honest enough to admit them to God, maintained my post in the area of ministry where He has positioned me, and trusted Him to either resolve my issue or to give me the strength to deal with it and still remain productive in His kingdom. Trouble is not allowed in our lives for us to surrender to the world, but so that we may learn how to totally trust in God and gain strength from His Word.

Our trouble is nothing more than a sure sign that the old, worthless things are being removed, while the positive and eternal things are being strengthened and made more evident to us.

January 5th

2 Corinthians 4:16

Therefore we do not lose heart. Even though our outward man is perishing, yet the inward man is being renewed day by day.

One of the most difficult lessons I have learned from God has been that what I desire from Him is not always what He is trying to develop in me. Psalm 37:4 says, "Delight yourself also in the Lord, and He shall give you the desires of your heart." Here, the word *delight* means to pursue those things that please God. When we do this, our desires will also be things that please Him. Paul tells us to "not lose heart." Don't give up! Why? Because the truth of the matter is, our outward man is going to perish with or without more materialistic possessions. God is not interested in developing what is perishing in our lives, but rather what is being renewed in our lives.

He allows us to go through what we go through because He is trying to make us better *every day*. Not weekly, monthly, or yearly, but daily.

January 6th

2 Corinthians 4:17

For our light affliction, which is but for a moment, is working for us a far more exceeding and eternal weight of glory.

Paul calls his troubles "light afflictions." Our problems are momentary; they seem longer, however, because we compare them to the wrong things. We compare our problems to what we feel and see around us. But Paul compared his problems to the promise God made for eternity, for when his problems had passed. Our oldest daughter Ayonna helped me to understand this so much better. A few years ago, she received a demotion on her previous job and did not tell me all about it. What she did was perform in the demoted position to the best of her ability without complaining. A few months later, one of her former co-workers moved on to another company and a position came open there. She recommended Ayonna based on how well she had handled her demotion at her present job, and Ayonna was hired making more money with even greater responsibilities, security, and benefits. The manner in which she handled her demotion determined her ability to receive a promotion. Indeed God has more in store for us than we can see right now.

Our troubles work on our behalf toward something that far exceeds anything we could ever imagine. And it all leads to a greater level of God's glory being revealed in our lives.

January 7th
Acts 1:8

But you shall receive power when the Holy Spirit has come upon you; and you shall be witnesses to Me in Jerusalem, and in all Judea and Samaria, and to the end of the earth.

While Jesus is no longer around us in the flesh, His presence is even greater because He now lives within us through the Person, Power, and the Presence of the Holy Spirit. His presence not only protects us, provides for us, and pardons us; it also gives us the ability to *publically proclaim* Him. He told the disciples of Jesus they would be filled with the Holy Spirit so that they would have power to witness about Him. How much witnessing have you done about Jesus this year?

Don't worry about what you don't know about Him. Begin, simply, by sharing with people what you *do* know about Him and what He has done in your life. Make it your goal for this year to lead at least twelve people to Jesus—one person each month. You are saved because somebody told you about Jesus; now you go and do the same for someone else.

January 8th

Acts 1:8

But you shall receive power when the Holy Spirit has come upon you; and you shall be witnesses to Me in Jerusalem, and in all Judea and Samaria, and to the end of the earth.

Have you taken the time to consider the fact that Jesus has chosen us as His representatives here on earth? Most companies and institutions look to employ people who have spotless backgrounds and impeccable pedigrees. But the Lord chose to represent Him a denier like Peter, and tax collector like Matthew, a doubter like Thomas, position-seekers like James and John, and even sinners who have made one mistake after another like you and I. He has done this because He knows it takes forgiven fallen people to reach other people who are still in their fallen condition.

We should not take our selection by the Lord lightly. He knows our faults and failures and He still wants to use us to represent Him. Let's not let Him down, because He has never failed us.

January 9th
Acts 1:14

These all continued with one accord in prayer and supplication, with the women and Mary the mother of Jesus, and with His brothers.

Occasionally it is wise to stop and ask yourself, "What does God want me to embrace so that I may have a greater level of spiritual effectiveness?" Many of us are so engulfed with things we think are important to us, and we take very little time to consider what is really important to our Heavenly Father. This first group of believers who were assembled in the upper room after the ascension of Jesus knew their ability to fulfill their assignments from Jesus was based on their commitment to prayer. These people prayed "consistently"; they prayed "collectively"; and they prayed "compassionately."

How much time do you spend in prayer with the Lord? Prayer goes beyond asking God to do things for us; it also involves us listening to Him as He gives direction and directions for our lives. Take a moment now to ask Him to forgive you for neglecting to talk to Him on a regular basis, and then make a commitment to Him and to yourself to correct that for the rest of your life.

January 10th
Acts 2:36

Therefore let all the house of Israel know assuredly that God has made this Jesus, whom you crucified, both Lord and Christ.

I was asked by a Muslim a few years ago why I thought Christianity was superior to all other religions. My answer was, "That is simple, we are the only religion who serves a Savior who is still alive, and if He is not alive, then just produce His body." Peter preaches this verse on the day of Pentecost, and he makes all those listening to him aware of the facts that Jesus had been crucified and that God had raised Him from the grave. He is both Lord and Christ. As our Lord, He directs us and provides for us. As our Christ, He has satisfied the payment owed to God for all of our sins.

Live this day with full assurance of the fact that Jesus has conquered hell, death, and the grave for you, so surely He can handle whatever struggles you may encounter from this day forward.

January 11th

Matthew 6:31-32

Therefore do not worry, saying, "What shall we eat?" or "What shall we drink?" or "What shall we wear?" For after all these things the Gentiles seek. For your Heavenly father knows that you need all these things.

"Don't Worry, Be Happy" was a popular song by Bobby McFerrin in the late 1980s. McFerrin borrowed those four simple words from Indian mystic and sage Meher Baba, who used the phrase with his own followers. My advice goes a step further.

Many of us worry because we seek happiness as opposed to seeking the joy of the Lord. Happiness is temporary, but joy is eternal. In this verse, Jesus makes us aware of the fact that He is our provider, and He is able to meet all our needs. He tells us not to worry about what we will eat, drink, or wear, because these are things that the Gentiles, or, the people who do not have a relationship with Him, are consumed with. Our Heavenly Father knows what we need, when we need it, and how much of it we need.

So, my advice to you is: "Don't worry, be filled with Faith." Trust God even when you cannot trace Him.

January 12th
Matthew 6:33

But seek first the kingdom of God and His righteousness, and all these things shall be added to you.

Many of us experience disappointment in our searches because we seek all the wrong things. Jesus tells us to seek the kingdom of God first. Instead, we are guilty of seeking jobs, relationships, promotions, acceptance, prosperity, and success, and we give little to no attention to seeking those things that are important to the Lord. Notice carefully the words Jesus uses. He says that when we seek first God's kingdom and His righteousness, all the other things will be added to us.

He will add what we cannot afford, attain, or attach to our own lives. And it will all take place when we make Him our number-one priority. Why work, struggle, and hustle for things He desires to add? When we seek Him, He will supply us.

January 13th
1 Corinthians 6:20

For you were bought at a price; therefore glorify God in your body and in your spirit, which are God's.

Most, if not all, of us purchase things to make our lives better and more complete. But when God purchased us with the blood of His Son Jesus, we were of no value to anyone else but Him. He has not forsaken us or broken His relationship with us in spite of the facts that we: 1) not only cost God the life of His Son to get us saved and 2) do things that have broken His heart since the moment of our salvation. This should be a tremendous incentive for each of us to live closer to Him, express a greater level of compassion toward Him, and spend more time communicating both with and about Him.

He purchased us when we were worthless, and now all He asks is that we surrender to Him so that He can use us to His glory. That's really not asking much at all. But that is just like Him: He always gives more than what He asks for in return. Let Him know how much you appreciate Him with a greater level of service both to Him and for Him.

January 14th
1 Corinthians 6:20

For you were bought at a price; therefore glorify God in your body and in your spirit, which are God's.

God gave the life of His Son in exchange for worthless sinners like you and me. That does not seem like a very wise investment. But the reason He did it was because He saw something in us that was worth an eternal redemption that we did not even see in ourselves. One of the best ways to express our gratitude to Him for that enormous sacrifice is for us to keep the temple (our bodies) clean where the Holy Spirit now lives. Don't force Him to live with the pollution of corrupt communication, carnal conduct, and cowardly conformity. We are now people of value, because we are God's children. Don't allow the devil to reduce that value, because Jesus paid too much for you. His blood has delivered us from all of our sins. So let's walk and live like delivered people.

Now that is really something to give glory to God about.

January 15th
Psalm 107:2

Let the redeemed of the Lord say so, whom He has redeemed from the hand of the enemy.

So many times I hear people say, "I try to keep my religious and Christian beliefs to myself." Yet those same people talk openly about their favorite clothing stores, their favorite movies, and their favorite sports teams. The writer of this Psalm does not just encourage us, but he commands every redeemed person to say something about the God we serve. Whatever we love and are proud of, we have no problem talking about. Sharing our redemptive story about what the Lord has brought us out of, and what He has brought us into, is not something we should feel forced, compelled, or coerced to do. It should be done willingly from our hearts.

We may not know everything about the Lord, but just share what you know He has done for you, and even more importantly, how much He means to your everyday life.

January 16th

Philippians 4:13

I can do all things through Christ who strengthens me.

Every child of God needs to be reminded, and in some instances informed, of the fact that our Heavenly Father has not set us up for failure, but rather to walk in victory in every phase of our lives. This does not mean there will not be challenges, temporary setbacks, and even seasons of disappointment. But it does mean that His will for us and through us will be ultimately accomplished when we learn the joy of totally depending on Him. Our encouragement verse for today does not just say, "I can do all things," but that we are able to do everything that God has assigned for our lives through the power and the person of His Son, Jesus Christ. The problem many of us may be facing lies in the fact that we are trying to do too many things that have not been ordained for our lives, and it only leads to one level of disappointment after another. Why not totally surrender all your plans—right now—to the authority of Jesus Christ?

Then just watch Him transform the gloom of defeat into the joy of spiritual victory. If He says you can do it, then you can! Just make sure you have heard from Him.

January 17th
Colossians 1:3

We give thanks to the God and Father of our Lord Jesus Christ, praying always for you.

If we are not careful we can spend the bulk of our time praying only about those things we think we need, want, and feel should be a part of our lives. By so doing, we miss out on one of the great aspects of prayer, which is called *intercession.* Intercession is when we place our needs, desires, wants, and problems aside, and focus instead on praying for others who may be going through things much worse than we are going through. Why not take just a moment right now and ask God to help someone else with a problem you know they are facing–and do so without also asking Him to do something for you in that same prayer. When we learn the importance of praying for each other, we discover how God can take our minds off our problems and teach us how to undergird each other with prayer. In this one verse, Paul prays with the right *Purpose*: He "gave thanks." He prayed to the right *Person*: the God and Father of our Lord Jesus Christ. And he prayed with Persistence: He kept praying "always."

If Paul had the wherewithal to take his mind off all his many struggles to pray for other people, then surely we can do the same.

January 18th
Psalm 18:30

As for God, His way is perfect; The word of the Lord is proven; He is a shield to all who trust in Him.

Upon whom do you depend to make decisions regarding the direction in which you will be traveling today? The Lord wants us to know that His plans for our lives always lead to productivity and progress even in the midst of what seem to be temporary setbacks. I hope you agree with me when I say that the Lord never leads us into an unproductive, evil or harmful place. Seasons of uncertainty almost always arise for us because we travel down our own roads and forsake the leadership that our Heavenly Father desires to give to us through the person of His Holy Spirit. The psalmist informs us of the fact that God has a *perfect pathway.* He desires to lead us in directions that improve our relationship with Him and our trust in Him.

Take just a moment to adjust your plans for today. If God is not leading them, surrender to Him, ask for His guidance, and watch Him add great joy to what was going to be a gloomy day without Him. He has more to say about His perfection, and, Lord willing, we will examine that of tomorrow.

January 19th
Psalm 18:30

As for God, His way is perfect; The word of the Lord is proven; He is a shield to all who trust in Him.

Hopefully, this day is starting with a tremendous amount of joy based on applying the principles from yesterday. Our God has a perfect pathway. But that is not all this verse has to say about our God's perfection. We also discover that "the word of the Lord is proven." His Word has stood the test of time. While we are walking on the path, we also need to be mindful to govern our lives according to His *perfect precepts.* God does not force us to stay on the right path; it is a choice we make. And one of the main reasons we make the decision to get off the *perfect pathway* is because we partner with people who pollute our minds with poisonous principles. The perfect precepts of God are found in His Word. This daily devotional is not designed to replace the Word of God, but rather to help us to appreciate the Word of God at an ever greater level.

We must desire His Word, have a discipline to read His Word daily, and then delightfully practice the perfect precepts of His Word. Then, we will watch Him give us the desires of our hearts.

January 20th
Psalm 18:30

As for God, His way is perfect; The word of the Lord is proven; He is a shield to all who trust in Him.

The Lord speaks once again from the same verse. We now walk on the perfect path and live according to the perfect precepts. We can now be assured of His *perfect protection.* The psalmist tells us that God "... is a shield to all who trust in Him." By this I understand that the more trust I place in Him, the greater my level of protection from Him. Trusting Him allows us to yield to Him, surrender to Him, obey Him, and depend on Him—which automatically leads to our being protected by Him. When we take matters into our own hands, we move ourselves from the protective umbrella of our Heavenly Father's shield.

We have learned to trust Him to lead us in the right path. He guides us with the right precepts. And now let's make today a great day as we walk under the shadow of our God's perfect protection. Don't settle for imperfection when God has perfection with your name written all over it!

January 21st

Psalm 9:1

I will praise You, O Lord, with my whole heart; I will tell of all Your marvelous works.

Whenever we do something nice for someone, especially when we have gone out of our way to make their life better, it's a pleasure when they stop to tell us, "Thank you," and let us know how much our deeds have meant to them. As this is true from a humanistic perspective, it also applies in our relationship to our Heavenly Father. The psalmist provides a great model to follow. He announces that he is going to praise the Lord, and that he is not going to do it in a half-hearted manner. He says, "I will praise You... with my whole heart..." In other words, "I'm going to give the Lord all I have and give Him my very best. He shares with us that one of the best ways to do this is by simply telling other people what the Lord has done for us. Can you agree with the psalmist and me when we say that the Lord has done some "marvelous works" in all our lives?

Why not make this day a day of praise, gratitude, and witnessing. Begin by singing a verse of a favorite praise hymn you know. If one does not come to mind, allow me to share a stanza from one of my favorites: "Amazing Grace, how sweet the sound that saved a wretch like me. I once was lost, but now am found; Was blind, but now I see." That should add a new level of joy to your soul.

January 22nd
Psalm 40:1

I waited patiently for the Lord; And He inclined to me, and heard my cry.

One of the most difficult things for people to do is to wait. We have a microwave mentality: we want things done right now and we want instant results. There are three reasons why the Lord allows waiting to be a part of our lives. One is to give us time to better evaluate why we are in the situation we are in. He does this so we will pray and seek His guidance before we find ourselves in this situation again.

The second reason God allows us to wait is to teach us the importance of listening to His voice. His Word always leads us into places where we know we have His divine approval.

The third reason He allows us to wait is to teach us patience. This involves trust, reliance, and confidence, and I hope you will agree with me when I say that none of those things can be established quickly. The Lord is interested in a long-term relationship with every one of His children. After all, we will be spending all of eternity together.

When we wait patiently, He will incline to us; He will lean over so that we feel His presence and He hears every one of our cries. Whenever a child cries from pain, a loving parent always picks them up. Get ready for God's lifting power to be revealed in your life—but remember, waiting is a part of the process.

January 23rd
Genesis 50:20

But as for you, you meant evil against me; but God meant it for good, in order to bring it about as it is this day, to save many people alive.

There will be times when the Lord allows some things to happen to us and to confront us, and we have no idea why all this misfortune has overtaken us. During those times we question our relationship with the Lord; we feel like giving up and throwing in the Christian towel, so to speak. But just when there seems to be no hope, you read your devotional for today, and you hear the Lord say, “Don’t worry. I’ve got it all in control. Cast all your cares upon Me, because I care for you.”

Joseph’s brothers expressed their hatred for him by selling him as a slave and forcing him to spend time in prison for crimes he did not commit. He did not give up, but he maintained his faith in God, and the Lord allowed him to be elevated to one of the highest positions of authority in all of the land of Egypt. When Joseph’s brothers experienced a famine, they came to him and he spoke the words of our devotion for today. Joseph did not try to get even; he did not try to figure out what God was doing; he just waited and trusted in the Lord. This may be just the thing the Lord wants you to do today. Don’t try to understand the difficulties that are facing you–just trust and wait on the Lord, and watch Him move.

Whatever the devil intends for evil against you, God is able to turn it around for good, and even give you an opportunity to bless the same people who have hurt you. Don’t seek revenge; seek for an opportunity to express the Lord’s unconditional love.

January 24th
Exodus 14:13

And Moses said to the people, "Do not be afraid. Stand still, and see the salvation of the Lord, which He will accomplish for you today. For the Egyptians whom you see today, you shall see again no more forever."

Feeling hemmed in with no way out? Wondering if this is the end of the road for you? To that I say, "Cheer up." After all, this is not your first time dealing with a situation beyond your control. The Lord brought you through the last one, and He is able to bring you through this one. Although, this one may seem more severe because the Lord is trying to teach new lessons: Release your panic (that is, do not be afraid); remain in your position (that is, stand still); and now, watch God release His power. You are about to see His salvation not just from your sins, but also from your circumstances, at a level unlike anything you have ever seen before. God often allows our enemies to overwhelm us so that they can see Him when He delivers us, and we can see when He destroys them, should He allow that. This day will be filled with both challenges and opportunities.

The good news is, every confrontation from the devil leads to new confidence in God, and every opposition the enemy sends leads to new opportunities for us to make it to the other side of that Red Sea which holds us back. It may be too deep to swim across, but just stand still and get ready to move forward. God will give you the grace and faith to walk across it on dry land.

January 25th
Exodus 3:14

And God said to Moses, "I AM WHO I AM." Thus you shall say to the children of Israel, "I AM has sent me to you."

Are you feeling as though you have a spiritual assignment that is too big for you? Well, you are exactly where the Lord wants you. This task is not about who you are, but about to whom you belong. God is getting ready to use you to impact some people for His kingdom and for His glory at a level you never thought possible. The Lord was getting ready to use Moses for a special assignment in our devotional scripture in spite of the mistakes he had made in the past, and in spite of his speech impediment. When we do only what we feel like we are able to, we get the glory for ourselves. When God does things through us that seemed impossible to us, He gets the glory.

Place all of those excuses in a trash bag and set them out for the garbage man to carry away. I simply say to the Lord, "Since You desire to use me, I make myself available." Now walk with the *I AM* of the universe, and watch Him use you to His glory.

January 26th
Psalm 1:1

Blessed is the man who walks not in the counsel of the ungodly, nor stands in the path of sinners, nor sits in the seat of the scornful.

We live in a time when we hear a lot of talk, and even a lot of music, about the favor of God and having a desire to be blessed by God. Most of the songs and the words have to do with God doing all of the providing of what we want, and all we need to do is just sit back wait for it, and when it shows up, enjoy it. This may all sound good, but in the words of the woman on the Esurance television commercial, "That's not how it works; that's not how any of this works."

The psalmist tells us that if we expect to receive God's blessings, God has requirements and expectations of us: We must not have intimate fellowship with people who are opposed to God's will; We must not become hindrances to those who strive to see what a real child of God is like; We must not become comfortable around people who are filled with disdain and criticism for the people of God and the Son of God.

When we make a purposeful effort to purge our lives of these things and these people, we are then ready to start enjoying and receiving the true blessings of God. Now go out and make it a *blessed day* by paying close attention to whose counsel you take, whose path you stand in, and who you become comfortable sitting with.

January 27th
Psalm 1:2

But his delight is in the law of the Lord, and in His law he meditates day and night.

Nothing can transform a gloomy day into a glory-filled day like the Word of God. The devil wants to fill our minds with countless doubts, distractions, and disappointments. God is just waiting to replace all that negativity with some delightful development from His Word. The Word of God is not the first thing most of us turn to in times of uncertainty. This is why our appetites must be adjusted. Our children did not want to eat vegetables when they were young, but as parents, we made sure they ate them because we knew they were essential for their proper physical growth. Now that our children are much older, we don't have to force or insist that they eat vegetables; they now desire vegetables because they have seen the positive results that have taken place in their bodies. When we develop a desire for God's Word, we will be brought to a point of realization that nothing we face is new to God. He has handled it for one of His children before, and He is well able to do it again.

God has allowed what He has allowed so as to cause you to develop a desire for His Word. Now pick up your Bible and "taste and see that the Lord is good."

January 28th
Psalm 1:3

He shall be like a tree planted by the rivers of water, That brings forth its fruit in its season, Whose leaf also shall not wither; And whatever he does shall prosper.

God has planted you in a special place. Not only has he planted you, He perfectly positioned you. Not only has God planted you and perfectly positioned you, He has also protected you. (Your leaf, which is indicative of your ability to fulfill His purpose for your life, is not going to wither.) I know you may not think it can get any better than this, but it does. God has planted you in special place, perfectly positioned you, protected you, and if you will just trust Him and maintain your faith in Him, He is getting ready to bring a new level of productivity to your life. This does not, however, mean that God is getting ready to add on more stuff and possessions. After all, this is about a tree, and trees don't grow fruit for themselves; they produce fruit to meet the needs of other people.

God wants you to know that on this day, He is going to use you to help meet the need of some person who is hungry for His Word and thirsting for His righteousness. So, prepare yourself so that no one will leave your presence today with an unfulfilled appetite. God has given you just what they need from Him.

January 29th
Psalm 8:4

What is man that You are mindful of him, And the Son of man that You visit him?

This is just one of the many verses in the Bible which helps us understand just how special we are to God. With all that He has to do in keeping this earth rotating on its axis, keeping planets in their orbits, and controlling the weather throughout the universe–to name just a few things God is responsible for–He has each and every one of us on His mind. As you begin or conclude your day, know that everything that will take place or that has taken place is all part of our Heavenly Father's divine master plan. While you may not understand all the events that take place, it's not your job to; it's His. He knows what, when, where, and how every need should be fulfilled in our lives. You will not face any slipups or surprises on the part of God.

Since He thinks about you, why not return the favor? Stop worrying or fretting, and just start thinking about Him. Because thinking about God always leads to thanking God. Right now would be a good time for a heartfelt, "Thank you, Jesus." Now, don't you feel better?

January 30th
Psalm 23:3

He restores my soul; He leads me in the paths of righteousness for His name's sake.

Think of a time when you felt tired and weary. Did it seem as though you had all you could take? No worries. God knows just what you need: restoration time–and He begins that process with our souls. The Lord knows that when we have healthy souls, we can make it through any and all adverse circumstances. David tells us that God does not sub this job out to an unskilled contractor; "He" restores my soul. God's restoration process includes the fact that He knows the problems with us and the potential within us. He has the power to fix us, and He has already paid the price for us. What a great God we serve. So, if you are feeling a bit down in the dumps, pull over into His repair-shop-of-prayer. Make a commitment to attend Bible study or a ministry meeting, or get up early and attend Sunday school and worship. The repairs cannot be done if you don't get your soul to that repair shop called the "House of the Lord."

Once the repair work is complete, He will lead you on some new paths you never would have been able to travel on in your previous condition, and it will all be for His name's sake. When God finishes what He is doing, you will tell people, "It was nobody but the Lord who made the changes in my life."

January 31st
Psalm 30:2

O Lord my God, I cried out to You, and You healed me.

We have made it to the end of the month. It seemed like only yesterday we were celebrating New Year's Day. Whatever this day holds, keep in mind the fact that God has already worked out some thirty issues this year, but He is just getting started. If you are feeling a bit overwhelmed, surrender those feelings of anxiety to Him. The psalmist says he cried out to the Lord. What's stopping you from crying out? He knows what you are thinking; now just allow Him to hear you verbalize it.

The Lord is aware of the hurts we encounter and the pains we face, and He is still able to provide healing either from or in every one of those situations. We have much more joy ahead of us this year, so let's cast our cares upon Him so we can approach every challenge with a healthy spirit and strong faith.

PRAYER

Thank You, Lord, for the joys and challenges of this month.
Thank You for Your peace in the midst of adverse situations, and
Thank You for teaching us how to totally trust in You.

In Jesus' name,
Amen.

Fruit from Our Father in February

February 1st

1 Peter 5:7

Casting all your care upon Him, for He cares for you.

Have you ever experienced getting out of your car and then trying to enter your home or place of business, but were unable to enter with ease because your hands were full? I'm sure we have all had that experience at least one time in our lives. Wouldn't it be nice to have an extra set of hands to help out during those times? Whether you realize it or not, we do have an extra set—His. And He is willing to help us not only with our bags, books, cleaning, purses, and briefcases, but He is also willing to help with every burden, difficulty, pain, and problematic situation each and every one of His children faces. Trying to carry the load of our daily struggles was never anything our Heavenly Father intended for us to deal with all alone. His hands are larger than ours; His hands are stronger than ours; and His hands are able to crush those things we have been carrying which seem to be crushing us.

Don't make the mistake of placing those cares in the hands of the wrong people—they will only drop them and disappoint you. He is waiting right now for you to take that concern out of your hand and prayerfully place it in His, and He is watching how much lighter your burden will instantly become. Once you place it in His hands, leave it in His hands.

February, 2nd

2 Corinthians 5:17

Therefore, if anyone is in Christ, he is a new creation; old things have passed away; behold, all things have become new.

One of the great distractions that the devil uses against the people of God in our efforts to make progress is to constantly keep us mindful of the terrible mistakes we have made in the past. Often, we make the tremendous mistake of focusing more on what we were than on what we are and on what we are becoming now that we belong to Jesus Christ.

Let's add this up right quick. What we were: 1 negative. What are now in Christ Jesus: 1 positive. What we are becoming in Christ Jesus: 2 positives. Wow! We win, 2 to 1! The past is behind us and we cannot change it. Asks God's forgiveness for those poor choices and accept the free grace that He offers by allowing us to be a part of His eternal family. Since God has forgiven our past and blotted out all our sins, why would we want to continue to hold onto them? Our remembrance of the sins may not instantly go away, but we don't have to allow any of that to stop us from being all that God has called us to be.

We are now in Christ; we have protection, permanence, and a secure position. Release the old, embrace the new, and live the life that God has called you to live in Him.

February 3rd
2 Corinthians 5:17

Therefore, if anyone is in Christ, he is a new creation; old things have passed away; behold, all things have become new.

I'm sure there have been times in all our lives when we were feeling as though we didn't measure up, that we just didn't have what it takes. At those times, we need to remind ourselves of the fact that Jesus has stepped in and made us the complete and whole individuals God first created us to be. This is a day for you to walk like the new creation God has made of you. The gloom, failure, and frustration you had from your past was all part of the "before" you. This day, people are going to have an opportunity to see the results of God's grace poured out in your life with the "after" you. I have some really good news for you: the "before" image of you was temporary; the "after" essence is permanent. The only way people will notice the difference is for you to allow them to see the change at every opportunity you get. Turn that frown upside down, and make up your mind that you are going to live, walk, act, and react like the new creation God has made of you.

Because the truth of the matter is, your "after" image looks so much better than your "before" image. Throw that old one away, and show the new one every time you get a chance.

February 4th

Matthew 5:13

You are the salt of the earth; but if the salt loses its flavor, how shall it be seasoned? It is then good for nothing but to be thrown out and trampled underfoot by men.

Your family, friends, flatterers, and foes all need your flavor. Jesus does not say you shall become salt; He says, "...you are the salt of the earth..." Whatever salt touches, it adds flavor to. The problem most of us have is that we keep our salt in the safety of the Sunday morning salt shaker. We only want to pour ourselves out on other salty people. But today you will face some whose lives are absolutely bland and distasteful. The only contact they may ever have to connect with the salt of Jesus Christ is through you.

Take that lid off. Get ready to shower someone with the flavor of your faithfulness and the potency of your praise. We don't want to be thrown out and walked on by people simply because we failed to use what God has given us to work with. Let's fill this day with the flavor we have been given by our Heavenly Father.

February 5th
Matthew 5:16

Let your light so shine before men, that they may see your good works and glorify your Father in Heaven.

Our Youth Pastor at Grace Tabernacle once came up with a simple theme for Youth Month: Light It Up! According to today's verse, spoken by Jesus Himself, this is not something we have to work to do, strain to do, or even prepare to do. We *are* light. All we have to do is show up, and things will light up! However, two problems exist: 1) We have allowed too many other people to define us and 2) we have overlooked what Jesus our Savior has said about us. Some dark areas of your places of employment, communities, friendships, and even family areas are in desperate need of light. You are that light, and you allow your light to shine when you express the love of Jesus Christ wherever you go. A Christian who does not shine is like a lamp with no bulb—they both look good while depending on the light from other sources, but they are absolutely helpless to anyone who is in the dark.

As you begin your day, make up your mind to "light it up" and glorify your Father in Heaven. Don't worry about your wattage; He knows what you can handle.

February 6th
John 14:1

Let not your heart be troubled; you believe in God, believe also in Me.

Release your stress right now. Let go of the anxiety, and surrender all your apprehensions to our Savior Jesus Christ. Whisper a word of prayer; share with Him your concerns–He already knows about them; He's just waiting for you to verbally release them to Him. Your heart was designed to be filled with praise, not with worry and agony. He endured all that for us over 2,000 years ago at a place called Calvary. He died and was raised from the dead for us, and now He gives us the freedom to place our troubles in His hands. God has created you, never forsaken you, and He will never renege on the promises that He has made to you. Take a deep breath; cry if you need to; kneel in His presence if you need to; lift holy hands in surrender if you need to.

Just release those worries and say to Him, "Jesus, since you love me enough to die for me, I know that you will see me through this also."

Now, don't you feel better? Well, if not, you will; the day is not yet complete.

February 7th
Joshua 1:6

Be strong and of good courage, for to this people you shall divide as an inheritance the land which I swore to their fathers to give to them.

One of the great privileges and responsibilities that God has entrusted to us is that of giving to other people what He has for them. We may have never given this idea much thought in the past, but the truth of the matter is that God blesses His people through other people. This is why we must be strong, faithful, dependable, and trustworthy. There are others who need you to be a blessing to them *today*. This is not limited to material possessions. You may cross paths with a person who needs the plan of salvation explained to them. What can possibly be more valuable than that? You may come into contact with someone whose hope needs to be lifted, their faith may need fortifying, or their self-esteem may need to be restored. When we apply for a job, someone hires us. When we apply for an auto loan, the person on the other side of the desk approves our application. Yet our tendency is always to say, "God granted those blessings in our lives." And He did—He simply provided us with what we needed through those people who could be trusted with our resources.

The people God used to bless us have done their part. Now it's time for us to do our part. Let this day be filled with strength, and courage, and interacting with other people on our Lord's behalf, because you have someone's land in your hand, and God is depending on you to make sure the delivery takes place.

February 8th

1 John 1:6

If we say that we have fellowship with Him, and walk in darkness, we lie and do not practice the truth.

There must be a level of consistency with our confessions and our conduct. We need to be mindful of the fact that we are representatives of Jesus Christ every day of our lives, and most of our representation come when we are unaware of it. People often look at those of us who have confessed Christ as our Savior with the intent of finding faults and weaknesses in us. Let's not do them any favors by giving them obvious sins to point out. I am by no means suggesting that we have the ability to live our lives filled with total perfection, but I do want us to be mindful of the fact that we are the only examples some people will ever see of Jesus Christ. And what they see in us is automatically what they will assume about the Son of God. Strive to make this day a day of fellowshipping with Jesus. Find your joy in Him, your worth in Him, and your purpose in Him. He has come to lead us out of the darkness, out of those areas of fear, uncertainty, and temptation.

Make practicing the truth of His Word a part of your everyday life and watch how your joy, both in and with Jesus, will continue to grow and expand.

February 9th

1 John 1:7

But if we walk in the light as He is in the light, we have fellowship with one another, and the blood of Jesus Christ His Son cleanses us from all sin.

We are about to embark on an exciting journey—at least for the next four days. We are going to take our time, because we can't handle too much spiritual excitement at once, or even all in one day. So, today, let's take the first step.

John says, "But if we walk in the light..." This small word *if* makes us aware of the fact that we have a choice in the matter. Therefore, *if* we choose to walk in the light that God has provided for us through His Son Jesus Christ, we can be assured of at least one prominent thing. By so doing, we will be making some progress. This day is about growing in our relationship with Jesus Christ. Grow in your *praise* to God—this is worship. Grow in your *participation* with God—this is your work. Grow in your presentations to God—this is your wealth. God has not created us for stagnancy, or to reside in stationary positions. We should be walking. (But don't try to run just yet.) Just walk with Him. Surrender to His will and make yourself totally available to Him. Let this day be a day of moving from the sideline of observation to getting on the field and engaging in participation.

After all, a good walk is good for the heart. Since that is true from a physical perspective, just try to imagine how much healthier we will become when we walk with Jesus spiritually.

February 10th

1 John 1:7

But if we walk in the light as He is in the light, we have fellowship with one another, and the blood of Jesus Christ His Son cleanses us from all sin.

We are now ready for the second leg of this wonderful mini-journey of spiritual calisthenics. If you are just starting with us, I give you permission to back up to yesterday's reading and catch up with us real quick.

How was your walk, whether you took it yesterday or today? While we walk in the light, we not only make progress, we also have His divine protection. Did you miss it? There it is. Let's look at it again. "But if we walk in the light *as He is in the light...*" We don't have to search for Him, we don't have to wonder about His presence, and we don't ever have to feel insecure. As long as we walk in the light, He is right there with us. He is going to walk with you throughout this day as you walk with Him. He does it by guarding you from danger, guiding you around difficulty, and governing you with His discipline. Let those feelings of fear go. Place all that apprehension behind you. Take a deep breath and release your anxiety. We do not walk alone; we have His presence.

Wherever He leads you today, you can take courage in knowing that He has already been there and is walking with you every step of the way. This is going to be a great day. Just keep moving in His will and don't allow anything or anybody to turn you around.

February 11th
1 John 1:7

But if we walk in the light as He is in the light, we have fellowship with one another, and the blood of Jesus Christ His Son cleanses us from all sin.

I can only imagine you must be sitting there with tiptoe anticipation wondering what is going to be next on our great journey. Well, let's get right to it. So far, the Lord has shown us our ability to make progress in Him, and He has assured us of His presence. But wait, there's more! *"...we have fellowship with one another..."* The Lord has allowed our lives to be connected to others who have gone through what we are going through, or who will go through what we are dealing with now or those things from which He has delivered us. His purpose for doing this is to give us some human partnerships. In other words, while Jesus walks with us on this journey, we also have other brothers and sisters in Christ who walk with us as we walk with Him. We encourage each other, gain strength from each other, and help each other when and if we should happen to fall. This is one of the reasons that being attached and committed to a Bible-believing and Bible-teaching-Bible-preaching church is so important. We need the support of each other.

This day will be not only one filled with the potential for you to find encouragement from other people in the Body of Christ through spiritual partnerships, but it could also be the day God uses you to encourage someone else with your spiritual partnership. Get ready; your opportunities await.

February 12th
1 John 1:7

But if we walk in the light as He is in the light, we have fellowship with one another, and the blood of Jesus Christ His Son cleanses us from all sin.

Here we go with the anchor leg of our trip. "...and the blood of Jesus Christ His Son cleanses us from all sin." Wow! On this trip we have made progress; we have been assured of His protection; and we have established new partnerships. Now we cross the finish line with our *purification.* I call this the finish line because Jesus, as He was hanging on the cross of Calvary, said, "It is finished." This statement does not mean that all of our assignments from God have been fulfilled. Rather, it means the work of atoning for our sins has been completed. Not by us, however, but by Him. We no longer have to worry about our guilt or our unworthiness. Jesus Christ has cleansed us from not some, but all of our sins: all past sins, all present sins, and all future sins. You should note that this does not give us a license to sin; it gives us freedom from sin. We should not abuse this gift from God. No one in their right minds would go out and purposefully have an automobile accident simply because they now have auto insurance. In the same vein, we should not go out and purposefully sin simply because we know that we have been forgiven by Jesus Christ.

We show our love and appreciation for Him when we walk with Him, and glorify Him in every phase of our lives. Make this a great day. God is waiting to use you to His glory.

February 13th

1 John 2:15

Love not the world, neither the things that are in the world. If any man loves the world, the love of the Father is not in Him.

This scripture holds a very special place in my heart. It was the verse that the Lord used to save me on December 6, 1973. I was a drug addict and living a rebellious lifestyle. It was not until the Lord revealed to me that I was in love with the wrong things that a real, positive, Christ-like change took place in my life. Many have suffered the hurts of broken hearts and shattered dreams because their love attachment has been misplaced and displaced. The Lord wants all His children to know that He does not want us to become attached and committed to the things of this world because they all pass away. Will you agree with me when I say that what we wanted three years ago is not the same as what we want now? Our desires for things are constantly changing. At the point in time I realized what Jesus was offering me was eternal, and what the world was offering was only temporary, my spiritual eyes were opened at last.

This day is going to be a day of release and letting go of old things, so we can get ready to receive the great things God has in store for us. After all, how can we receive His good things, if our hands are filled with worthless worldly things? Go out and make it a productive day.

February 14th

1 John 3:1

Behold what manner of love the Father has bestowed on us, that we should be called the children of God! Therefore the world does not know us, because it did not know Him.

No candy or flowers yet on this day of lovers? Don't sweat the details. Candy adds calories and flowers soon wilt. Your Heavenly Father has a love gift for you that will never fade, tarnish, or droop. Love expressed to us from a human perspective has limitations. But God's love is without limit. It is because of His love that we are called the "children of God." We have a new identity. Can you even wrap your mind around that? God loves us enough to call us His children. And He does not do it in the privacy of some bedroom or the secrecy of some restaurant, but He does it while hanging on a cross at Calvary with the words, "Father, forgive them for they know not what they do." He then dies for us to make sure the love is secure. But that is not the end of the story. Early one Sunday morning He rose from the grave all powerful, and now intercedes to His Father on our behalf every time we pray.

So, if you don't get a gift today, remember, yours arrived over 2,000 years ago. If you do get a gift, don't get too attached to either it or the giver, as neither will last too long. Instead, celebrate the fact that the world did not and could not give you what you deserved, because they don't know who you really are. You are a child of God. Happy "Calvary-tines" day to you. You are loved by the universe's greatest lover, Jesus Christ Himself.

February 15th
Proverbs 3:5

Trust in the Lord with all your heart, and lean not on your own understanding.

Are you facing any major decisions today? Have you been spending time trying to get every aspect of your life figured out? If so, take a deep breath and surrender those things to our Heavenly Father. He can handle them much better than we can. It is part of our human nature to work things out for ourselves and to prove that we don't need assistance from anyone else. The greatest problem with that line of thinking is that we fail to realize we are no longer just human beings. We are now spiritual new creations in Jesus Christ. Our relationship with Him is one that is based solely on trust and faith. Solomon tells us to "trust in the Lord with all our heart..." When we surrender to Him, we are not being irresponsible or derelict in our behavior; we are doing what His Word commands us to do and what our Father loves for us to do. He knows there will be issues in our daily lives which are beyond our finite comprehension. During those times we should not lean on our own understanding, which is too weak and will crumble and cause us to fall and hurt ourselves.

Trust God's guidance with the decisions that need to be made, and watch Him work out all the details for your good, and for His glory.

February 16th
Proverbs 3:6

In all your ways acknowledge Him, And He shall direct your paths.

Many people make the mistake of asking God for directions only after they have started their personal journeys. Then, when the details and the troubles of the trip seem to be more than they can handle, they cry out to God. Rather than travel along the paths God blesses, we make the mistake of asking God to bless whatever paths we happen to be traveling on. Everything about our lives is important to God. Every detail, every aspect, and all of the highs and lows that we experience are significant to Him. Don't ever feel as though you are troubling God with the minute details of your life. He is waiting to hear from you, and He offers us the freedom to acknowledge Him not just in our difficult ways, our problematic ways, or our confusing ways, but in all ways—we have an ongoing invitation to acknowledge Him. The assurance comes in knowing that He shall direct our path.

We can save ourselves a lot of unnecessary pain and frustration if we would just consult our Savior first and then travel in the direction in which He leads us. His path always leads to His purpose for our lives.

February 17th

Proverbs 15:1

A soft answer turns away wrath, but a harsh word stirs up anger.

In the book of James we are told the tongue is just a small part of our biological make-up, but it has the ability to do some powerful and destructive damage. Once we speak harmful words, we can apologize and ask for forgiveness, but we can never take those words back. Make up your mind that this is the day you will not speak before taking the time to consider what impact your words will have on the person or group you speak them to. If we really want to end the arguments that come in our direction, we are given the formula to do so right here. We are certainly not told to be sharp witted or condescending, or to exercise our levels of grammatical expertise.

Solomon says, "A soft answer turns away wrath..." Isn't it ironic that we overlook the first part of this verse and cling to the second part that says, "...but a harsh word stirs up anger." Challenges await you today. The devil will tempt you to say things that are harmful and will cause people to become alienated from you. Don't take the bait! Surprise those people who are expecting a combative verbal battle from you with some loving words of politeness and genuine Godliness.

Speak softly, even if you feel the other person does not deserve it. After all, our Heavenly Father gives us His abundant grace on a daily basis and none of us deserve that. Surely we can hold our tongue and speak kindly to people as His representative.

February 18th
Proverbs 16:3

Commit your works to the Lord, And your thoughts will be established.

God does not want this day to be filled with any unnecessary angst or frustration. He is aware of all the demands before us, and He also knows that He is capable of handling them much better than we are. This verse begins with a strong, attention-grabbing word: commit. It means to assign, trust, hand over, and whole-heartedly release. This is exactly what the Lord wants us to do. Not just with those issues that we don't think we can handle on our own, but with everything. Have you ever noticed that, when we are certain we can handle a given situation, it often becomes the one that completely overwhelms us? We need to commit all of our works, worries, and wishes to the Lord, and then watch Him establish our thoughts. This simply means that God will fill our minds with His directions and His plans, and we will never have to deal with the frustration of wondering if we have made the correct decision. When He leads, we always arrive at a place that helps us mature in our relationship with Him.

If you feel uncertain and ambiguous about the responsibilities you face today, commit all of that to Him, and He will establish your life on a solid foundation.

February 19th
Jeremiah 1:4

Then the word of the Lord came to me saying...

Perhaps you're sitting there wondering where the rest of the devotional scripture reading is for today. You're probably saying, "This isn't all of it, Pastor Brackins, is it?" Well, yes, it is, and we are about to discover that it is more than enough to equip us for whatever challenges and responsibilities face us today. One of the main reasons I find so much comfort in this verse is because it reminds us of the fact that God is willing to keep speaking to us even in spite of our weaknesses, failures, and unwillingness to totally trust and follow Him. Allow me to explain it like this. Whenever I become displeased with people, or they become displeased with me, one of the first things that happens is we stop speaking to each other. Sound familiar? But God is not like that. He continues to communicate and speak with us, and He does so in at least three ways:

- Through His written Word called the Bible. If you are feeling that God is silent in your time of struggle, it just may be because you have not taken the time to read His Word and hear His voice.
- Through His human representatives. He uses people to share His Word with other people. There just may be a Word of hope and comfort awaiting you on Sunday at your local church or at that ministry meeting you have not attended in several weeks.
- Through His Holy Spirit. He whispers words of assurance to us during our times of joy as well as in the painful moments.

Feeling a bit lonely and forgotten? Do you think the Lord is angry with you and has no desire to talk with you? Nothing could be further from the truth. He is speaking right now, reminding you of His love, His forgiveness, and His restoration. He has just spoken, are you listening? Make it a great day.

February 20th

Daniel 6:10

Now when Daniel knew that the writing was signed, he went home. And in his upper room, with his windows open toward Jerusalem, he knelt down on his knees three times that day, and prayed and gave thanks before his God, as was his custom since early days.

Have you ever received news or a report that was not as positive as you expected? It may have left you wondering what to do next. Well, Daniel helps us with these kinds of dilemmas. He has just been told that if he prays again to any other deity than King Darius, he is going to be thrown into a den of lions. (Surely your report is not as severe as his.) Even in the midst of this life-threatening situation he maintains his composure and does what has always worked for him in the past: He prays. He does not argue; he does not try to prove his innocence; he does not lash out at his accusers–he simply goes home, opens his windows, and prays to his God.

When Daniel prays, he does not do it without knowing how extreme the odds are. The verse says, *"Now when Daniel knew that the writing was signed..."* It appeared final. In other words, it was not a promotion, but a firing. Not just a lump, but cancer. Not reconciliation in the relationship, but a termination of it. The writing was signed for him, and it may look like the writing has been signed for you. But Daniel goes home and prays. This is what God wants all of us to do when the events of our lives are totally beyond our ability to repair. By praying, we release our cares to God; we remove the burden from ourselves, and we replace our fears with faith.

The next time you are in the car driving, turn the radio off, open the window, and spend some time in prayer to God. Daniel prayed and God delivered him, and He will do the same for each of us. This is no time to panic; this is time to pray! Just as God can calm lions, He can also calm your situation.

February 21st
Luke 18:1

Then He spoke a parable to them, that men always ought to pray and not lose heart.

Jesus knew how important prayer was to the spiritual survival of His disciples, and He also knows how vital it is for each of us today. As we pass through our daily lives, we should always do so in a prayerful frame of mind. We should not limit our prayer time to God by only asking Him to eliminate or undo bad things and add better things to our lives. We should spend time in adoration and praise to Him. When was the last time you simply told the Lord how much you loved Him, and did so without asking Him for anything? We don't like people in our lives who are always begging. We want people to let us know how much they appreciate what we have already done for them without asking for even more. Let this be a day you spend all your time thanking God.

I know there are things you need, but He just may grant those things without you asking for them—that is, if you take some quality time to thank Him for what He has done, and for any difficulty He has not allowed you to confront without His constant power and presence. Thank you, Jesus! Now, don't you feel better?

February 22nd

Psalm 150:6

Let everything that has breath praise the Lord. Praise the Lord!

Take a deep breath and hold it for three seconds. One, two, three. Okay, exhale. Are you still there? I expect you are, which means you qualify to participate in today's devotional. We are not told for every rich person to offer praise to the Lord. We are not told that every well-educated person should praise the Lord. We are not even told that every healthy person should praise the Lord. But if we are breathing, we owe the Lord what I call "oxygen praise." The very fact that our God has kept us alive and breathing is more than enough reason to give Him praise. Have you taken time to consider what good new houses, cars, clothes, and careers would do for us if we could not breathe to enjoy them? While we sleep, and in the very image of death, He still keeps us breathing.

Start this day by celebrating the presence of God in your life and the glory of God around your life. He is alive; He has kept us alive, and we should be filled with rejoicing. Now, take another deep breath. Didn't that feel good? Praise Him for it and go out and have yourself a praise-filled day!

February 23rd
Psalm 139:23

Search me, o God, and know my heart; Try me, and know my anxieties.

I start today's devotional by asking a simple, yet profound, thought-provoking question. "Which is more important to you: God granting you the things you ask Him for in your limited time of prayer with Him, or God fixing you so that He can use you to His greatest glory?" Our honesty in answering this question determines our commitment to, compassion toward, confidence in, and communication with, God. When you talk to the Lord, what does the conversation consist of most: things you are requesting from Him, or things you are releasing to Him?

I have grown and given a great deal of attention to my prayer life for the last sixteen years or more, but a study I engaged in during late summer 2013 took my prayer time with God into a dimension I did not even know existed. I am not talking about a lot of emotional outburst and the appearance of heavenly visions on a daily basis, but rather about a dramatic shift from praying about those things I thought were important to me in making my life better to praying about what is important to God so that I can be used to bring a greater level of glory to Him.

I ask my question again. Which is more important: God giving you what you think you want and need, or God fixing you so that He can use you at a greater level to His glory? Notice carefully the last part of the question. I did not say simply, "God using you at a greater level to His glory," but, "God *fixing you,* so that He can use you at a greater level to His glory." The fixing part is the part we don't like, because when we hear the word *fix* in connection with God, we automatically think personal pain is involved. Truth be told, there is! In fact, we all need some fixing. So, will we choose to remain in our broken and wounded condition and continue to ask God to add brief, Band-Aid blessings to our lives, or will we pray as David did in Psalm 139 for God to purify us so that He can add value to our lives and get greater glory out of us?

February 24th
Luke 23:46

And when Jesus had cried out with a loud voice, He said, "Father, into Your hands I commit My spirit." Having said this, He breathed His last.

When you trust someone completely, you have no trouble totally surrendering to them. It is only when we are uncertain about the strength of the relationship that we hesitate to remove all the barriers that may hinder us from placing complete confidence in a person. In our devotional scripture for today, Jesus is hanging on a cross at Calvary. He is just moments from death—a sacrifice made for guilty sinners like you and me. From a humanistic perspective, the physical suffering was more than He could bear. But notice what He does: He surrenders everything to His Father even though He did not deserve anything that was happening to Him. When our lives seem filled with perplexities that are more than we can bear or understand, that is not the time to try to figure out what God is doing—that is the time to totally surrender to Him. Even if every event of this day does not turn out the way you planned it, if you can muster up the faith to surrender everything to God, it will turn out the way *He* planned it.

I hope we can all agree on the fact that God's end results are always better than ours. Calvary lasted six hours; the grave lasted three days; but His resurrection has lasted more than 2,000 years. Surrender your cares to Him—the sooner you do, the closer you can move to your resurrection reality over everything that has been holding you back and causing you pain.

February 25th
John 14:6

Jesus said to him, "I am the way, the truth, and the life. No one comes to the Father except through Me."

Let me remind you of what you already know. This day is going to be filled with uncertainties and unplanned difficulties. But the good news lies in the fact that we don't have to face all those situations alone. Thomas, one Jesus' disciples, wanted to know how he could be certain he was traveling in this right direction after the death, burial, and resurrection of Jesus Christ. Jesus wanted him, and He wants us to focus more on the Person traveling with us on the journey than on the path where He is leading us. The paths are filled with uncertainty, but the Person is filled with comfort and reassurance. When my children were small, they never complained about where I would carry them as long as they felt my presence while in my arms. It was not until they got older and started to walk on their own that they became hesitant to follow my directions. The Lord has allowed us to mature, and many of us now want to second-guess His leadership by using our human intellect. Jesus wants us to know that He is the way—not *a* way, but *the* way—the only truth and the only life.

We arrive at our destination, which is His Father's perfect will, only by following Him moment by moment. This day is not only about the direction God will lead your travels in, but also, and more importantly, about knowing that He walks with us every step of the way. This day is a new journey for you, but Jesus has traveled that road more times than we can count. Trust His leadership, and make it a great day.

February 26th
Genesis 18:14

Is anything too hard for the Lord? At the appointed time I will return to you, according to the time of life, and Sarah shall have a son.

Whenever the Lord tells us to wait, we usually have only one question: "How long?" No matter how long we have to wait, the God of creation, salvation, and sanctification reminds and reassures us of the truth that there is nothing too hard for Him to accomplish in the lives of any of His children. In today's scripture, the Lord makes a promise to Abraham and Sarah that He will bless them with a child. At the time the promise was made, Abraham was 99 years old and Sarah was 89. They were 100 and 90, respectively, when the promise was fulfilled. This should give us all hope and encouragement. It is never too late for God to make good on His promises. Don't allow your dreams and aspirations to dissipate simply because you feel you are past your prime. God's timetable is not the same as ours. He moves in your direction to confirm every promise He has ever made to you.

Take your eyes off your condition, and focus on His provisions. After all, His provisions have always been greater than our conditions. There is nothing too hard for God, and we are never past our prime for a miracle.

February 27th
Ezra 3:10

When the builders laid the foundation of the temple of the Lord, the priests stood in their apparel with trumpets, and the Levites, the sons of Asaph, with cymbals, to praise the Lord, according to the ordinance of David, King of Israel.

A good friend of mine, Pastor A. C. Stapleton, always poses the following question: "Are you able to shout and give God praise on credit?" His reasoning behind this question is to motivate God's people to learn the importance of praising God for His promises even before we realize the possessions. The people in our verse for today did not wait until the temple was completely rebuilt; they started shouting and praising when the foundation was laid. This day is going to be filled with many things we need from God. As opposed to focusing only on what we have not yet received, why not rejoice about the foundation He has already laid by allowing us to rise this morning to see another day? The bricks of this day are not yet all in place. The furnishings we need for our lives have not yet all been arranged. Let's leave those details to God; He is the Master builder and the Master architect.

Stand fully dressed in your garment of praise and refuse to allow the devil to steal any aspects of this day's joy from you. Praise God for the foundations of family, faith, forgiveness, and a secure future. Those are the things that will hold us. After all, the foundation holds the house in place; the house does not hold the foundation in place. Just as David gave directions to Israel concerning their praise, I want to take the liberty to give you some directions: Rejoice, bless the Lord, and thank Him for your foundation!

February 28th
Nehemiah 6:3

So I sent messengers to them, saying, "I am doing a great work, so that I cannot come down. Why should the work cease while I leave it and go down to you?"

Distractions, distractions, distractions. The devil is the master of distractions. Feeling a bit distracted today? Well, allow me to encourage your heart. The devil only distracts those of us he knows are making great progress for God. Your wall of commitment is getting taller; your wall of sacrifice is getting stronger; and your wall of praise is reaching new heights. My advice to you is, "Don't come down!" God is being glorified; don't allow even those well-meaning and well-intentioned people to distract you. God is using you to glorify Him and to bless the body of Christ.

Force the devil to get a crook in his neck while looking up at your progress, and don't you dare stop building on the firm foundation where God has planted you. This is the end of the month, and we need to enter the joys and the responsibilities of March knowing we are fulfilling our God-given tasks. Stay up there, because God is doing a great work through you.

PRAYER

Lord, Thank You for allowing us to walk with You and discover the plan, purpose, and protection You have for our lives. We surrender every care to You and embrace every assignment from You.

In Jesus' name,
Amen.

Muffins from the Master in March

March 1st
Job 1:20

Then Job arose, tore his robe, and shaved his head; and he fell to the ground and worshiped.

You really don't have to know a whole lot about the Bible to be familiar with the story of Job. His pain, suffering, the death of all ten of his children, and even being tempted by his wife to curse God and die were just a few of the things he faced. But he refuses to waver in his faith, determined to trust and wait on God. Job's steadfastness is based on the positive disposition he had when his suffering first started. It is here in chapter one that we find him doing something remarkable even in the midst of calamity. After tearing his robe and shaving his head, he falls to the ground and worships God. This is a great lesson we all need to learn. Even when we are confronted with seemingly catastrophic circumstances, we need to be reminded of the fact that God is still worthy of our worship. Praise allows us to enter into the presence of God, where His will becomes clear to us as we are drawn closer to Him.

Although you may be going through a painful period in your life, your eyes filled with tears and your heart aching, don't complain. Don't question God—just get on your knees and worship Him, and now watch Him change your situation just as He did for Job.

March 2nd
Job 14:14

If a man dies, shall he live again? All the days of my hard service I will wait,
Till my change comes.

I will not even attempt to offer a message of unbiblical nonsense by trying to make us think that being a Christian exempts us from all our troubles. Nowhere in the Word of God is that promise made to us. But I will share with you both Biblically and confidently that those of us who have been washed in the blood of the Lamb are headed to a place in eternity called Heaven, where trouble and pain no longer exist.

When we awake in the morning, we are faced with a new set of challenges because this world we live in is filled with sin. But the good news reminds us of the truth that we are headed to a place where trouble, sickness, and disease are completely eliminated. You may be wondering what we should be doing in the meantime. I'll tell you. We must continue to serve God, praise God, focus on God, and, most importantly, trust God.

Whatever this day may hold, be encouraged. Your change is on the way. God will either make changes in you to handle your struggles, or He will make changes to the struggles so they will not overwhelm you. You have a whole lot of living left to do. So go out and make this a Heaven-preparation day by focusing exclusively on the Lord.

March 3rd

Job 42:10

And the Lord restored Job's losses when he prayed for his friends. Indeed the Lord gave Job twice as much as he had before.

Friends: They can be some of the most encouraging people, and yes, they can also be the very ones who bring heartache, betrayal, and pain to our lives. When Job was going through the most painful period of his life, his friends constantly accused him of committing secret sins. He did not lash out at them; he simply maintained his position of integrity with God. After Job's extreme suffering as relayed in the first forty-one chapters of this book, the Lord reverses all of Job's negative misfortune by converting it into a positive blessing and giving him twice as much as he had before. But, according to today's verse, it did not happen at once; in fact, it did not happen until he prayed for his friends. The Lord uses this passage to teach us the importance of forgiving and praying for those we believe have caused harm to our lives.

What are you waiting for the Lord to restore in your life? Are there any people who have hurt you and you have not forgiven them? Today is the day to release that bitterness. As soon as you finish reading this paragraph, pray for them. If you feel led by the Lord to do so, call them and tell them all the bitterness of the past is released, without feeling the need to discuss any of the painful details. Now, get ready for the Lord to deposit into your life all that He wants you to have.

March 4th
Psalm 37:1

Do not fret because of evildoers, Nor be envious of the workers of iniquity.

Just let God handle it! That is our lesson for today. Short, sweet, and to the point. Just let God handle it. Don't waste another minute worrying about what negative people are doing in their attempts to prevent you from being all that God desires you to be. May I tell you why? Because, if you do, it is proof we have more confidence in what they can do to harm us and hold us back than we have in our God who is the only one who can promote and elevate us. Stop giving your naysayers so much attention. They are evildoers and they are simply doing the only thing they know how to do. Release that pressure from yourself. God has placed you on this earth to please Him and to serve other people. Not everyone appreciates our service, but they are not the ones who pay our salaries.

God is our provider and our protector. Say goodbye to fear, hello to your faith, and let the evildoers do what they do. In the meantime, we will allow the Lord to do what He does best: make all our enemies fall at our footstool.

March 5th
Psalm 107:1

Oh, give thanks to the Lord, for He is good! For His mercy endures forever.

Today is a day of thanksgiving. There's no need to wait for the fourth Thursday in November. Every day is a day of thanksgiving. Are you wondering what we should be thanking the Lord for? Read the verse again. "...for He is good!" He has no "was," or "will be" attached to His goodness. (I know my editors are going to try to delete this phrase, but I meant what I said, and I said it like I meant it!) The Lord *is* good. Regardless of what confronts us, He is still good and His goodness demands a great level of verbal gratitude from His people. If we need even more to thank Him for, it is right here in this same verse: "For His mercy endures forever." Most of us focus only on the grace of God. Through His grace He gives us things we do not deserve. But through His mercy, He holds back the punishment both He and we know we deserve.

Begin this day with a thankful heart and a voice filled with gratitude. Tell Him, "Thank you, Lord" right now! Because of His mercy, our sins were not dealt with in the manner they deserved. Now that's a lot to thank God for.

March 6th

Isaiah 6:8

Also I heard the voice of the Lord, saying: "Whom shall I send, and who will go for Us?" Then I said, "Here am I! Send me."

Many times we make the mistake of wanting the Lord to only do impossible things *for* us, and we fail to make ourselves available for Him to do impossible things *through* us. God is about to do something through you that you never dreamed possible, if only you yield completely to Him. Our verse for today was spoken by the prophet Isaiah, and he is presenting himself totally to the Lord with no strings attached. The Lord has a special assignment for you today, just as He had for Isaiah. He is just waiting for you to speak the same words Isaiah did: "Lord here am I. Send me." We need to know that when God sends us, He already knows where we will arrive. But He does not always tell us what the destination is because He wants us to walk with Him by faith. It matters not where the journey of this day may lead you; what really matters is knowing that God walks with you every step of the way, and ensures your safe arrival at your destination.

Whisper a word of surrendered prayer to the Lord and tell Him you are ready to go wherever He desires to send you. Now get ready for the most exciting journey you have ever been on in your life.

March 7th

Habakkuk 3:19

The Lord God is my strength; He will make my feet like deer's feet, And He will make me walk on my high hills.

Just when you were feeling down in the dumps and ready to throw in the towel, God once again shows up with a wonderful verse of scripture filled with encouragement. The first six words of this verse really provide all the spiritual B-12 nourishment we could ever need: "The Lord God is my strength..." You are going to not only traverse today's difficulties, but you are going to run with feet like a deer's. This simply means the trouble that confronts us won't last very long. God is strengthening you right now through His Word. This verse is just what you need for *today*. Take you mind off tomorrow's and next week's responsibilities. Let's focus instead on the strength God provides today. Go ahead and face those challenges, confront those responsibilities, and get ready to overcome every one of those obstacles.

High hills await you. (And I'm not talking about high "hill" shoes!) God has new ground He wants you to cover today, and He has a new perspective He wants you to visualize. Don't stop now. Ascend those hills. Release your weakness to His strength and get ready to move at His marching orders.

March 8th

Zephaniah 3:14

Sing, O daughter of Zion! Shout, O Israel! Be glad and rejoice with all your heart, O daughter of Jerusalem.

Okay, let's make up our minds right now that this is going to be not just a good day, but a *great* day. We start this day off with two very important things: the precepts of God (His Word) and the praise of God (His Worship). Now, really, what more do we need? Sing! If you are at your desk at work, hum. You are a child of God, and God loves to listen while His children sing His praise even while we walk in the rain of a storm. Make up your mind to have a glad heart. Sadness did not help yesterday's problems go away, and it surely will not make today's issues any more bearable, but worship and praise will.

I remind you of the fact that, after all the preaching, teaching, and evangelizing have concluded, we spend eternity offering praise to our God. Now would be a great time to get some much needed practice in. So, go out and make it a praise-filled day.

March 9th
Psalm 121:5

The Lord is your keeper; The Lord is your shade at your right hand.

Whenever we are feeling vulnerable and susceptible to troubles beyond our control, we need to remember that we are covered by the all-protective hand of our Heavenly Father. He is a keeper. This means that God not only owns us, but He also provides constant protection for us. Even during times of trouble, He is right there to place limitations on those who would seek to destroy us. While God has never promised to keep us from trouble, He has promised to always be with us when we are in trouble and to lead us through those troubles.

Is the sun beating down a bit too hard? Just raise the umbrella of your faith and allow His shade to give you the covering you need right now. "The Lord is your shade at your right hand." I just felt a cool breeze blow in our direction.

March 10th

Psalm 133:1

Behold, how good and pleasant it is for brethren to dwell together in unity!

The Lord has made us a part of His forever family. As Christian believers, we are not to be isolated from each other, but instead, we should be supportive of each other. We all need to be attached to others both *to* whom we give strength and *from* whom we receive it. God never designed us to handle all of our frustrations alone. We place them at His feet in prayer then receive comfort and encouragement from other believers until God reveals to us His perfect plan for our lives.

If you are not connected to a church family, get connected this week. Remember, relationships take time, and you must work to grow and improve them. Surround yourself with people whose walk and relationship with the Lord is stronger than your own so you can be strengthened by them. Then, as you become stronger, do the same for someone who needs your help. Let's dwell together in unity.

March 11th
Psalm 55:22

Cast your burden on the Lord, And He shall sustain you; He shall never permit the righteous to be moved.

The Lord uses this day to teach us a greater level of dependence on Him. During those periods in our lives when we feel as though we walk alone and have no one who really understands what we are experiencing, know that nothing could be further from the truth. The Lord not only comes to our rescue; He walks with us every step of the way, waiting for us to release our cares into His mighty hands. Those burdens which weigh you down mentally and emotionally don't have to be carried alone. Our Father is waiting to show you His sustaining power.

Don't worry about being shaken out of place, because today's verse also says, "...He shall never permit the righteous to be moved." The key to unlocking our full understanding of this verse is found in the fact that if we would only maintain a righteous walk with God, we will also experience His sustaining power.

March 12th
Titus 3:5

Not by works of righteousness which we have done, but according to His mercy He saved us, through the washing of regeneration and renewing of the Holy Spirit.

I'm excited. I know it may be early when you are reading this, and perhaps you're wondering what I was so excited about when I wrote today's devotional, but I can honestly say I'm excited about the truth that is housed in today's verse. This verse informs us of the truth that we do not, and cannot, work for our salvation–it is a free gift from God. He saved us through His mercy and made us brand new because the power and the presence of the Holy Spirit live within every believer. Listen to me carefully: We do not work to be saved. We work for the Lord because we have already been saved. Our work does not earn us more of God's grace, but rather, is an expression of our appreciation to God for His undeserved mercy and His unmerited grace.

I hope you, too, are excited by now, in the knowledge you are saved, sealed, and secure in the Lord because you have been born again. Let this be a day of just thanking God for saving us and cleansing us from all our sins.

March 13th

Matthew 4:20

They immediately left their nets and followed Him.

What are you holding onto that prevents you from following Jesus wholeheartedly? Most of us want to keep those things we feel we cannot live without, just in case the Lord does not come through the way we expect Him to. I have discovered that the Lord never reveals His best for our lives as long as we have a plan B. The men referred to in this verse, Peter and Andrew, were professional fishermen. But when they met Jesus, He had such a profound impact on their lives that they abandoned everything that was important to them to follow Him.

Please don't miss the fact that they had just met Jesus and yet they left everything for Him. Many of us have known Him for years and still have not released those things which hold us back. This is a day of purging. Let it go! Now just watch as He moves you to a position to which you would never have been able to ascend with all that negative baggage.

March 14th

Matthew 6:11

Give us this day our daily bread.

It's only the 14th of the month and some of you are already concerned about the responsibilities for the 15th through the 31st. Take a deep breath. For today, all we need is bread. The Lord wants us to utter this prayer for three simple yet profound reasons. When we ask Him to give us this day our daily bread, we can be assured of receiving *fresh* bread. He does not want us to eat anything stale. What is more, He gives us the *Father's* bread. Jesus does not want us eating from the hand of the devil. We are also assured of *faith* bread. He provides for us, but we don't even know where it comes from.

Worry bread costs a lot and most of us can't afford it. But fresh bread—the Father's faith bread—is free; it's already been paid for by Jesus Christ. All we really need is just enough for today. Relax, clear your mind, and go out and make it a great day. God has a loaf with your name on it!

March 15th
Psalm 20:7

Some trust in chariots, and some in horses; But we will remember the name of the Lord our God.

I remember vividly the first time I read this verse of scripture in the Bible. One reason I remember it so well is because it reminded me of an old song that I grew up singing in Church and I still sing now. The name of the song is simply "I Will Trust in the Lord." Does that bring back any memories? This verse helped me realize that whenever I place my trust and confidence in any inanimate object or any other human, I will always face letdown and disappointment. The chariots spoken of here symbolize those things we feel add a greater level of protection for our lives. The horses represent the shortcuts we take to speed up our plans and desires. But at the end of the day, the only way we will have lives full of the peace of God is to forget about all those other things and concentrate on remembering the name of the Lord our God.

He is our protection; He is our pacesetter; and He is our provision. Trust totally in Him–He will last longer than any chariot, and He will transport you more smoothly than any horse. Remember His name and join with me in singing "I Will Trust in the Lord."

March 16th

Psalm 147:11

The Lord takes pleasure in those who fear Him, In those who hope in His mercy.

When God finds a life that is pleasing to Him, that life will be filled with His constant presence and provisions. This does not mean we will not experience times of difficulty and days of temporary defeat. But it does mean that we have Him at the forefront of our lives. Many times, we make the mistake of asking God to give us more from His hand, and we fail to ask Him to draw us in closer to His heart. The word *fear* as it is used in this verse does not mean to be frightened or terrified of God. Rather, it means to reverence Him, to respect Him, and to give Him the adoration He deserves. When we do this, we discover He takes pleasure in us. He will be pleased with our desire to get closer to Him to discover who He is rather than be concerned with what He has.

Let this day be a day of reverencing God. Just tell Him how much you honor, adore, esteem, extol, and magnify His holy name. Then find hope in the fact that He is a merciful God; He has not held our past transgressions against us, but instead has washed away all our sins.

March 17th
Mark 4:9

And He said to them, "He who has ears to hear, let him hear!"

I just ended a call with someone concerning a problem I was having with our automobile. This person went on and on telling me about the tests that had been done and the results of those tests. I politely interrupted and made him aware of the fact that he had not listened carefully to my explanation of the problem when I first brought the car in. I could have saved us both about ten minutes of talk, if he had just taken the time to listen. (I know you see where this is headed.) So often we spend time giving God a grocery list full of our needs and a lengthy laundry list of things that need to be cleaned up in our lives, but little-to-no time listening to Him. Jesus says, "He who has ears to hear, let him hear." Ears have only one purpose–for us to hear. We have only one mouth, but two ears. God wants us to listen to Him and then heed His directions before spending time telling Him what we need to make our lives better or what should be added and removed.

If you must speak, then begin by saying, "Speak, Lord, I'm listening." Now let's obey what He tells us to do.

March 18th

Matthew 4:4

But He answered and said, "It is written, 'Man shall not live by bread alone, but by every word that proceeds from the mouth of God.'"

There is nothing better than having a healthy, yet satisfied, appetite for the Word of God. What we eat physically sustains us physically. What most of us fail to realize is that we need spiritual nourishment much more than we need physical nourishment. Often the devil defeats us because we are malnourished of the Word of God. Let this be the day you begin each day by reading at least one chapter or passage from both the Old and the New Testaments. I know we will not totally understand all that we read every day. But it will help us develop an appetite for the voice of God that we hear through His Word. After all, most of us didn't like broccoli, green beans, or asparagus as kids, but our parents fed them to us because they knew we needed them to grow and become healthy.

Make God's Word a part of your daily routine and it won't be long before you feel starved if you go even a few hours without having it. Purchase a small Bible, keep it with you, and read it during lunch and break time. Those text messages can wait. God wants to you read His text.

March 19th
Matthew 5:4

Blessed are those who mourn, For they shall be comforted.

We all have those days, weeks, and even seasons when it seems as though we face one issue after another that pulls us down emotionally and spiritually. We don't plan to feel that way; we don't like it when we feel that way; and sometimes, we don't even know why we feel that way. But when we see the sin that has polluted God's world and the violence that confronts us on a daily basis, before we know it, we can't help but take on a mournful spirit. Well, cheer up! Jesus knows all about it, and He has promised us some relief. But listen carefully. We do not experience relief by the elimination of the mourning, but rather in the entrance of His comfort. Whenever the Lord sees us mourning, that is, speaking about Godly sorrow, we can then rest assured of His comfort.

The comfort of Jesus does not always remove the mourning, but His presence always eases the pain to the point that we shift our focus more on who is with us than on what is going on around us. Mourn if you must, but be assured, if the mourning is Godly in nature, we have His blessings and His comfort. What more can we ask for?

March 20th

Matthew 5:8

Blessed are the pure in heart, For they shall see God.

When I was growing up in Houston, a lot of Christian children recited this verse right before eating their meal. In our house, our parents taught us to quote a Bible verse and then say a prayer before we ate. Most of us picked the shortest verses and said the shortest prayers so our food would not get cold. "Jesus wept" was the most popular one. But now that I am older, I have come to realize there is so much more contained in today's verse than simply a few words spoken before a meal. Jesus teaches us the importance of doing at least three things. We must regularly *check our hearts*; we do not know what condition they are in if we fail to check them. We must regularly *cleanse our hearts*; whatever is not from God and not like God must be removed. At that point, we will be able to *concentrate on God.*

Check your spiritual condition right now. Cleanse anything that is not of God through prayer. Now go out and make this day a day of *Godly* concentration. I can see better already.

March 21st
Matthew 5:9

Blessed are the peacemakers, For they shall be called sons of God.

Today you will likely experience some stressful situations. They may not be aimed at you, but you have the ability to diffuse them. The Lord wants all His children to be known as people of peace. We need to know that peace is not the absence of confusion. Rather, peace is the infusion and the inclusion of God's presence. We do not create peace by avoiding negative and hostile people; we create peace by allowing God's presence to be felt through us and reacting in a way that is totally unexpected and unpredictable. The devil has set things up that he thinks will cause you to react in a negative and ungodly way.

Surprise him and throw him in a tailspin while loving people not with your love, but with the love of God. Jesus did say that the peacemakers will be called the sons (children) of God. People may not know your wit, your level of educational attainment, or any other personal fact about you, but through your peaceful disposition they will know you are a child of God!

March 22nd
Galatians 1:4

Who gave Himself for our sins, that He might deliver us from this present evil age, according to the will of our God and Father.

At times, it seems our world and society are becoming more corrupt and wicked with each passing day. When we look at the conditions in which we are forced to live, the outlook can occasionally be pretty bleak. But the good news lies in the fact that these troubles, sins, and wickedness will not last forever for those of us who are believers in Jesus Christ. We must never forget that we were once part of the problem of polluting God's world with sinfulness, but now we have surrendered to Him and been saved by the blood of His Son Jesus Christ. I find hope and encouragement in knowing that Jesus was not forced to die for us; He was not assassinated—He willingly and freely gave His life for us. He came to deliver us from this present evil age. Even though we are still in this world, we are not of this world.

We find comfort in knowing that God has a new life of eternity prepared for us after this life of sinfulness has ended. We don't subscribe to the when-you-are-dead-you-are-done philosophy. We know that we have been set free from sin so that we might be prepared for our forever life with God, the Holy Spirit, and His Son Jesus Christ. Don't allow the things around you to bring sadness to your heart. Look up, because that is the direction in which we are headed—soon, very soon.

March 23rd
Galatians 1:11

But I make known to you, brethren, that the gospel which was preached by me is not according to man.

One of the mistakes many believers make in our effort to witness to people is to talk more about our opinions and ideas than about the Gospel of Jesus Christ. One of the reasons we do this is because many of us know more about our ideas and opinions than we do about the Gospel of Jesus Christ. Our opinions need support, validation, and verification. But the Gospel of Jesus Christ will always stand on its own. In our verse for today, Paul makes clear the fact that he has not preached a "manly Gospel" but a "Christ Gospel."

Whenever we witness to people, portions of the Word of God must always serve as the foundation for our testimony. This is one of the reasons regular and systematic Bible reading and study are so important. Our experiences must be based on His Word, and we must not seek to reverse the order. As you witness throughout this day, a good place to start would be to just say about Jesus what His Word has already validated and verified. A good place to start is with the fact that He is a loving God (see John 3:16). That needs no props or humanly support.

March 24th

Romans 1:16

For I am not ashamed of the Gospel of Christ, for it is the power of God to salvation for everyone who believes, for the Jew first and also for the Greek.

Our relationship with the Lord should not be a private matter. I know that we now live in a time when it is not politically correct to talk about Christianity and the Bible among our friends and peers. News flash! We have not been saved by the Lord to be politically correct, but to be *spiritually responsible*. When it comes to the Gospel and our Savior Jesus Christ, we should never be ashamed or timid to let people anywhere and everywhere know that we are children of God. The Gospel has power to *magnetize* people. It has the power to *mold* people. And it has the power to *mend* broken people. Has it not dawned on you that our fear to share Christ and the Gospel with people who desperately need Him may be what prevents them from being magnetized, molded, and mended by Him?

The message God has given us is nondiscriminatory in nature. Paul said in our verse for today that the Gospel of Christ will save the Jews. This represents the people who have at least heard about God. And the Gospel of Christ will also save the Greeks. This represents the people who may have never been introduced to Christ and who have been trusting in their own human intellect. This day is going to be filled with opportunities to share your faith. So rid yourself of that shame and embrace God's holy boldness instead.

March 25th

Psalm 37:25

I have been young, and now am old; Yet I have not seen the righteous forsaken, Nor his descendants begging bread.

God is our provider. No matter what you are faced with today, keep that truth at the forefront of your mind. He has been doing His job of taking care of His children for a long time, and He has been doing it without any failure. We often want to figure out how God is going to do what we feel needs to be done in our lives. We want all the details and the time frame. But this is not how God works. He makes promises to us and then expects us to wait and to trust in His word. In our verse for today, David shares his testimony with us about God's provisions for His children. David was not a perfect man; his life was filled with mistakes and sins, yet God continued to take care of him. He will do the same for us.

This day should not be filled with worry and grief about your basic needs being met. This is a day of trust, a day of Godly confidence, and a day of expectation. By the way, didn't you have some concerns yesterday? Well, He brought you through those, and He will take you through whatever this day may hold.

March 26th

Psalm 119:105

Your word is a lamp to my feet and a light to my path.

Ever had a season in your life when you were having trouble seeing what God was doing in your life? Maybe you are experiencing one of those seasons right now. Well, I've got good news. It may just be that you are trying to see what God is doing by using the wrong lighting system. Our finite human minds will never be able to clearly understand the things of God. But when we use the lighting system of His Word, things begin to clear up. The psalmist gives us two very important components about the Word of God: He says it is a "lamp" and it is a "light." The "lamp to our feet" helps us see where we are now. This is important because we can never move in the right direction until we are honest with ourselves about where we are now in our relationship with the Lord. Many people stay away from the lamp because they don't want to confront themselves with the condition of their present surroundings. The Word is also a "light to our path." This aspect helps us see the direction in which we should be traveling.

If today's journey leads you down some dark paths, turn around, follow His light, and you will begin to walk in His will for your life.

March 27th
Psalm 23:4

Yea, though I walk through the valley of the shadow of death, I will fear no evil; For You are with me; Your rod and Your staff, they comfort me.

You are not in this alone. If this is a season of great joy in your life, praise the Lord for it, for you are not in that glorious spiritual atmosphere without His presence. If you seem to be facing some of the darkest days of your life, you are not walking through that season alone. You are not going through the valley of death; you are going through the valley of the *shadow* of death. When preaching this at Grace Tabernacle, I say, "Now lean in real close." Wherever there is a shadow, there has to be some light, and Jesus is the light of the world. Even in those dark valley parts of our world, His light still shines to give us hope. Don't panic, don't fear, and don't quit–He is with you. He does not have to come and find you–He is with you. Even when you cannot feel Him, or hear Him, know that He is right there.

Make the next step, keep walking, and don't worry about those things that try to overwhelm you. His rod and His staff are there to comfort you, give you courage, and make sure nothing conquers you. You are not walking *to* the valley; you are walking *through* it. And, in case you are wondering how to get out of this, it is simple: just keep walking.

March 28th

Romans 5:1

Therefore, having been justified by faith, we have peace with God through our Lord Jesus Christ.

There are at least two important aspects of peace of which every Christian must be assured. One is the peace of God. This is what happens when our faith is firm and our confidence is strong and secure. Because we have the peace *of* God, we no longer worry or get stressed. The second aspect is peace *with* God. When Jesus died at Calvary to remove us from being at enmity with God, we gained peace with God, as we became His children and His friends. This is what is spoken of here in this verse. Our faith has justified us. In other words, because of our faith, God now loves us as if our sins never stood between us and Him. He has not ignored our sins; He has forgiven us and set us free from the penalty of them. Because of this, we now have peace with God, and it all came through His Son our Lord Jesus Christ.

We are forgiven. We are loved. And we are at perfect peace with our God. Release that guilt. Why do you want to hold onto it, when He has disregarded it? Make this a peace-filled day of intimacy with our Heavenly Father.

March 29th
2 Corinthians 9:7

So let each one give as he purposes in his heart, not grudgingly or of necessity; for God loves a cheerful giver.

Many Christians are always looking to receive more from God, while few of us are willing to give more to the Lord. Take a moment to think about all the Lord has done and what He continues to do for you on a daily basis. Now ask yourself, "How much is that worth?" Our giving to God should never be forced, coerced, or compelled. We should give to Him willingly. When you arrive at your place of worship this week, give the Lord a special offering. Take an envelope, write the Lord a note, and say to Him, "This is just my small way of thanking You for all You have done for me." When you place it in the offering receptacle, do it with an honest, sincere smile on your face. He loves a cheerful giver. A word of caution: Don't wait until you think you can afford to do it; it may never get done. Make the sacrifice and bless the Lord who has blessed you with so much.

After all, you are reading with His eyes, breathing His oxygen, turning the pages with His hands, and His Son has washed away your sins with His blood. Isn't that worth a special gift? That's right. Write the check out now, put that special offering to the side, and give it cheerfully to the Lord.

March 30th

Ephesians 5:1

Therefore be imitators of God as dear children.

My father, Mr. Leroy Brackins Jr., died and went home to live in the presence of the Lord in 2003. His memories are still fresh and encouraging in my heart and mind. Whenever I returned to Houston to visit where we lived and where I was raised, people would say to me, "Roy Elton, the older you get, the more you look like your father." I still make return trips to Houston, but lately, people have been saying, "Roy Elton, the older you get, the more you *act* like your father." I realize I cannot control my looks, but my actions are different; they reflect the principles my father taught me over the years.

Wouldn't it be wonderful if people noticed that we not only look like what they expect of Christians, but also that we act like Jesus Christ? Imagine if more people said, "Child of God, the older you get, the more you act like and imitate your Heavenly Father." We have a tendency to mimic the habits of others, but seldom spend quality time trying to replicate the characteristics of our Lord. Paul says in our verse for today that we should be imitators of God as dear children. Allow this day to be one you put forth a special effort to be more like Jesus from this day forward. Love like Him, forgive like Him, and serve like Him. I thank God when people see my biological father's traits in me, but my soul is lifted to an entirely different level when people see my Heavenly Father's traits in me. Let's imitate the One who has liberated us.

March 31st

Ephesians 5:2

And walk in love, as Christ also has loved us and given Himself for us, an offering and a sacrifice to God for a sweet-smelling aroma.

If we are going to imitate the Lord effectively, at least two things must take place. We must spend time walking with Him, and we must learn the importance of walking like Him. When we walk with Him, we need constant communion and fellowship. When we walk like Him, we need to monitor our conduct and walk by faith. To "walk in love" means to live according to the principles and guidelines of God's Word. This calls for us to make sacrifices and place our plans on the back burner. But God is worth whatever adjustments we need to make. He has loved us and given Himself for us. When we walk with Him, the aroma is wonderful. What was once a vile and repugnant odor at Calvary has been transformed into a sweet-smelling aroma by the power of God's love for all His children.

Let's make that walk a daily walk. Not just during times of desperation, but also during seasons of celebration.

PRAYER

Dear Lord, We thank You for bringing us through the third month of this year. We acknowledge our faults and failures, and we thank You for Your amazing, keeping Grace.

In Jesus' name,
Amen.

Apricots of Assurance in April

April 1st
Psalm 14:1

The fool has said in his heart, "There is no God." They are corrupt, They have done abominable works, There is none who does good.

Only the fool believes God does not exist. This is not a day for acknowledging fools or participating in foolish behavior. This is a day of setting the record straight and letting everybody we come into contact with know that our God is real, He lives, and He lives in us. We begin this month with the assurance of God's presence in this world and His presence in our lives.

Don't waste time playing jokes and deceiving people today; offer them the real, authentic truth about God's Son, our Savior Jesus Christ. People don't need an April fool's joke; they need some *April Fresh Faith* from our Father in Heaven. Give them what they need and not what they want.

April 2nd
Psalm 137:4

How shall we sing the Lord's song in a foreign land?

When this Psalm was written, the people of God had been carried away as captives from their home land of Jerusalem and were now being forced to live as slaves to the Babylonians. Their captors wanted some entertainment so they asked a group of them to sing one of the songs of praise that they used to sing back in Jerusalem. Their response to this request was, "How shall we sing the Lord's song in a foreign land?" They made the same mistake that many of us make today. We allow our position, the people around us, and the problems we are experiencing to either limit or eliminate our praise to God. The question in the psalm is valid. How can we sing the Lord's song when we seem to be in a strange land? The answer is relatively simple. We need to do three basic things. First, never lose sight of the Person to whom our song is being offered: God. Second, don't allow your position to postpone your praise. There are some storms we must shout and rejoice our way through. Third, don't lose sight of the purpose of your song. We, as Christian believers, don't sing just to please ourselves and other people; we sing to get closer to our Heavenly Father.

You may not have been carried away to Babylon, but your job or being around some of your associates may sometimes seem like being in a strange land. Regardless, don't allow your position or other people to stop or limit you from singing praise to our Father God.

April 3rd

Ecclesiastes 11:1

Cast thy bread upon the waters: for thou shalt find it after many days.

We all seem to have needs—needs we perceive must be met by obtaining material goods. And, the more material goods we obtain, it seems the more we need. When we "up level" our cars, we need more money to pay the monthly notes. When we get larger homes we need more money for the insurance and higher utility bills. Today, however, is a day of casting and blessing other people. Not because they deserve it, but because God has commanded us to do so. He has given us what we have, and none of us deserves His grace. Let this be the day when you look for an opportunity to bless someone else in the name of Jesus. Place your personal needs to the side. You will feel so much better if you do.

There is a great promise at the end of this verse. When we cast our bread upon the waters, which means to bless the Lord and the people who are a part of His world, we are assured we will find it after many days. A seed planted near a plentiful source of water will grow into a healthy, productive tree. Release your own seed, and watch God grow it into a bountiful harvest.

April 4th

Acts 20:35

I have shown you in every way, by laboring like this, that you must support the weak. And remember the words of the Lord Jesus, that He said, "It is more blessed to give than to receive."

I hear songs on the radio and sermons from the pulpit about how much people desire to be blessed by God. Well, if we really want to be blessed by God, doesn't it seem rational that we should be willing to do what the One we want to be blessed by tells us to do? (Now *that* was a mouthful!) Paul the Apostle spoke these words and he was a hard-working man. He labored as a tentmaker for his personal needs to be met, and he labored as a preacher of the Gospel for Jesus Christ. He tells us the pattern to follow and the steps to take if we really want to be blessed by God. He says, "It is more blessed to give than to receive." Most of us focus only on receiving more, but we need to learn the real joy of giving.

Don't wait for someone in need to ask you for something; go ahead and bless them, and watch the Lord change your own classification from barren to blessed. When we give, we align ourselves with God. And any time we align with God, something extremely good is bound to happen. Give and watch God give back to you.

April 5th

Psalm 3:3

But You, O Lord, are a shield for me, My glory and the One who lifts up my head.

We are not in this all alone. The Lord is a shield for us. He guards us and makes sure nothing can come upon us until it first passes His divine inspection. This does not mean that this or any other day will be problem free, but it does mean that God knows just where you are and exactly what you need. The shield of the Lord ensures that we are aware of His comfort. It gives us the source of reassurance we need during the assailing attacks launched by the devil against the people of God. The shield of the Lord also makes us aware of His correction. You may be wondering how this process works. At times, God is so gracious that He hides and corrects us behind His shield so that His chastisement of us will not be open to everyone around us. The shield of the Lord then makes us aware of His commitment–He is not going to leave us exposed to our troubles, but remains committed to us no matter what we face.

Approach this day knowing the Lord protects you with His shield and lifts your head so you can see the great things He has planned for your future.

April 6th
Psalm 3:4

I cried to the Lord with my voice, And He heard me from His holy hill.

God is listening, and He never ignores or disregards the cries and petitions of any of His children. At times, it will seem as though the Lord is silent, and we often wonder if He has forgotten about us. The truth that always helps me process these seasons is when I evaluate my own expectations from the Lord. There were times in the past when I made poor choices; I knew then that those plans were not God's will for my life and I wanted Him to be silent during those times. But when I was in agony, I wanted Him to respond to all my requests—quickly. The Lord allows us to cry out to Him as a means of showing us how futile it is to cry out to others who are totally inadequate at coming to our rescue.

Does it seem as though God does not respond to your petitions? Maybe you are not crying loud enough. He is still on His holy hill. Take time to steal away alone and be with the Lord. Pour your heart out to Him. He may not answer in the way or as quickly as you want Him to, but when He does, it will always be the right answer at the right time. He is on His holy hill waiting to hear from you right now.

April 7th
Psalm 3:5

I lay down and slept; I awoke, for the Lord sustained me.

In Psalm 121:4, we are told the Lord neither slumbers nor sleeps. The Lord never goes to bed and He never takes a nap. A friend of mine says God does not even have eyelids to blink with. The eye of the Lord is everywhere. I mention all this because it helps us understand He remains awake all day every day and every night. As a result, there is no need for His children to lose any sleep. A lack of sleep and the difficulty many have in getting a good night's sleep can be a serious matter and can negatively impact so many areas of our lives. Before you rest your head on the pillow, surrender all the day's cares and concerns totally to Him. Surrender, too, those of the next day. Remember, we have a shield that protects us. We have a God who hears our cries. Now it's time for us to rest safely and securely in His arms and sleep.

The Lord is our sustaining power. The word *sustain* means literally to lift up. In this case, God lifts us up, holds us in place, and keeps us from falling apart. What more could we ask for? Sweet dreams. Leave those cares in His hands. He is going to be up all night, so get some peace, sleep, and rest. Tomorrow will be another day for us to show the world His sustaining grace in our lives.

April 8th

Jeremiah 33:3

Call to Me, and I will answer you, and show you great and mighty things, which you do not know.

You have not seen all that God has in store for you. Your present season is one of "holding on." The Lord has great and mighty things—ones that have not yet been revealed to you. Anything gained too easily is appreciated too lightly. Call to Him. The promise from Him is that He will answer. Not only will He answer, but He will show you great and mighty things. We often miss experiencing God's great and mighty things because we settle for easily attained mediocre, weak things. While they may not be demonic things, they just may be that which God does not plan for your life. The key to understanding today's verse is held in the final words: "...which you do not know." The Lord has things in store for you—things about which you know nothing just yet. Here is where our faith in Him must be strong. I always receive hope and clarification when I ask myself, "Am I willing to settle for the first thing that comes along, or do I have enough faith to wait for God's best for my life?" The answer is a no-brainer to me!

Don't settle for good when best is attainable, and don't settle for the right-now when mighty things from God are moving in your direction. God's best is worth the wait.

April 9th

Daniel 1:9

Now God had brought Daniel into the favor and goodwill of the chief of the eunuchs.

God is able to give favor to His people even in some unfavorable circumstances. In our verse for today, Daniel has been taken away from his homeland. He has been separated from family and friends. In spite of it all, we read that God brought Daniel into favor. Look carefully at the verse again. The Lord brought Daniel into the favor and goodwill of the chief of the eunuchs. If Daniel had never been carried away from his homeland, he would never have been escorted into what would be God's best for his life. Perhaps God has *you* at this point in your life. Don't complain about your present condition. Celebrate your position. That person, the one you think is trying to harm you emotionally and financially, just may be the person God uses to bestow His favor upon you. If you move too soon and relocate without God's approval, you could quite possibly miss your favor from God.

Now let's make it a real good today with this bit of information from the verse. The favor of God and the goodwill of the Lord was brought into Daniel's life from the "...chief of the eunuchs." God used the person at the top to be a blessing to Daniel. Since the Lord did it for him, He can do it for each of us, too. Take your eyes off your circumstances, and get prepared for the awesome favor of God.

April 10th
Psalm 73:26

My flesh and my heart fail; But God is the strength of my heart and my portion forever.

There is no need to worry or be troubled about any area of your life where you feel you have encountered or experienced a breakdown. We have a Heavenly Father who makes up for every one of our failures. The automobile I drive has an "Extended Factory Warranty." This gives me a calm assurance in the event a warning light comes on or when there is a temporary malfunction. The Lord has given every one of His children an "Extended Heavenly Warranty"—paid for in full over two thousand years ago at Calvary by His Son Jesus Christ. All we need to do is to take our broken, fractured, and wounded lives to Him in prayer, and He will make all of the necessary repairs. So, if your bodily "warning light" has come on or your heart is experiencing some malfunction, there is no need to worry or fret. The Lord is our strength and our portion—on not just a temporary basis, but forever.

The Lord does not give us a loaner or substitute life to make it through hard times. But he walks with us every step of the way. He travels with us moment by moment and makes the necessary adjustments. This verse gives us the good news that we can live victoriously over whatever we are confronted with both internally and externally.

April 11th

Mark 2:5

When Jesus saw their faith, He said to the paralytic, "Son, your sins are forgiven you."

I hope you agree with me when I say we live in a time when most people only want to use their faith to make their lives better or to remove any difficulties they may be experiencing. In today's verse we see the opposite: We see how the faith of four men helped the sick man among them receive exactly what he needed from Jesus without asking the Lord to do anything for them personally. This just may be the season when the Lord presents opportunities for you to use your faith to help ease the pain of others and redirect your attention from those issues you feel need resolving in your life. These men acted compassionately. They picked their friend up and took him to Jesus. They worked collectively; everybody played their part. They worked courageously; they climbed to the top of the house with their sick friend. At that, Jesus gave the paralytic the cure he needed for his condition.

The Lord will present opportunities for you throughout this day to show your compassion. Lift someone with a kind word. You will have an opportunity to work collectively with other believers. When that happens, don't try to do it all by yourself; the assignment is too heavy. You will be presented with the chance to show your Christian courage by doing jobs that don't have "easy" attached to them. When you do your part by faith, watch the Lord bring on the cure and the change that is needed in the lives of people who are hurting.

April 12th

Mark 2:11

I say to you, arise, take up your bed, and go to your house.

After the Lord frees you from the pain of your past and delivers you from the shackles of your old surroundings, don't make the mistake of lying back down in that same old environment. Get up, pick up, look up, and move up. Jesus is speaking to you today. He is saying, "I have delivered you; I have set you free, and I have eliminated the shackles of your past; now it's time for you to accept personal responsibility for moving forward." Jesus has done for us what we could not. And now, it is time for us to do that which we can. The friends of the man Jesus speaks to in our verse for today had brought the man to Jesus. Now that the man is healed, he is able to walk on his own.

The Lord does not want us to walk empty handed. He tells the man to take up his bed, which the man then used as his testimonial badge. Everywhere the man went, he was able to tell people who saw him with his bed what the Lord Jesus had done in his life. Leave your old environment, but don't leave behind the testimonial badge. Jesus wants you to move forward–He now has a new and better assignment for you in the future.

April 13th
John 1:29

The next day John saw Jesus coming toward him, and said, "Behold! The Lamb of God who takes away the sin of the world!"

I've got good news for you. No, wait, that's too restrained. I have *great* news for you! Jesus is moving in your direction. In our verse for today, John the Baptist, forerunner of Jesus Christ, makes an announcement upon seeing Jesus move in his direction. Today, more than 2,000 years later, our faith helps us realize that Jesus is *still* moving in the direction of His people. If you have been feeling lonely and forsaken, those feelings are about to change. Jesus is just waiting for you to open your eyes of faith and embrace Him into your heart. Don't just welcome Him when things seem to be rocky and turbulent–he wants to reside as a permanent resident at all times.

John was expecting Jesus; he was excited about Jesus; and he embraced Jesus. The Lord always finds joy when he resides in places where His people love and treasure His company. Make your heart one of those places and watch how that loneliness evaporates moment by moment.

April 14th
Hebrews 11:1

Now faith is the substance of things hoped for, the evidence of things not seen.

People who do not have a personal relationship with Jesus Christ live by a totally different set of standards than those by which people of faith do. Those who are unsaved must first *see* things in order to believe in their existence and reality. As Christian believers, we don't need to see to believe; we first believe, then our faith in God allows us to see at His own set time. Faith in God is to simply believe in the promises of God. This is one reason why it is vitally important for us to have a level of educated insight concerning what God says to us in the Bible. It is impossible to believe in the promises of God if we don't even know what those promises are. Don't allow what you see throughout this day to have a greater impact upon you than what God has said and promised in His Word. No matter how the odds may seem to be stacked against you, fear not; your faith and His power can conquer every one of them.

Faith is not a blind leap into the dark just hoping something good will happen. Rather, faith is a step into the light walking with full confidence and knowing that God has everything working together for His glory and for your good. Make this a faith-filled day.

April 15th

Hebrews 11:3

By faith we understand that the worlds were framed by the word of God, so that the things which are seen were not made of things which are visible.

I hope you agree with me when I say most, if not all, of us do not walk out of our homes each morning fearing that the earth will crumble beneath our feet. Perhaps you are wondering what that statement has to do with our inspiration for the day. In reality, everything! Just as we put full trust in God to hold up the earth beneath our feet each day, we must also trust Him to hold up all of His children who walk on top of what He has created. His word spoke this world into existence, and His word is what holds our lives in place. He has framed the earth and all that is directly and indirectly connected to it, and He has the same power to make sure that each one of His children has everything we need.

Remove from your mind your fear about what you think you need that you cannot yet see. God made the world you live in from nothing; surely He is able to handle whatever problems you face by bringing into your life just what you need when you need it the most.

April 16th

Hebrews 11:6

But without faith it is impossible to please Him, for he who comes to God must believe that He is, and that He is a rewarder of those who diligently seek Him.

Have you ever heard someone make an amazingly truthful, insightful statement and then thought to yourself, "Wow, I wish I had said that"? Well, I have, and one time in particular had to do with an insight I received concerning today's inspirational verse. Many years ago, while preaching from this passage, Reverend John Bowie I said, "The reason it is impossible to please God without faith is because faith is the only thing God does not have and does not need." When we bring our faith to the Lord we give to Him all of our trust. God, on the other hand, does not need to trust in anyone because He is self-sufficient–the proper term is *sovereign.* When we begin our relationship with the Lord, at least three things must take place. We must believe in His *existence.* We must believe in His *effectiveness.* We must believe in His *endurance.*

This day should be focused on pleasing the Lord and not about pleasing ourselves. The best way to do that is to bring all our faith and trust to Him, and then watch Him reward us for diligently seeking Him. If you have not found everything you feel you need from God, keep seeking Him with a diligent heart. He has your reward in His hand.

April 17th
Romans 6:23

For the wages of sin is death, but the gift of God is eternal life in Christ Jesus our Lord.

Whenever we, as children of God, hear the word *sin*, sadness and guilt automatically come into our minds, as they very well should. But our inspirational verse for today gives us some much needed hope about what the Lord has done to cover and forgive us of our sins. Let's get things straight, first. We are all guilty and deserve nothing more than the punishment of God. But because of His amazing grace, He has abundantly blessed us–not just here on this earth, but also by securing our eternity. Consider the word *wages*. This word causes me to think of the pay I receive for work I have done. Paul makes us aware of the fact that the devil works us our entire lives to live in sin. The devil then pays us off in death and causes our eternal separation from God. But Jesus Christ, in the very moment we accept Him, cancels our sin tab and gives us eternal life. He does not place us on trial or probation; instead, we are assured of living with Him forever. This is absolutely amazing. In the words of my mother Mrs. Lucy Brackins, "Now, who wouldn't serve a God like that?"

You may have failed in the past, but this is a day of recovering from those sinful errors and preparing to live forever with the King of glory. Don't take His grace for granted, but live daily for His glory.

April 18th
Galatians 6:9

And let us not grow weary while doing good, for in due season we shall reap if we do not lose heart.

Most people typically weary of doing things that are pleasing to God before tiring of those activities that dishonor and disrespect Him. It is just a part of our human nature to turn and go back to some of the very things that caused us harm, those from which the Lord has delivered us. In our scripture for today we are told to not grow weary while we do good. Doing good pleases God. When we strive to please the Lord, however, there will always be opposition from the devil. The deceiver wants to delay us, defeat us, depress us, and he even attempts to destroy us.

When you feel attacks from the devil, be steadfast in two things: Don't give in, and don't give up! Your season of reaping the rewards for the labor you have done is just around the next corner. A mother giving birth must keep breathing, pushing, and pressing through the pain. The final product will be worth it all. Don't lose heart. Your season of reaping is on the way.

April 19th

Titus 2:1

But as for you, speak the things which are proper for sound doctrine.

The Lord wants us to always be mindful of the words we allow to come out of our mouths, especially when those words are related to His Church, His Kingdom, and His Word. Be careful to not allow things you hear other people say which are not Bible-based become part of your everyday vernacular. Before you attempt to speak for the Lord, make sure you are speaking what He has already spoken.

Let this be a day you speak words of *edification,* to build up those with whom you come into contact. Let this be a day you speak words of *exaltation,* or quote or read from one of the Psalms about the majesty of God. Let this be a day of *expansion.* Ask the Lord to use what comes out of your mouth to help enlarge the Kingdom of God rather than turn people away from a desire to get to know Jesus Christ. Speak those words which are proper for sound doctrine, and God will be pleased.

April 20th
Philemon 1:18

But if he has wronged you or owes anything, put that on my account.

Tucked away in the latter half of the New Testament is a great little book called *Philemon.* Paul writes to this brother concerning a man who had wronged him before he surrendered his life to Jesus Christ. At the time of the letter, the man who had caused Paul's pain had become a born-again Christian, and Paul was seeking to heal and restore their relationship with each other. He goes as far as to tell his brother, "Whatever my friend owes you, put that on my account." This may just be the day the Lord wants us to take our eyes and focus off what we feel we need, and focus instead on helping to heal broken relationships we see all around us. Reach out to people who were once close to each other but who allowed differences to separate them. It matters not who was right and who was wrong. Just tell them you want to do in some small way in their lives what Jesus has done in all our lives in a grand way: bring about healing and reconciliation.

Don't try to fix the problem; just focus on reconnecting their lives. Oh, and by the way, this works regardless of if you are the hurt person in the relationship or the one who caused the hurt. Jesus still heals broken hearts and broken relationships.

April 21st
1 Peter 3:8

Finally, all of you be of one mind, having compassion for one another; love as brothers, be tenderhearted, be courteous.

Your acts of genuine kindness and love throughout this day can mean more to people who are hurting than you will ever know. On a daily basis we come into contact with people who are emotionally wounded, mentally bruised, and on the verge of completely giving up on life. Don't focus on speaking nicely to only the people you feel deserve it. Show compassion to that person who may have been rude to you in the past. Use the water of God's love to douse the fire of their negative demeanor. Love them with the brotherly love of Jesus Christ.

Be tenderhearted; be courteous–you won't regret it, and God will bless your efforts. Don't forget: It's not about how they receive our love and compassion; it is about the fact that we obey the Lord and extend love and compassion to them. God will be pleased, and everything after that takes a back seat.

April 22nd

James 2:26

For as the body without the spirit is dead, so faith without works is dead also.

There has been a tremendous amount of debate concerning whether salvation is a free gift from God or if it can be attained by our good works. Allow me to simply respond to that confusion by saying: Salvation is a free gift from God that we cannot earn and we do not deserve. We do not work to be saved; we work because we love the One who has saved us and we work to bring glory to Him. Our inspirational verse for today informs us that just as a body cannot claim life if it has no spirit, we cannot claim our faith if we have no works as a sign of God's power working in and through us.

Faith is not designed to be admired; God has given us faith so that we may use it. Step out of your comfort zone. Allow the Lord the opportunity to honor His Word in your life. Then, when you do, don't give credit to the work you have done; instead, give glory to the One who has worked through you. Are you alive? Well, go out today and use your faith.

April 23rd
1Timothy 4:12

Let no one despise your youth, but be an example to the believers in word, in conduct, in love, in spirit, in faith, in purity.

People learn how to do what is wrong and displeasing to the Lord so much faster than they learn, or are willing to learn, how to do what is right. The reason people learn wrong so quickly is because they have so many examples of wrong to follow. The Lord presents you with a challenge to break that cycle today. Don't worry about what everyone else is doing or not doing. Take the lead. Even if you are a young convert—perhaps saved for just a few weeks, months, or years—"Let no one despise your youth..." Set a good example in not just your actions but, more importantly, your reactions. People are paid to be good actors, but Christians are saved to be holy reactors. Allow the love of God and the life of Jesus Christ to be heard and seen in your words, conduct, compassion, sensitivity, faith, and in the purity of your lifestyle.

Whether you realize it or not, someone is always watching you. Lead them in the right direction; this is the day God wants someone to follow your Godly example.

April 24th

Philippians 3:14

I press toward the goal for the prize of the upward call of God in Christ Jesus.

The Lord's command and challenge for you today is to "Keep pressing forward," no matter the odds or the obstacles. Just keep on pressing. Make up your mind right now and know there will be things this day that you will have to press your way through. Those things were not designed to overwhelm you, overtake you, or out-power you. They are there to give you an opportunity to use your God-given power to overcome. The goal that exists before you is to live in such a manner that God is well pleased. Your journey does not head in a downward direction. Rather, you move toward a prize as you press your way on the upward call of God.

God allows what He allows to move you to higher ground. Isn't that good news? On level ground you can't see the whole picture, can you? But press on, and God will elevate you. Then you will understand things a bit better. This upward call is "in Christ Jesus." Being in Him means we do not climb all by ourselves.

April 25th

John 10:27

My sheep hear My voice, and I know them, and they follow Me.

Have you ever found yourself lost and in need of directions? Well, if you have, welcome to the club. Being lost can be a frightening experience, but it's not as bad when you know you have someone who is willing to lead you out of your confusing surroundings and to the place you are trying to get to. Jesus leads us with His voice, but not to those places where we want to go. Instead, he leads us to those places He has destined for our lives. People suffer when they are lost because they are unable to get to their intended destination: the places, people, and possessions they thought would make them happy and bring contentment to their lives. Most cars today come equipped with what is called a GPS system that gives voice driving directions. We never see the person whose voice we hear. (I hope you see what direction I'm headed in.)

If you are feeling lost and as though you are in a strange environment, slow your life down, pull over, and pray. Wait for the Lord to speak, and then follow His directions explicitly. He speaks even though we cannot see Him. If you can trust your vehicle's GPS to help you reach your destination, surely you can also trust your Jesus!

April 26th

Jeremiah 29:13

And you will seek Me and find Me, when you search for Me with all your heart.

Today's verse informs us of the fact the Lord wants us to passionately pursue Him at all times. When I first read it, the question that came to mind was, "Why would the Lord tell us to pursue Him as opposed to Him always being at our beck and call?" The Holy Spirit spoke to me in response and said, "Whenever a child of God pursues the Lord it automatically causes them to move farther and farther away from ungodly people and ungodly practices." When we seek the Lord we must begin our search for Him in areas of holiness. We should not be upset when we are told that God wants us to seek after Him. All He is doing is moving us a greater distance away from things that can bring irreparable harm to our lives.

In our seeking of the Lord, His promise to us is that we will find Him as long as we search for Him with all our heart. Don't half-heartedly search for God; give it all you have. Give Him your best praise, your best prayers, your greatest passion, and He will reveal His presence. What more could we possibly ask for?

April 27th
John 8:12

Then Jesus spoke to them again, saying, "I am the light of the world. He who follows Me shall not walk in darkness, but have the light of life."

Do things around you seem a bit cloudy or hazy in your life right now? Not certain about what decisions to make or what path to take? Who are you following? Allow me to make a strong recommendation. Jesus is not only the light of your life, the light of the city, state, and country, but He is the light of the whole world. There is no need for us to wander in a meaningless maze of mundane mediocrity when the Master wants to give meaning, purpose, and direction for our lives. He does not force us to follow Him; He gives us a choice. Let's make the decision to follow the Lord who does not need a light because He is the light.

He always leads us in the right direction and takes us to our destiny. Let's make this a light-filled day by following the Lord of Light, Jesus Christ Himself.

April 28th
Acts 11:9

But the voice answered me again from Heaven, "What God has cleansed you must not call common."

Too many of us make the mistake of getting bogged down in trivial matters that really have nothing to do with our spiritual growth. Many of these things wind up causing us to focus more on trying to please people than trying to please the Lord. In our inspirational verse for today, the Lord makes a correction in the mind and heart of Peter. He was more concerned about keeping the Old Testament Law which told him what not to eat than he was about receiving his blessing from the Lord who was making him aware of the fact that everything being given to him was already clean. The Lord does not want His people to be shackled with a lot of "don'ts" and things we cannot do. Instead, He wants our lives to be filled with positives and focused on what He has given us.

The best way to determine whether or not a person or possession should be part of our lives is relatively simple. We must ask ourselves where this person or possession came from. If it came from the Lord, He wants us to embrace it and enjoy it. If it did not come from the Lord, then immediately release it and remove it from your life. If you are not certain, don't touch it until God gives you clearance. Just enjoy and be thankful for the people and things you know He has added to your life.

April 29th

Colossians 1:17

And He is before all things, and in Him all things consist.

Even though you may have been feeling a little shaky lately, there is no need to worry or fear. God has assigned His Son Jesus the responsibility of holding everything in place. He has an impeccable track record and has never failed His Father or us in an obligation. Jesus was here before we arrived, He walks with us through our earthly journey, and He will still be here long after we are gone from this earth.

All things consist in Him. This simply means all things are held together by Him. I don't need to say any more; that would be tampering with perfection. Have a great and steady day.

April 30th
1 Thessalonians 5:18

In everything give thanks; for this is the will of God in Christ Jesus for you.

I know it may seem to be humanly impossible to thank God for everything that happens in our lives. But life becomes so much sweeter when we learn how to thank God while we are *in* everything. This is not a suggestion, a recommendation, or a proposal. This is a command. God's will for all His children is for us to trust Him no matter how bleak and dismal the surroundings. Don't just thank the Lord for things that are good and pleasant. Thank Him also for trusting you with trouble and for developing you through difficulties.

God's will is for us to be totally dependent on Him, totally trusting in Him, and always thankful to Him. Even if you are going through a painful period right now, just lift your hands toward Heaven and tell Him, "Thank you, Lord." Tell Him you don't understand it all but you do know that He has it all in control. Don't you feel better now? That is what gratitude will do for your heart.

PRAYER

Lord, We thank You with all our hearts for allowing us to see the end of the fourth month of this year. We were faced with many challenges during January through March, and we had no idea how You were going to work those matters out. They have not all been resolved, but we are still here and our hearts still depend on You. We love You and look forward to what You have in store for our lives during next few days, weeks, and months.

In Jesus' name,
Amen.

Melons of Mercy in May

May 1st
Psalm 32:8

I will instruct you and teach you in the way you should go;
I will guide you with My eye.

Whenever we feel a bit perplexed and unsure of which way to turn, it is human nature to be upset with ourselves. Well, don't be so hard on yourself. Lighten up; God is already aware of our human frailties and our intellectual weaknesses. The Lord wants us to learn the importance and the joy of waiting until we hear directly from Him before we make any decisions in our lives. Wouldn't life be wonderful if we never had to ask God to bail us out of a bad situation or relationship? Well, one of the ways we can watch that happen is by listening attentively to His instructions at all times. He wants to teach us, and we all know that teaching takes time. We often make the mistake of moving and traveling on the paths that we, ourselves, have selected. Our inspirational verse for today makes us aware of the fact that the Lord wants to teach and instruct us in the way we *should* go, which is not always the way we want to go.

We can depend on His eye to guide us, and we know that He holds our hand and we hold His; we will arrive at our destination safely and according to His timing. He is teaching. Are we paying attention and learning?

May 2nd

Psalm 143:8

Cause me to hear Your loving kindness in the morning, For in You do I trust; Cause me to know the way in which I should walk, For I lift up my soul to You.

Our inspirational verse for today is part of an urgent prayer and a plea from David for the Lord to provide guidance and direction for his life. The words "Cause me to hear Your loving kindness *in the morning*" really opened my eyes and blessed my heart. In the morning–before the day gets off to a rough and rocky start. In the morning–before we are bombarded with demands, responsibilities, and difficulties. In the morning–before we are confronted with news about wars, crimes, death, and disease. We desperately need to pursue the voice of God every morning.

Hearing from Him and talking both to and with Him automatically builds our trust in Him, and it removes the stress for us to plan and map out our own daily agendas. Surrender those cares to Him; lift up your soul and allow Him to embrace you with His presence and flood your heart with His peace. Wow, I feel better already. How about you? Now go out and make it a great day.

May 3rd
John 15:14

You are My friends if you do whatever I command you.

Okay, let's get right to the meat of the matter. Today's verse lets you know where the rubber meets the road. Is there any doubt in your mind about God not leading you to a place where you will encounter more harm than good? If not, why is it so difficult for many believers to totally trust and obey the Lord? We discover something incredibly heartwarming and encouraging in our inspirational verse for today. Jesus not only desires a salvation relationship with us, but He also desires to be our friends. Can you even wrap your mind around that? I can understand how we would want to be friends with Him; but Him wanting to be friends with us is almost beyond comprehension. He tells us, however, that the primary contingency for this friendship is for us to do whatever He commands us to do. That is why I asked that question earlier. We should have no problem obeying the Lord's commands, no matter how difficult they may seem to be.

His commands always lead to a brighter future, a bolder faith, and a better friendship with Him. Come on now, who could ask for anything more? Let's make this a day of proving our friendship to Jesus by following all of His commands for our lives.

May 4th

Matthew 5:5

Blessed are the meek, For they shall inherit the earth.

Many people make the mistake of confusing meekness with weakness. The first clarification to make about this misinformation is what Jesus says in our inspirational verse for today: that people who are meek are blessed. The Lord never told us to exhibit weakness, so these two cannot be one in the same. Meekness is simply *power under control.* One problem we face in the Body of Christ is using our God-given power for the wrong purposes and at the wrong times. We should never "flex our spiritual pecs" to harm or belittle another person or cause their self-esteem to take a nose dive. The Lord wants us to specialize in the areas of edification and encouragement. Many opportunities will present themselves today for you to display your God-given meekness. Use each and every one of them wisely and passionately. Always keep in mind the fact that when you use your meekness, you position yourself to be blessed in a greater way by our Savior, Jesus Christ.

Allow this to be a day of controlled power usage. There will be times when you will need to address matters of concern and correction with other people. Do it with *power under control.* If you do, Jesus already has a blessing with your name on it.

May 5th

Matthew 5:44

But I say to you, love your enemies, bless those who curse you, do good to those who hate you, and pray for those who spitefully use you and persecute you.

Let's be honest and admit that this is one of those verses many of us wish were not in the Bible. Okay, we said it. We got it off our chest. But the fact remains, it *is* in the Bible, and the truth of this commandment given to us by Jesus cannot be diluted, avoided, or wished away. When we love only the people who love us, and express kindness to people who are kind to us, we are simply using our human abilities. But at those times we extend love, forgiveness, mercy, and grace to those we know would not care less if we fell dead and left the face of the earth, God's love is being revealed through us. The devil expects us to retaliate, get even, and settle the score. But Jesus says, "Love your enemies, bless those who curse you, do good to those who hate you, and pray for those who treat you spitefully and persecute you." The bottom line to the whole matter is, the devil tells us to do one thing; Jesus tells us to do the complete opposite. Who are we going to listen to and obey?

I know this is not easy, but sacrifice never is. This day is not about taking the easy way out, but about showing the love of Jesus Christ to undeserving people, and bringing joy to the heart of our Heavenly Father. Love those you think don't deserve it–you just may be the only representative of the love of Jesus they will ever meet in their lives.

May 6th

Acts 3:6

Then Peter said, "Silver and gold I do not have, but what I do have I give you: In the name of Jesus Christ of Nazareth, rise up and walk."

I feel quite certain when I say most, if not all, of us feel we either need or could use more money. Often, we focus too much on what we don't have and completely overlook and ignore the vast spiritual wealth God has given us in the form of His power—power that is manifested when we use His name properly. In our inspirational verse for today, Peter shows us the importance of taking our minds off what we feel is lacking in our lives, and instead being ready at all times to use what God has given us. When Peter left his home that morning on his way to the House of the Lord, he was aware of at least two things: First, he did not have any money, and second, he had the power of Jesus Christ. Remove from your mental faculty those thoughts that surround the notions of lack and insufficiency. Now, focus on the fact that you are an over-comer, a victor, and a powerful, spirit-filled child of God.

We may not have all the money we think we need, but this verse shows us that we do have all the Jesus we and, in fact, someone whose life is in much worse condition than ours, truly needs. As we use what is in us to meet the needs of others, the Lord will also make sure all our needs are met.

May 7th
Psalm 9:9

The Lord also will be a refuge for the oppressed, A refuge in times of trouble.

Most of us pray more—a lot more—when we are going through seasons of struggle and suffering. Then, when those seasons have passed, our time of praying to the Lord becomes less and less. I have discovered that God often allows trouble to confront us because He has a great desire to hear from us, talk to us, and spend time with us. A refuge is a place where people in trouble run to and feel safe. Have you also noticed that, when the trouble is over and the storm ceases, we leave the shelter of the refuge and go right back to the norm of our daily routine? My challenge to you for today is to not just use God as a person to run to when trouble begins and then leave after the trouble has subsided. Instead, walk with Him daily; commune with Him moment by moment; and find joy basking in His presence.

When trouble comes it would be so much better to simply jump into the arms of God because we are already in His presence, rather than try to find Him because we have become distant from Him. If you are feeling oppressed, cheer up—He is your refuge. If you are in trouble, be encouraged—He is your strong tower. Now go out and make this a day filled with courage, confidence, and comfort, both in and with our Christ.

May 8th
Psalm 16:7

I will bless the Lord who had given me counsel; My heart also instructs me in the night seasons.

Too many of us simply settle for good advice when what we truly need is Godly counsel. The advice we receive even from well-intentioned, well-meaning people is often flawed, because it is based on their experiences or their personal feelings, rather than being based solely of the truth found in the Word of God. In our inspirational verse for today, the Psalmist not only appreciated the counsel He received from the Lord, but he also blessed and praised the Lord for it. This helped me understand the positive effectiveness of the Lord's counsel. It provided a foundation for every area and timeframe of his life. The counsel of the Lord penetrated his heart and helped him while he was going through some seasons of darkness in his life.

The Lord wants us to trust in His Word, and allow it to fill our hearts to the degree that it will instruct us even in our night seasons. There will be times when our nights last longer than from 9:00 p.m. to 11:59 p.m. We will have true "night seasons." But if our hearts are filled with the counsel of the Lord, we can handle them with full assurance and patience knowing that the morning is soon to come.

May 9th

Ecclesiastes 12:1

Remember now your Creator in the days of your youth, Before the difficult days come, And the years draw near when you say, "I have no pleasure in them."

The wise man Solomon speaks to us today about the importance of being mindful of God while things are well in our lives. The reason this is so important is because, if we neglect to establish a pattern of intimacy with the Lord, it will not be long before the devil tempts us with bitterness and resentment about life as a whole. When I first read this verse I erroneously assumed that he was speaking only to people who were biologically young. But the broader truth is found in the fact that we are being instructed to remember the Lord during the early days of our relationship with Him, no matter how young or old we were chronologically when we accepted Jesus Christ.

Many of us know people who have grown old and bitter, and who feel they have nothing worth living for. This sentiment occurs because they focused more on themselves than they did on Jesus Christ. In the song entitled "Because He Lives" there is a line that says, "And life is worth the living just because He lives." Allow this to be a day you remember the promises and protection of God, and one that leads you to giving constant praise to God. Difficult days will come, but remembering His goodness and His grace will take us through every one of them.

May 10th

Isaiah 6:1

In the year that King Uzziah died, I saw the Lord sitting on a throne, high and lifted up, and the train of His robe filled the temple.

I want to give you a snapshot of what our inspirational verse for today encompasses, and hopefully it will move the joy of your day to a paramount level. A man who was near and dear to the life of Isaiah had died. After Isaiah's period of grieving, he goes into the temple to worship the Lord. There, he was able to experience the Lord's presence at a level unlike anything he had ever experienced before. God has a way of allowing us to sense, and even spiritually see, His presence when we view Him through the pain of teary eyes. I want to encourage you today by signaling an important truth from this one verse. This episode took place in the year King Uzziah died. It was a *painful period* in Isaiah's life. The Lord was seated on a throne, high and lifted up. That was His *prominent position.* The train of His robe filled the whole temple. That was His *perfected presence.*

Whatever you face today, just remember, God is present during your most painful periods. He is seated in a prominent position (seeing everything that you can't). His presence is perfect. All you need to do is look up and get a glimpse of God, even if you have to view Him through teary eyes.

May 11th
Psalm 29:2

Give unto the Lord the glory due to His name; Worship the Lord in the beauty of holiness.

When we are confronted with perplexing issues in life, our tendency is to spend more time groaning about our problems than to give glory to our God who is able to lift us above and bring us through our problems. Our verse for today commands us to "Give unto the Lord the glory due to His name." How would you like to establish an excellent credit score with the Lord? I know you may be wondering what on earth I'm referring to. Well, the verse says there is glory "due," or "owed," to God. When we pay Him the glory we owe Him, our credit score goes up and He will approve our prayerful applications in a timely manner. Many of us suffer through seasons of overwhelming frustration because we have "past-due" glory bills with God. Allow this to be a day of worship, a day of praise, and a day filled with genuine Godly appreciation. Don't make pity payments or complaint compensations. Let's get caught up with the Lord on our *account of adoration.*

After all, it is much more pleasant to behold His beauty than to focus on the burdens that confront us. If we pay Him what we owe, He will take care of all of those other matters.

May 12th

Isaiah 6:3

And one cried to another and said: "Holy, holy, holy is the Lord of hosts; The whole earth is full of His glory."

Today, share your praise report with someone. Tell a friend about the great things God has done, is doing, and, according to His Word, that He has promised to do. In our inspirational verse for today, the angels were sharing with each other about the holiness of God. Since the angels were able to tell each other about God's greatness, and they have never been redeemed, then surely the saints of God should be sharing our testimony with one another.

I declare this to be a no-complaint day. Let's just fill the entire earth with His glorious testimonies. The glory is already there; He just wants to use His people to bring it to the attention of others who may not know Him and who desperately need Him. Don't let Him down. Have a "glory-filled" day!

May 13th

Psalm 46:1

God is our refuge and strength, A very present help in trouble.

In truth, most of us don't realize how much we desperately need the Lord–that is, until we desperately need the Lord. Even though we often take His presence for granted, He never takes His protection of us lightly or flippantly. Our verse for today informs us of the constant, ever-present help of our God. Throughout this day you may find yourself in some depleted situations. You may feel humanly drained, weak, and frail. But just know that God is there to fill you during your times of weakness. As you face the opportunities and the oppositions of life, remind yourself over and over of the promises God has made to you. Don't allow the voice of the devil to drown out the voice of God.

God is a "very present help in trouble." If you feel as though you might be in trouble, take heart. God's presence was there even before you made your arrival to it. He simply uses what you are experiencing to draw you closer to Him.

May 14th
2 Timothy 1:7

For God has not given us a spirit of fear, but of power and of love and of a sound mind.

Whenever I check my emails, I am careful not to open any messages from addresses I do not know or am expecting any communication from. I do this is because, if I open every message, one or more of them could contain a virus and cause my computer to crash. I simply send those unrecognizable communications to spam and delete them. Whenever our minds receive messages of fear, weakness, bitterness, and confusion, I strongly suggest we not open those messages, because they have the potential to spread a venomous virus through our lives. Delete those thoughts of defeat. Even if they keep coming, show the devil that every time he sends one, you are going to delete it. Do this, and keep moving forward to receive God's best for your life.

We cannot prevent the thoughts that enter our minds, but we can determine what actions we will take on them. Those messages of negativity simply represent satan's ploy in trying to hinder us from moving to the level of spiritual excellence where the Lord desires we abide. You have the power to overcome the devils' plots; you have love to overcome his animosity; and you have the mind of Christ to help you overcome whatever confusion he sends in your direction.

May 15th
1 Peter 2:2

As newborn babes, desire the pure milk of the word, that you may grow thereby.

I am confident you will agree with the following statement: If we do not eat, we cannot grow. This is true in the natural and physical realms as well as in the spiritual realm. In our devotional verse for today, Peter portrays the image of a hungry baby who, in order to survive, has a desire and a craving for milk. Without realizing it, what the baby craves will help it not only survive, but also to thrive and grow. On a scale of one to ten, how much do you crave the Word of God? Peter wants us to know how vitally important it is to our spiritual health that we have and maintain a healthy, consistent diet of the Word of God. His Word is *pure*, His Word is filled with *promises*, and His Word is *powerful*.

When we don't eat, we get weak and become frail. We allow ourselves to be defeated by the devil because we have no energy. Fasting from the Word of God is something we should never do. But many of us do it without even recognizing it. Adjust your appetite and fill yourself with His Word on a daily basis. By the way, don't worry about overeating; you will never get too full.

May 16th
Luke 10:2

Then He said to them, "The harvest truly is great, but the laborers are few; therefore pray the Lord of the harvest to send out laborers into His harvest."

Few, if any, will not agree when we say our world is in a terrible, sin-infested condition. Yet it is also true that few of us spend little-to-no time praying and asking the Lord to use us and to send others as evangelists to win the lost to Jesus Christ. Many of us love to complain about the condition of things, but we seldom offer ourselves as solutions to changing those conditions. Jesus gives us a command in our inspirational verse for today. The command is to make some much-needed adjustments in our prayer lives. Instead of praying for things we feel we need to make our lives better and more comfortable, we should be asking the Lord to partner us with people who are willing to share the sins.

Today, share your faith with another. Encourage other Christians to join you in sharing their faith. Just know that people will be watching our ways to see if they match our words about Jesus Christ.

May 17th
1 Samuel 16:7

But the Lord said to Samuel, "Do not look at his appearance or at his physical stature, because I have refused him. For the Lord does not see as man sees; for man looks at the outward appearance, but the Lord look at the heart."

Because we have trouble living up to the expectations of other people, discouragement often sets in and overwhelms us. This can be frustrating, especially when, in our minds, we never seem to measure up to their standards. The Lord wants all of those thoughts to be removed from our minds this very moment. Our main concern should be to make sure the Lord is pleased with our motives, our efforts, and the purity of our hearts. Many appear to be able to fill the responsibility, just as the oldest son of Jesse in our inspirational verse for today did. Samuel was about to anoint him as the king of Israel based on his appearance. But the Lord had to correct that thought pattern. You need to be encouraged today, because even though you may not look as though you have all it takes for your assignments and opportunities, God lives inside you.

People look at the fading façade of our outer appearance, but God looks at the purity of our hearts. After all, He is really the One we should strive to please.

May 18th
Psalm 111:2

The works of the Lord are great, Studied by all who have pleasure in them.

When we take the time to consider the vastness and the superiority of this world that our God has created, it is mind baffling. His works are great! However, the truth that truly endears me to the Lord is when I also consider the fact that this world is fading and passing, but we are His eternal children. Since He went to great detail in making this world, then surely He invested so much more into each of us.

When we realize the greatness of our God, we should study, ponder, and meditate on the great things He has done. This will lift us to a new level of pleasure both with Him and in Him. Don't be one who just gazes at the stars; instead, be grateful for the stars and everything our Heavenly Father has placed beneath them. Our Lord has done great works. Now go out and have a great day in this great world He has created.

May 19th

Proverbs 9:9

Give instruction to a wise man, and he will be still wiser; Teach a just man, and he will increase in learning.

We need to ensure we never close our hearts or our minds from good, sound, Godly wisdom. The Lord desires to surround us with people who can help us during critical decision-making periods in our lives. We reveal how wise we are by our ability to surround ourselves with other Godly-wise people. Notice, I said, "Godly-wise" people. A person may have intelligence but still lack Godly wisdom. We can determine a person's level of Godly wisdom by their conversation, their conduct, and their commitment. All three areas must be filled with Biblical holiness. When we are offered advice from people filled with Biblical holiness, we would do well to embrace and heed it. Their wisdom shared with us leads to a greater level of wisdom being birthed in us.

Leave your heart and mind open—not for new truth, but for Godly clarity on the truth that has been here since this world was created. It will lead to greater levels of learning, which automatically lead to a greater level of living.

May 20th
John 3:3

Jesus answered and said to him, "Most assuredly, I say to you, unless one is born again, he cannot see the kingdom of God."

Our main responsibility as Christians is to be not politically correct, but Biblically correct. In our inspirational verse for today Jesus speaks directly to Nicodemus and tells him that man's greatest need is to be "born again"—not a spiritual awakening, not a change in behavior, not even to become more charitable. Instead, we need to make sure the world and every person we come in contact with knows Jesus Christ is the only way to see the kingdom of God. Don't be timid and don't be ashamed to share the truth about our Savior. You may not win any popularity contests, but you will bring great delight to the heart of our Heavenly Father.

Without being rude, offensive, or compassionless, use this day to share the real truth about God's Son who died and was raised from the grave for our sins.

May 21st

Proverbs 11:28

He who trusts in his riches will fall, But the righteous will flourish like foliage.

Many people make the mistake of thinking that if they just had more money, life would be great and all their problems would cease. Nothing could be further from the truth. In our inspirational verse for today, the wise man Solomon offers each of us some profound advice. God has intended for His people to place all our trust in Him, and not in those things He blesses us with. It is easy to become more attached to what comes from God's hand than to what connects us with God's heart. Our money and possessions do not sustain us during those crucial periods in our lives. Rather, the righteousness of God which has been given to us through His Son Jesus Christ upholds us and even causes us to flourish. The thinking behind this statement lies in the fact that righteousness serves as the root for every believer. When we have roots of righteousness, we will bear fruits of stability.

Thank God for the things He has added to your life. They are gifts from Him. Just don't become distracted from Him by your problems, possessions, or personal pleasures.

May 22nd
John 2:5

His mother said to the servants, "Whatever He says to you, do it."

Many of us feel we must be able to understand and rationalize what the Lord tells us to do before we are willing to obey Him explicitly. This is nothing but an attempt by the devil to prevent us from positioning ourselves for the Lord to work a miracle through us, for us, with us, or right before us. I write today's devotion while traveling on a plane from Houston, Texas, to New York City. I was told to fasten my seat belt, turn off my cell phone, store my carry-on luggage, and put away my laptop (I'll come back to that in a moment). I obeyed all the commands that were given because I knew the pilot and flight attendants had my safety and well-being in mind. I am not an expert in the laws of aeronautics, so I obeyed the people who have a greater level of expertise. In our inspirational verse for today, Mary the mother of Jesus totally surrenders to Him with this advice to the men who were serving at this wedding feast in Cana of Galilee: "Whatever He says to you, do it." The Lord just may challenge your faith today with a task you don't understand or to which you might not be willing to submit.

My advice to you is the same as the advice Mary gave: Whatever He tells you to do today, just do it, and then watch and wait for Him to reveal His Master plan. Oh, by the way, the only reason I'm using my laptop is because after we were airborne, the flight attendants gave me permission to do so. The Lord will let you know when the time is right for you to return to your regular activities. Until then, just obey His commands.

May 23rd
John 7:5

For even His brothers did not believe in Him.

Doubt and discouragement often come from the very people we should be able to look to for support and encouragement. Do you ever feel forgotten or overlooked by people you thought would be there when you needed them most, but they were not? Well, cheer up. I have great news. You are in the same company as Jesus Christ. The Son of God had brothers who grew up with Him, were raised in the same home with Him, yet did not completely believe in Him. Jesus did not allow their doubts about Him to discourage, dissuade, or defeat Him—we need to learn to do the same thing. The devil knows that if he is going to discourage us, he must use someone close to us.

The Lord, however, makes us aware of the fact that He is closer to us than any family member will ever be. His love for us is unconditional, and His plan for us is unstoppable. Don't allow anything or any person's doubt about your relationship with the Lord and your assigned responsibilities from the Lord stop you from representing the Lord.

May 24th

Psalm 119:67

Before I was afflicted I went astray, But now I keep Your word.

I know it may seem and sound ironic, but the truth of the matter is that God often allows trouble to become part of our lives to keep us from harming ourselves and to move us closer in our relationship with Him. No one welcomes trouble; no one in their right mind prays for difficulties; and no one looks forward to seasons of problematic situations. But our inspirational verse for today informs us of at least two benefits that come into our lives as a result of the troubles God allows. First, God keeps us from going even further astray from Him. Trouble has a way of stopping us. Whenever people fail to stop their ungodly behavior, it is only because the trouble has not become severe enough to them. The second thing trouble does is move us into a closer relationship with the Word of God. His Word shows us where we have gone wrong, and His Word also shows us how to get back on the path of righteousness.

Whatever problems confront you today, instead of asking God to move them, ask Him to reveal what needs to be removed and what needs to be added to your life. If God has allowed it, He will teach you while you are in it, and He will see you through it.

May 25th
Matthew 5:10

Blessed are those who are persecuted for righteousness' sake,
For theirs is the kingdom of Heaven.

Whenever we strive to live Godly, holy, moral lives, we seem to be the brunt of people's jokes, and we receive a lot of criticism and judgment. Jesus has already informed us things would be this way, so we should not be surprised when it happens. One of the main reasons this occurs is because people have distorted value systems and priorities. They feel we should blend in with the crowd when the truth of the matter is that we are preparing ourselves for Heaven. When you pray before you eat, refuse to go to Happy Hour, and never miss weekly Bible Study or Worship, people will say negative things about you. Just be encouraged, receive it with a smile, and keep your focus on your eternal destination, for yours is "the kingdom of Heaven."

In this verse, Jesus was referring to actual life-threatening, life-ending persecution. We, on the other hand, deal with mere criticism and verbal disapproval. Just make sure the attacks come as a result of your righteousness, and not due to unrighteous behavior. God will be honored and you will be rewarded. Now, go out and make it a righteous day.

May 26th
Luke 5:28

So he left all, rose up, and followed Him.

Matthew Levi, the man who wrote the Gospel that bears his name, shows us what a life committed to Jesus Christ should really include. In our inspirational verse for today, he has just been confronted by Jesus to come and follow Him. As a result, he does three basic things which should be incorporated into every believer's life: 1) he "left all," which represented his *elimination* of the past; 2) he "rose up," which represented his *elevating* his position; and 3) he "followed Him," which represented his *embracing* of God's purpose for his life. What have you left behind to follow Jesus more closely? What positions have you changed in your life as a sign you will not allow the devil to walk over you while you are horizontal when the Lord wants you to live vertically in victory? Have you truly embraced God's purpose for your life, or do you spend time asking Him to bless your plans?

This day is a day of spiritual readjustments. This is a day of living according to His will, not ours. Jesus is worth whatever we leave behind to follow Him. He will show us His best for our lives only when we rise up and make a commitment to follow Him. He always leads us on paths of His divine development and purposeful productivity.

May 27th
Psalm 113:3

From the rising of the sun to its going down The Lord's name is to be praised.

The Lord's name is to be praised—all day and all night. This should be the mindset and the practice of every child of God. Praise should be the dominant factor in our lives—not just when we are in corporate worship with other people, but all day, every day. We don't always have to be overtly emotional to praise the Lord. We can honor Him with praise by taking a few moments out of every hour just to tell Him how much we love and esteem Him, and how thankful we are to Him for just saving us and protecting us.

When you awake each morning, spend time praising the Lord even before the sun rises. Map out a few moments during lunch as your personal praise time. Then before you lay down to sleep, don't just ask Him for a good night's rest, but praise Him for His keeping of you all day long. Your life will be better, and your soul will be lifted to a new level of spiritual elevation.

May 28th
Matthew 7:18

A good tree cannot bear bad fruit, nor can a bad tree bear good fruit.

Many are familiar with the old proverb that says, "The fruit does not fall far from the tree." The proverb implies that whatever falls off a person's life is a good indicator of what that person is truly made of. Those of us who are children of God must keep in mind our responsibility to always bear good fruit. When the things that fall from our lives look more like the world than our Savior, we need to check our connection. The Lord wants us to bear fruit of righteousness and holiness so that people around us will know that we are connected to a holy and a righteous God.

This includes our actions, our reactions, our words, and our thoughts. Ask the Lord to fill your life with His presence so that you may bear good fruit to His glory. When people see us, they need to know beyond a shadow of a doubt that we are connected to the life-producing tree, Jesus Christ Himself.

May 29th

Psalm 119:71

It is good for me that I have been afflicted, That I may learn Your statutes.

God has a way of producing something good out of every bad situation. We don't always see it or understand it when it takes place, but He reveals it to us mostly after we have been in it for a while or after we come out of it. In our inspirational verse for today, the Psalmist is honest enough to admit that the afflictions he experienced were actually good for him. He gives testimony about what I like to call the "advantage of afflictions." There were benefits in his afflictions. There were behavior changes from his afflictions. There were blessings after his afflictions had ended. The great blessing he received was not a new car or home, or any material possession, but rather an elevated understanding of the Word of God.

Most of us take fresh insight from God's Word too lightly. But the Lord allows us to go through stormy seasons just to reveal to us principles and promises in His Word that we have not yet discovered before the trouble arrived. Your afflictions are not designed to move you further from God, but to bring you *closer* to Him and His Word.

May 30th

Luke 5:32

I have not come to call the righteous, but sinners, to repentance.

Are you feeling somewhat guilty about things you did that were contrary to God's will for your life? If so, worry not; all hope is not lost. I've been in your shoes as has every person ever born on this planet except for Jesus Christ. I do not want to make light of our sins, because all unrighteousness is repulsive to the Lord. But I do have good news. Jesus came looking for people just like us. He did not come to earth for those who feel as though they have no need of forgiveness and no need of a savior. Rather, He came for those of us who recognize that we are sinners and are willing to repent and accept His forgiveness. Perhaps one of the most difficult things for us to do is to forgive ourselves. The Lord wants us to know that when we confess and repent our sins, He will forgive and cleanse us of all those sins.

He came looking for us, and He knew He would find us. His heart is filled with acceptance, and He wants us to live free from the painful mistakes and sins of our past, and walk in the newness of life. Jesus is *calling.* If we *confess*, He will *cleanse.*

May 31st
Matthew 7:11

If you then, being evil, know how to give good gifts to your children, how much more will your Father who is in heaven give good things to those who ask Him!

May 31 is a special day to me; it was my father's birthday. He was a man who sacrificed for his family, loved his family, and led his family in worship. My father prayed for us and with us, and he provided for us. My father died and went to live in the presence of the Lord in June 2002. He was a Godly father, but not a perfect man, as not one of us is. Even with his imperfections, he always provided for his family. In our inspirational verse for today, Jesus tells us that if evil people provide for their own children, how much more will our Heavenly Father provide and meet every need in the lives of His children? Many of us spend a lot of time worrying about how we are going to meet our needs. In reality, we will never be able to. That is God's job. Perhaps you are unable reflect on fond memories of your biological father; maybe you don't even know him. No need to worry; the Lord has stepped up to the plate to fill that void.

Whatever you need, ask Him. If what you desire is according to His will, He will grant it in His own timing. Thank Him for being there not just when you needed Him, but for never leaving you even when you took His presence for granted.

PRAYER

Lord, we praise and we bless Your holy name. Our hearts are lifted to You in genuine gratitude. We thank You for bringing us through this fifth month of the year and we look forward to Your future blessings and Your protection. Please forgive us if we failed to take advantage of any opportunities to represent You. Please forgive us if our lives brought shame to Your name in any way. Now prepare us for the things You have in store for our lives.

In Jesus' name,
Amen.

Juice of Joy in June

June 1st

Proverbs 27:1

Do not boast about tomorrow, For you do not know what a day may bring forth.

The wise man Solomon encourages us to make sure we learn the importance of taking and living our lives one day at a time. We have no right to boast about anything over which we have no control. This verse warns us of the sin of bragging and becoming filled with pride about what we plan to do and how we feel we control our own future. The fact is, our lives are in God's hands. Solomon is by no means suggesting we fail to make plans, but he warns us of the danger of making those plans without consulting the Lord first. As you begin your day, there may be meetings and deadlines to accomplish. But you need to surrender those thing to God; He can handle them a whole lot better than you can.

When we acknowledge our dependence on Him, He has a way of giving us more than we expected and removing the trouble we thought we were about to encounter. We don't know what tomorrow holds, but we do know who holds all of our tomorrows, and that is really all that matters.

June 2nd
Philippians 3:7

But what things were gain to me, these I have counted loss for Christ.

In our inspirational verse for today, Paul acknowledges he was willing to lose what was once important to him so that Jesus Christ would be magnified through His life. Most people have only one question on their minds, “What am I going to get out of this?” Paul was willing to make a small sacrifice of his personal desires to allow the love of Christ shine through his life. This is a day when the Lord is going to give you an opportunity to place your personal desires on the back burner. People need to be able to look at our lives and see the sacrifices we are willing to make as a result of the great sacrifice Jesus made for us at Calvary. He died for us—all He asks in return is that we live for Him.

When we place our gains to the side, the eventual benefits reaped from Him will overshadow them into oblivion. Make this a day about His glory rather than your gain.

June 3rd

2 Thessalonians 3:16

Now may the Lord of peace Himself give you peace always in every way. The Lord be with you all.

At least two prominent things are capable of brightening each and every day of our lives. One is being assured of God's *presence*; the other is being aware of God's *peace*. Our inspirational verse for today gives us some very comforting and reassuring information. We are told that our peace comes from the Lord of peace. He is the One who controls all peace. He is willing to give His peace to us not just at isolated times, or on special occasions, but "...always in every way." This simply means His peace is available to us at all times and for every situation we may face. One thing we all need to do is make sure we have the peace of God while life is calm and tranquil, so we won't become frantic when things go wrong, as we know they surely will.

This verse also makes us aware of the fact that God offers us not only His peace, but He also offers all His children His presence. It is comforting just to know God is with us in spite of our faults, failures, and faithlessness. We may forget about Him, but He never forgets about any of us. This is going to be a great day because you are filled with His peace and surrounded by His presence.

June 4th

Romans 8:28

And we know that all things work together for good to those who love God, to those who are the called according to His purpose.

I know what you face may not seem good, may not feel good, and may not even look good. But today's inspirational verse informs us that everything we face works together for our good. God has a way of using what, to us, are horrific, negative incidents, and transforming them into opportunities for us to grow in our relationship with Him. Paul says we must know all things work for our good. This speaks to our *confidence* in the Lord. And to whom does this apply? It applies "...to those who love God..." Our confidence is based on our *compassion* for the Lord. The other important thing this verse helps us understand is that we have been *consecrated* for a purpose in the kingdom of God. That is, God has consecrated us for a specific purpose. Whenever He has an assignment for us, He always makes sure we are prepared and equipped to fulfill those assignments.

While what you encounter today may not seem good, feel good, or look good, be confident that it all works together for your good.

June 5th

Galatians 6:7

Do not be deceived, God is not mocked; for whatever a man sows, that he will also reap.

We hear a lot of talk these days about sowing and reaping, and much of it has to do with acquiring, amassing, and attaining material possessions. There is nothing wrong with desiring the best for our lives; but there *is* something wrong when we feel that is all there is to life. God is not pleased when, if we don't own a lot of stuff, we think we have failed. Our inspirational verse for today helps us realize there is another side to this matter of sowing and reaping. It has to do with our ability to recognize that whatever we invest into the kingdom of God will also determine what we receive back from the kingdom of God. Paul is warning us; in essence, telling us to not fool ourselves, for God is not to be ridiculed, taken for granted, or overlooked. He is aware of what we sow, and He allows our sowing to determine what we reap.

The Lord wants to use our lives as instruments of investing and sharing our best seeds into the work of the kingdom of God. Look for an opportunity today to bless someone who is doing a great job in promoting the work of the Lord. Don't wait to be asked to give; just plant the seed and watch God bring forth a great harvest in your life. After all, He has given much more to all of us than we have asked for, and surely more than we deserve.

June 6th
Proverbs 29:18

Where there is no revelation, the people cast off restraint; But happy is he who keeps the law.

Helen Keller was once asked if she could think of anything worse than being born blind. Her response was, "The only thing worse is to have sight with no vision." The wise man Solomon tells us in our inspirational verse for today that all of God's people need vision for their lives. But he also adds a disclaimer by noting that our revelations and visions should be based on the Law of God or the Word of God. Many people get frustrated when mapping out the plans for their lives. That is because they do so without consulting the Life-Giver, Jesus Christ. When our lives don't go according to plan, we cast off our restraints, which means we then do things that are not part of God's will, all simply in order to satisfy ourselves. Does this sound familiar?

Make sure this and every day that follows is filled with vision from God. When we do, we gain a level of internal joy and peace we cannot begin to explain or duplicate. When we get a good look at His Word, then His will becomes clear to us and our visions fall in line with His voice. Now go out and have a Godly, vision-filled day.

June 7th
Psalm 94:14

For the Lord will not cast off His people, Nor will He forsake His inheritance.

Those times of feeling alone, forgotten, and abandoned can be some of the most difficult periods a person experiences in their life. There is a part of our human nature that causes us to desire the attention and affection of at least one other person. We often make the mistake of going through life doing things in an effort to cause other people to like and appreciate us. When, in fact, we overlook the knowledge that we are loved, treasured, and appreciated by the greatest person we will ever come to know—God Himself. It does not matter what we have done, what we will do, or where we find ourselves right now; His love for us is unfailing. Today's inspirational verse makes us aware of the fact that the Lord will not cast off or discard His own people.

Even during painful periods in our lives when we have failed or disobeyed Him, He will never fail us, nor will He forsake us. There may be times today when you feel unappreciated. Quickly shake off those sentiments and focus on the fact that the God of the Universe is both proud and pleased to call you His child. He will never leave you.

June 8th

Psalm 94:17

Unless the Lord had been my help, my soul would soon have settled in silence.

Let's rearrange things a bit for today. First, place the challenges you face on hold for a while. And then, instead of using this time to receive more comfort and assurance from the Lord, we will take time to thank Him for the multitude of things He has already done for us. Notice the first clause of today's inspirational verse: "Unless the Lord had been my help..." Think about the many times you know the Lord has helped you and you were truly undeserving of His help. (If you are anything like me, then that includes *every* time He has helped, because I have never deserved it!) Without His help, our souls would have wasted away. Let's just praise and thank Him for being a source of constant help, a source of compassionate hope, and a source of corrective healing.

The good news from this verse lies in the fact that since He has done it before, we know He is well able to do it again. Rejoice in your soul right now for all the help He has already provided you. This will be your small way of thanking Him for not allowing your soul to settle in silence.

June 9th

Galatians 6:2

Bear one another's burdens, and so fulfill the law of Christ.

I have discovered that the best way for me to take my mind off my problems is for me to help someone else with theirs. In our inspirational verse for today, Paul admonishes us to help others with the loads they may be carrying. While there may be issues in your life which need to be resolved and settled, don't overlook the fact that there are people all around you whose burdens are twice as heavy as yours. When we help each other, we fulfill the command Jesus gave us that said we should love our neighbor as we love ourselves. Look for opportunities to help someone else with their issues today.

When we undergird others we also bring joy to the heart of Jesus Christ. That should be our greatest pursuit. Share words of comfort with someone whose heart is hurting. Take a few moments to listen to their struggles. Pray with them and for them, and then watch the Lord settle your issues while you help others with theirs.

June 10th

Galatians 6:5

For each one shall bear his own load.

Take a quick look back at yesterday's verse. Today's appears to be in contradiction to what Paul told us yesterday. In reality, though, they do not contradict each other; rather, they complement each other. Burdens are things we need help with, things that are too difficult for us to handle alone. Loads, on the other hand, are things for which we must take personal responsibility. We cannot expect others to do all the praying or sacrificing for us, or adjust all their plans just to make life more comfortable for us. Paul wants us to know that, even though we are not equipped to carry the *same* thing, we can all carry *some* thing.

Make sure you put forth an effort to do your part to advance and glorify the kingdom of God. The only way our spiritual muscles will grow and expand is for us to use them on a regular basis. Whatever load you have to carry, don't worry; you won't have to carry it alone. Jesus walks with you every step of the way.

June 11th

Matthew 10:39

He who finds his life will lose it, and he who loses his life for My sake will find it.

If you are over the age of 50 I'm sure you remember the expression "Finders keepers; losers weepers." Its meaning is fairly clear: Whenever someone finds something that does not belong to them, they can keep it; and if a person loses something that was initially theirs, they weep as a result of their loss. In our inspirational verse for today, Jesus completely reverses the order. He says those who seek to find their lives and live according to their own rules will one day weep because they will lose out in the end. But those of us who surrender our lives and hide our identity in Jesus Christ will find the true meaning and purpose God has for us. The Lord wants us to totally surrender to Him. We will never be able to satisfy ourselves because nothing this world has to offer will be able to fill that void.

At the time we lose ourselves in Him and for His sake, we discover the plan and the purpose He has with our name already written on it. Whisper a word of prayer to the Lord now, and ask Him to take full control not just of today's responsibilities, but every day from this day forward. This is when we really find out what great joy He has for all His children.

June 12th
2 Corinthians 5:21

For He made Him who knew no sin to be sin for us, that we might become the righteousness of God in Him.

Everything Jesus endured at Calvary was for us; He had absolutely nothing to gain personally from it. He died so that we would live. He suffered so that our burdens would be removed. He surrendered to the pain so that we could walk and live in victory. God placed our sin label on His Son Jesus Christ, who wore it and bore it without one word of complaint. All this was done so that we could transform from stained and sinful to righteous and redeemed. There is nothing we could or can do even now that will make us eligible for the righteousness of God. We have been made, declared, and proclaimed righteous by God, not because of our works, but because of God's grace. This should elevate our love for the Lord and increase our loyalty to Him. Take a moment to consider the fact that God lifted us from our lowest sinful condition and placed us on the highest plateau of righteousness–and we have absolutely nothing to offer Him in return.

Don't allow His sacrifice for you to be taken for granted. Live at a level that honors and pleases Him, and allow His love to be seen in everything you do and say.

June 13th
Philippians 2:9

Therefore God has highly exalted Him and given Him the name which is above every name.

There is power in the name of Jesus. There is passion in the name of Jesus. There is purpose in the name of Jesus. There is also promotion in the name of Jesus. Our God has given His Son a name which is above every other name. We should testify about His name. We should trust the person who has the name, and we should treasure His name and never use it lightly, flippantly, or in vain.

The closer we are to the man who has this name will determine our position in life. God has highly exalted Him, and when we are attached and committed to Him, we will also be exalted and lifted. Don't throw the name of Jesus around like you would the name of one of your old classmates or neighborhood friends. He is our Savior, our Lord, our King, and our God. His name is more valuable than any other name, and we should all treat both Him and His name accordingly.

June 14th
Proverbs 15:16

Better is a little with the fear of the Lord, Than great treasure with trouble.

We seem to be living at a time when most people, including the people of God, always desire more than they have. In our inspirational verse for today, the wise man Solomon shares priceless insight and wisdom. He says it is better to have little in life along with great reverence for the Lord than it is to have vast treasure and the accompanying troubles of holding onto them. The Lord gives us the power and the ability to obtain wealth. God is not opposed to His people living comfortable, even prosperous lives. But He is opposed to us pursuing those things at the price of risking and jeopardizing our relationship and respect for Him.

Take a few moments to thank God for what you have. Thank Him for what He has trusted you with. Thank Him for how He has not only blessed but sustained you. You may not have all you want, but you have no idea how much heartache the Lord has prevented you from by not allowing those added things and people to come into your life.

When you revere Him, He will make sure every need in your life is met. And the retirement package He has for us is literally "out of this world."

June 15th
Matthew 13:16

But blessed are your eyes for they see, and your ears for they hear.

In today's inspirational verse, Jesus is speaking to a crowd of people about their spiritual condition. He informs them of the fact they have blessed eyes and blessed ears. The reason their eyes and ears are blessed is because they have not only seen, but spiritually perceived what Jesus was doing in their midst. These people were also attentive in listening to His teaching and preaching, heeding every word He spoke to them.

When we reach a point in our lives where we see God's hand at work all around us, and hear His voice with clarity, we also become part of those who are blessed. Thank God for the wonderful things He has allowed you to see. Thank God for the pain you have seen but not been allowed to experience. Thank God for the preached and taught word to which He has allowed you to be exposed. His word helps us grow, and when we grow in Him, we are automatically blessed by Him. Now go out and have a blessed day.

June 16th
Luke 7:50

Then He said to the woman, "Your faith has saved you. Go in peace."

A woman with a sinful past and a terrible reputation went to a dinner where Jesus was present. She was not invited and she was not expected. But she went and poured her best perfume on His feet. The people at the party did not think Jesus should have allowed this to happen. In spite of what the others thought, He pronounced a spiritual blessing on this woman.

Today you may be faced with a situation where people don't think you fit in with the crowd. Maybe they think you don't measure up to their standards. Push those thoughts out of your mind. Jesus helps us recognize we don't get His attention by the size of our financial portfolio, but by our faithful positions. This woman acted out of faith, and she was willing to express her love for Him even among people who did not think very highly of her. The Lord wants us to express our love for Him at all times. When we do, it reveals to Him that we are more interested in Him seeing our faith than we are in meeting the approval of others. You are saved because of your faith. Now go and make this day one filled with His peace.

June 17th
Isaiah 54:10

"For the mountains shall depart and the hills be removed, But My kindness shall not depart from you, Nor shall My covenant of peace be removed," says the Lord, who has mercy on you.

One of the many reasons the love of our Lord continues to amaze me is because He is so faithful in loving us even when we have trouble loving ourselves. He forgives us long before we have released ourselves from the sins of our past. Our inspirational verse for today informs us of the fact that, even after this world as we know it has crumbled to pieces, the Lord's kindness will never leave us. He has made us an everlasting and eternal covenant of peace. Wherever the peace of God is, so is God's presence.

Regardless of what you face or encounter today, His peace and His presence will sustain you and see you through it. This does not mean you will have a problem-free existence, but it does mean we are never alone or uncovered. His mercy covers us. His mercy walks with us because He already knows what we deserve, but He holds back our punishment and gives us His peace and His presence instead. What more could we possibly ask for or need?

June 18th

Ephesians 5:15

See then that you walk circumspectly, not as fools but as wise.

Years ago, there was an R&B band (now don't tell me you're not familiar with that kind of music) who had a hit single entitled "Walking in Rhythm." Our inspirational verse for today shares with us the importance of walking not just in rhythm, but of *Walking in Wisdom.* To walk circumspectly means to walk carefully and to be attentive to each and every step we make. The direction in which we travel can either lead us closer to Jesus Christ or cause us to become distracted and dissuaded from our Lord. The Lord gives you an opportunity today to show the people He places around you what a wise walk looks like.

Don't allow the devil to defeat you with foolish steps and behavior. Walk in wisdom, and lead people into a closer relationship with Jesus Christ.

June 19th

Ephesians 5:16

Redeeming the time, because the days are evil.

The Lord wants us to take full advantage of every moment of life He gives us. Don't be wasteful with your talents, your treasure, or your time. When we walk according to the principles of God's Word, we place ourselves in a position to make full use of the time He has given us to live. Someone once said that God does not measure our life by how long we are here on this earth, but by how well we live and the positive contributions we make while here.

Savor every moment God gives us. Don't waste time with foolish people, practices, or pursuing foolish possessions. Evil days are all around us, and the only way we can make sure they do not overtake us is for each of us to use our time wisely. You have started your day off well by using your time to receive inspiration from His Word. Now go and make the rest of your day as productive as this part has already been.

June 20th
Ephesians 5:17

Therefore do not be unwise, but understand what the will of the Lord is.

I'm certain there have been times in your life when you made a decision you wish you could take back and do again. If given the opportunity, perhaps the second time you would act differently as a result of your growth in the Lord and your spiritual maturity. The truth of the matter is, we cannot repair or replace our past, but we can be redeemed from it by the blood of Jesus Christ. The Lord loves us enough to give us opportunities to act and walk in wisdom. When we do this, we prevent ourselves from experiencing a lot of unnecessary heartache and pain. Paul's admonishment to us in today's inspirational verse is to avoid unwise choices. The only way we will be able to do this is to make sure we understand and implement God's will for our lives. Spend extra time today in intimate prayer with the Lord. Ask Him to reveal His will to you and then make up your mind to surrender to Him and follow His directions.

When we understand His will, we are enabled to walk along His path and learn the importance of studying and applying His Word.

June 21st
Ephesians 5:18

And do not be drunk with wine, in which is dissipation; but be filled with the Spirit.

People who become inebriated often do and say things they would not normally do and say when they are sober—things which lead to negative activity. Paul shows us the positive side of being influenced by a power greater than alcohol. That power is the presence and the person of the Holy Spirit. When He controls our lives, we do and say things in a positive way, helping to build people up and teach us His importance in our lives. People who daily depend on alcohol to survive are called alcoholics. For the purpose of better understanding today's message, I am going to invent a new word. And, while you will not find it in your dictionary, I think it is a most appropriate fit here. Those of us who daily depend on the Holy Spirit's presence should be known as *Spirit-holics.* When we accepted Jesus Christ as our Savior, we were baptized with His Spirit. But we also need a daily filling to accomplish the spiritual assignments He places before us.

Alcohol and drugs cost money; they lead to unwise choices, and they never solve our problems. But when we yield to the Holy Spirit, we are charged nothing; He has already paid for us. Ask Him to fill you now for this day's responsibilities, and every day in your future. He will do it. I am a living witness!

June 22nd
Ephesians 5:20

Giving thanks always for all things to God the Father in the name of our Lord Jesus Christ.

Many people think that the only time we should offer thanksgiving to the Lord is when we think something good has happened to us. Well, if that is true, we should change that thinking and take Paul's advice for today to thank God at all times. You may be wondering how we can thank God at all times if everything that happens to us does not always seem to be a good thing. The answer is found in another of Paul's statements: "And we know that all things work together *for good* for those who love the Lord and those who are called according to His purpose." Even when we are unaware of the final product God is molding us into, our hearts should still be filled with genuine gratitude. Giving thanks to God changes our focus; it strengthens our faith and it helps us to know that our future is fixed by our Heavenly Father. Even if things are not perfect in your life right now, just thank Him for the things He has done in the past and the amazing things He has promised for your future. This is a day of no complaints, no grumbling, and no objections. Just thank God, and do it in the name of His Son Jesus Christ. "Thank you, Jesus." Wow, that made me feel so much better.

June 23rd
Matthew 11:28

Come to Me, all you who labor and are heavy laden, and I will give you rest.

How many times have you said, or heard others say, this familiar statement: "I am so tired and stressed out from my job and my daily responsibilities–I could sure use a vacation"? And then, upon return from vacation, you say again: "I need a vacation from my vacation." Is it possible the reason we often still feel tired even after a few days or weeks of vacation is because we spend that time with the wrong people? I wonder how many of us look forward to spending our vacation time in the presence of Jesus, and Him alone. We cannot overlook the profundity and the invitation Jesus offers us in today's inspirational verse. Jesus is looking for people who have labored, who are tired, and who are heavy laden. Do you fit any of those categories? If so, He promises to provide what we all claim we look for: true rest.

You may not be able to take time off your job or remove yourself from your daily activities, but block off some spiritual vacation time to spend with Jesus–with Him alone. He is the only One who can relax, refresh, and restore us. That is what you need right about now, isn't it? Well, He has it, and He's just waiting for you to come to Him to receive it.

June 24th
Romans 8:26

Likewise the Spirit also helps in our weaknesses. For we do not know what we should pray for as we ought, but the Spirit Himself makes intercession for us with groanings which cannot be uttered.

Most of us feel vulnerable only when faced with a challenge that is too difficult to handle by ourselves. But, on the contrary, if we know we have more than sufficient help, we don't really worry too much. In our inspirational verse for today, the Lord wants to make us aware of the fact that, in addition to having help in times of trouble, we also have help during those times we find it difficult to pray. The Lord is so gracious. He has put a divine interpreter at our disposal. When we are unable to get the right words out because of confusion in our minds or pain in our hearts, the Holy Spirit takes control. He communicates with God on our behalf. Pain and pressure result in our inability to speak in Heavenly language because we are in a different country. But our Divine Tour Guide–the Holy Spirit–goes to God and intercedes while we are in some of the weakest moments of our lives.

I know there are times when you feel all alone. Don't allow your feelings to deceive you. You are not alone. The Holy Spirit is with you, and He speaks even when you are unable to. He just informed our Father about your struggles for today. He is preparing you, now walk in His favor and abide under His protection.

June 25th
Matthew 6:21

For where your treasure is, there your heart will be also.

Jesus wants us to surrender our entire self to Him—not just the spiritual things, but also the material things. When our treasure is in one place and our affections and devotions in another, we are trying to live a divided life. Jesus wants us to know that, when that happens, we are literally doing ourselves more harm than good. We need to be reminded that whatever we have has come from His hand. The Lord will never bless us with anything that will cause us to become separated and isolated from Him. His blessings should draw us into a closer relationship with Him. Giving to the Lord should be a joy and a delight. When we invest in Him and His kingdom, we are investing in eternity.

Redirect your focus away from the here and now. When giving, we should put our hearts into it. Wherever you worship this week, set a special offering to the side and give it as a tangible token of your love both *for* Him and *to* Him. After all, He has given so much to us. He more than deserves something extra from us.

June 26th
Luke 5:4

When He stopped speaking, He said to Simon, "Launch out into the deep and let down your nets for a catch."

Today Jesus is about to give you a challenge which, if you obey Him explicitly, could lead to a greater level of spiritual productivity. We sometimes overlook the fact that Jesus desires to move us away from what we call the "shores of safety" to the "deep waters of development." He does not command us to move so as to drown or harm us, but to expose us to something we would never have been able to discover in shallow territory. It may be moving to a new level of ministry. It may be joining a ministry, or increasing your level of activity in His kingdom. Whatever the Lord calls you to do, just be obedient to Him. "Launch out into the deep, and let down your nets..." Oh, by the way, did you notice He said, "...let down your nets *for a catch*"? He has given you the nets–just release them again, no matter how many failures you may have experienced in the past. He has something for you to catch, but it will never be caught on the banks of unbelief. It is in the deep water. Jesus wants to take you deep-sea faith fishing. Trust Him, and watch Him fill your empty nets with His abundant blessings.

June 27th

Psalm 48:14

For this is God, Our God forever and ever; He will be our guide even to death.

I praise the Lord for the assurance He gives us on a daily basis. He assures us of His favor, His forgiveness, and in our inspirational verse for today, of His forever relationship with us. The Lord does not embrace us only when things are going well in our lives, and then discard us when we have sinned and fallen. He walks with us on a daily basis, whispering in our ears how much He loves us and reminding us of His constant presence. He is our God forever and ever. He has owned us as His children, and all He asks in return is that we trust and obey Him as our loving Heavenly Father.

People, positions, and possessions are temporary. They come and go, and today will attempt to fill your space. Take a moment to push them to the side and make room for the person who will be with you throughout all eternity. Don't worry about death, because He will be our guide even until our dying day. And remember, our dying day is when the real living begins. Now go out and have a reassuring, rewarding day as you walk with our Lord.

June 28th
Jeremiah 33:14

"Behold the days are coming," says the Lord, "that I will perform that good thing which I have promised to the house of Israel and to the house of Judah."

Our God is amazing. He reveals this aspect of His personality in many ways—not just in the things He does, but even more so in who He is. He is not like natural, biological parents, as we have the tendency to cancel promises we have made to our children based on their poor behavior. In our inspirational verse for today we see that our Heavenly father does not respond in that manner. At times His promises are delayed, but they are never denied. You may be feeling empty, depleted, defeated. The good news is that God knows just what you need and exactly when you need it. He has good things in store for your future. It is only a matter of our trusting Him, following Him, and waiting on Him. While our poor choices and sins cause His promises to be postponed at times, according to our inspirational verse for today they will never be completely canceled.

Throughout this day, remind yourself of His promises. Read His Word and become more familiar with His promises. Then just walk by faith and wait for every promise that He made to be fulfilled.

June 29th

Hosea 6:1

Come, and let us return to the Lord; For He has torn, but He will heal us; He has stricken, but He will bind us up.

There is a high price to pay when we walk contrary to God's Word and His will for our lives. Our personal desires often cause us to become estranged from God. Not because He has left us, but because we have left Him. Even in the midst of all of this He still passionately pursues us and welcomes us back into His tender-loving care. You may feel torn and splintered as a result of doing things your way rather than God's way. You may feel stricken and beyond repair. Our inspirational verse for today helps us understand that God may have caused those things to happen so as to get our attention, to stop us in our tracks, so that he may reveal His healing power. He has torn, but He will heal. He has stricken, but He will bind us up.

No matter how broken and unworthy you may be feeling, the Lord is about to lay you on His divine surgeon's table and perform His spiritual healing on you. There is only one thing you need to do: "Come, and let us return to the Lord..." If we do, He will repair. If we come back to Him, He will bind up our wounds and fill our hearts with the joy and peace He had in mind when He first created us. Come back right now. He's waiting to hear from you, with bandages already in hand.

June 30th
Joel 2:12

"Now, therefore," says the Lord, "Turn to Me with all your heart, With fasting, with weeping, and with mourning."

We don't hear much preaching and teaching these days about repentance and confessing our sins to God. When we overlook this very important aspect of our relationship with the Lord, sin piles up in our lives, and results in us taking God's grace for granted. The Lord wants us to see how we have allowed so many other things to come between us and Him, and blind us from seeing His plan and will for our lives. He wants us to then go back to Him with a pure, sincere heart.

You may need to set aside a time of fasting to focus your mind exclusively on Jesus Christ. You may need to go before His throne of grace shedding tears of confession and pouring out your heart to Him, asking Him to repair your relationship with Him. Whatever it takes, it is worth it. Turn away from distractions and toward the one who desires to develop you. When we cry, we simply give the Lord another chance to touch us with His tender care. He has promised to wipe every tear from our eyes. If you have not felt His touch in a while, perhaps you have not cried tears of repentance in a while. A good cry is good for the purging of the soul, and fasting brings us closer to our Heavenly Father.

PRAYER

Dear Lord, How we thank You for allowing us to experience Your grace and favor for these first six months of the year. We ask that You purge us of those things that hinder us from being all that You desire for us to be. We also ask that You deposit within us the ability to live for You on a daily basis, prepare us for the assignments before us, and to receive the blessings that await us.

In Jesus' name,
Amen.

Jujubes of Justification in July

July 1st

Psalm 37:7

Rest in the Lord, and wait patiently for Him; Do not fret because of him who prospers in his way, Because of the man who brings wicked schemes to pass.

One Saturday after Men's Ministry meeting in our church, I was speaking to one of the brothers, and he said something that is referenced in today's inspirational verse. He said, "Pastor it seems like everybody else is being blessed except me." At times we feel as though the blessings of God are passing us right on by. One of the reasons we feel this way is because we fail to properly evaluate the true value of God's blessings. We also fail to realize that, while there are people who have more material goods than we do, they do not necessarily have more blessings from God. The psalmist David tells us to "Rest in the Lord and wait patiently for Him..." This simply means to find a place of peace in our relationship with the Lord, and trust Him to provide the resources we need. Most of us become frantic over things we want, and we fail to realize the value of God giving us what we truly need.

Don't focus on the person who seems to prosper by doing things his own way. Don't compromise your principles or your character just to get ahead in the materialism line. The Lord knows where you are and what you need, and He is able to take care of every one of His children. Surrender your cares to Him, and just wait. He will provide you with His best for your life.

July 2nd

Daniel 3:17

If that is the case, our God whom we serve is able to deliver us from the burning fiery furnace, and He will deliver us from your hand, O king.

Our sickness leads to God's healing. Our troubles lead to God's resolutions. Our problems lead to God's peace. Our pain leads to God's soothing. And our shackles lead to God's deliverance. Three young Hebrew men were being threatened with being placed into a fiery furnace because they refused to bow down to an idol God. They believed God would deliver them, and gave collective testimony: "...our God whom we serve is able to deliver us from the burning fiery furnace..." At least three things leap from this story about the faith of these young men. These three things can be our own source of strength when we are faced with adverse circumstances.

1) "Our God." The men had a personal relationship with the God from whom they expected deliverance. The Lord allows trouble to strengthen our relationship with Him.
2) "Whom we serve." They were passionate about their responsibilities under the Lord. They not only worshipped Him and believed in Him; they also served Him. It is possible the Lord allows things to happen to increase our level of service to Him.
3) "Is able to deliver us" speaks to the men's public representation of the Lord. They wanted this king to know exactly in whom they trusted.

Whatever you are faced with today, keep in mind that God may have allowed it so as to exhibit His delivering power in your life.

July 3rd
John 12:32

And I, if I am lifted up from the earth, will draw all peoples to Myself.

Have you taken the time to consider where you would be if Jesus had not loved you enough to go to Calvary and die for you? Our hearts should be filled with joy just knowing we have someone who was willing to save us when we had absolutely nothing of value to offer Him in return. It amazes me how people receive all that the Lord offers them, then constantly ask Him for more, while failing to remain loyal and devoted to Him. He died for us, was buried for us, and rose from the grave with all power in His hands–not for Himself but for unworthy sinners like you and me. He loved us and was willing to save us, even when we did not love ourselves and did not know we needed to be saved or that we were worth saving. There were many times when Jesus talked about His death, sharing it only with His disciples. Here He shares this insight with a crowd of people. These were some of the very people He was willing to die for and redeem from their sins.

He speaks to us now more than 2,000 years later to call our attention to at least three important factors: 1) We are saved because of His sacrifice; 2) We are sealed because of His suffering; and 3) We are sanctified because of His subjection. He has drawn us to Himself. This means no matter what confronts us today, we are in His all-protective care.

July 4th
John 12:32

And I, if I am lifted up from the earth, will draw all peoples to Myself.

Jesus has given us our *spiritual independence.* He was lifted at Calvary because He wanted that to be the number-one attraction and focus of every Christian believer. When we look carefully at Jesus at Calvary we see the *gore* He endured for us, the *guilt* we caused which led Him there, and the *glory* He revealed while hanging there. No man took His life; He, himself, laid it down. And before He lay down in a hidden grave, He died a publicly gory, guilt-substituted, glory-filled death. When we allow something to blind us from looking daily at the pain Jesus endured for us, we begin to take His mercy and His grace for granted. Jesus was lifted up because He wants us to take our attention off those things which are beneath and around us–those depressing, defeating, and disruptive things. While some of them may seem innocent on the surface, if they blind us from Calvary, they are destructive. Insipid and seemingly innocent things can cause us to compromise our relationship with the Lord.

He was born and He lived *among* us. When He died He hung *above* us. He was buried *beneath* us. And now He lives *within* us. All this was done so that He would be the main attraction in our lives. You have been lifted; now start living on a higher spiritual level. If you don't have the red, white, and blue spirit of national independence today, just thank God you have spiritual independence, for you have been washed in the red blood of the Lamb; your sins have been made white as snow; and you no longer have to suffer from the sinful blues.

July 5th

John 12:32

And I, if I am lifted up from the earth, will draw all peoples to Myself.

Jesus says, "And I, if I am lifted up, will draw all peoples to Myself." He lifts us to love us more affectionately than we have even been loved before. He knows we need to be repositioned to receive His level of love. "I will draw all peoples to Myself." He *elevates* us, to *embrace* us! Jesus wants to lift us to protect us from people who would cause harm in our lives. Whenever we enter into a love relationship with another person, we run the risk of that relationship being only temporary. But this lifting that Jesus does for us and that He offers us is a permanent and eternal relationship. What more does Jesus need to do before you become willing to offer Him a greater amount of your *time*, *talent*, and *treasure*? We cannot pay for His love. But we must ask ourselves if our response to His love is appropriate for the level of affection He has showered us with.

Make this day one filled with assurance. He has raised you to use you to His glory. He would not have done all that He has done if He did not have a specific plan and purpose for our lives. You have been magnetized to the Master. What more could you possibly ask for?

July 6th
John 12:32

And I, if I am lifted up from the earth, will draw all peoples to Myself.

In the Old Testament Book of Numbers, the people were guilty of sinning in the wilderness. The Lord then sent fiery serpents to bite the people. God told Moses that a serpent had to be lifted and the people had to look up before they could be healed of their disease. The serpent had bitten them, and what the people had to look up to was the very thing that had caused them harm. When we look up at Jesus, we should be able to see that He who knew no sin became sin for us who were filled with sin. He allowed sin to bite Him on our behalf, and He died in our place. We must never lose sight of the amazing atoning work Jesus did for us at Calvary.

He was lifted so that we are able to do more than just exist. He wants us to live and to have life more abundantly.

July 7th
Hebrews 11:29

By faith they passed through the Red Sea as by dry land, whereas the Egyptians, attempting to do so, were drowned.

When we exercise our true faith in the Lord, it is manifested in such a way that no one can counterfeit it. The Lord brought His people through the Red Sea, but when the Egyptians tried to cross in the same manner, they drowned. The Lord often allows us to go through difficult struggles so that we learn deliverance is difficult. On the other hand, deliverance from easy dilemmas can be easily duplicated, and does not lead to any learning. In this case, the Lord led them to this place so they would learn how to use their energy more wisely. The physical strength that would have been needed to defeat the Philistines was not what God required of them. He only wanted them to keep walking for one night without stopping. How many battles have we initiated and prolonged because we took matters into our own hands and were traveling in the wrong location? I don't know of any one-day war, but this victory was won in one night because these people obeyed the Lord.

Whatever faith challenge confronts you, the Lord knows He has given you the ability to face and conquer it. But we often make the mistake of using our energy in all the wrong places. The Red Sea was two miles wide, and God held the waters back until all of them passed over. This word from God in today's verse has the power to deliver us all from whatever the devil uses to hold us captive. The only question is, "Do we have enough faith to walk through it?" A faith walk is not as difficult as a sight walk because on a faith walk we do not walk alone.

July 8th

Psalm 103:12

As far as the east is from the west, So far has He removed our transgressions from us.

The times we have sinned and fallen short of the glory and the grace of God we feel as though God is distant and far removed from us. The truth of the matter, according to today's verse, is the exact opposite. He has not removed Himself from us, but when we confess and repent, He removes our sins so great a distance from us that we will never be able to retrieve them. I have heard that when God casts our sins into a sea of forgetfulness, He then puts up a sign that says "No fishing." No matter how many so-called righteous deep-sea divers may be around us, the Lord wants us to know we are forgiven. Not because we deserve it, but because of His grace.

To be clear, this does not give us the right to go out and repeat ungodly behavior; it does, however, let us know we must walk with Him daily so that we will not have that guilt hanging over our heads. You are forgiven. Now walk and live like a child of God.

July 9th

Acts 20:24

But none of these things move me; nor do I count my life dear to myself, so that I may finish my race with joy, and the ministry which I received from the Lord Jesus, to testify to the gospel of the grace of God.

If there is one thing we can say about the Apostle Paul, it is that he was focused and determined to fulfill the ministry assignments the Lord gave him. Will you agree with me when I say that most of our stress comes from things related to the here and now, with few stressors related to our afterlife? The devil's job is to stress us out over the minor details of our lives, even if we perceive them as major. We must reach the point of completely trusting in the Lord to take care of us so that we may focus our attention on completing the assignments He has placed before us. This day is going to be filled with opportunities for us to move closer to completing and finishing those things that bring joy to the heart of God. He has given us each a special ministry. It may not include standing behind a podium preaching on Sunday, but it does include representing Him on a daily basis. I don't mean to rain on your parade, but this day is about more than just your personal happiness; it is about God's glory radiating through you.

We have received His grace; the very fact that we are still alive gives credence to that truth. Now, let's go out and testify about His affection for us, His attention toward us, and His atonement of us.

July 10th
Isaiah 43:1

But now, thus says the Lord, who created you, O Jacob, And He who formed you, O Israel: "Fear not, for I have redeemed you; I have called you by your name; you are Mine."

Today's inspirational verse is filled with comfort, assurance, and redemption. The Lord does not have to say much to get His message across. In this one verse, God reveals His *creative* work in our lives. He reveals His *constructive* work in our lives. He reveals His *comforting* work in our lives. He reveals His *consecration* work in our lives. He reveals His *compassionate* work in our lives. And He reveals His *completed* work in our lives.

As I write this, my eyes fill with tears. I think about the many times I have failed the Lord, yet He has entered into a relationship with me and brings all of these assurances–and I have absolutely nothing of value to offer Him in return. He made us. He has formed us to be able to handle whatever comes in our direction. He wants to remove fear from our lives because He has so much more work for us to accomplish. We are enabled to be successful in whatever assignment is before us because He has redeemed us. We do not have to wait for His approval, we already have His anointing. He has called us by our name. He knows the potential in each of us and He has a purpose for each of us.

We are His! We are owned by eternity. We belong to the creator of the Universe. When we meditate on these truths, we realize today can be nothing less than an absolutely wonderful day.

July 11th

Psalm 103:14

For He knows our frame; He remembers that we are dust.

Having grown up in a Christian church, I am accustomed to hearing the following cliché over and over: "The Lord knows just how much we can bear." Cliché or not, this statement rings completely true. Another cliché, however, is filled with only partial truth: "The Lord will never place more on us than we are able to bear." The Lord will, indeed, allow us to be confronted with pressures which are too difficult for us. Those are the times we are forced to seek His help and guidance. The assurance we find in today's inspirational verse is "He knows our frame..." He has made us and He knows how much each of us can handle. This is why we should never compare our lives and struggles to those of anyone else. The Lord has not constructed us the same. What may be too heavy and ultimately destroy another person may be just the amount of weight to develop and strengthen you. God has not forgotten you. He knows where you are, and what challenges are before you. He remembers we are dust. The good news is found in the fact that our dust combined with His divinity leads to determined development.

Don't complain about the weights you may have to carry today. Thank God for trusting you with them and for teaching you how to call on Him when they are too heavy for you to bear alone.

July 12th
Psalm 104:33

I will sing to the Lord as long as I live; I will sing praise to my God while I have my being.

I declare and decree that today is an official Day of Praise. I know I don't have any judicial power to make such a declaration, but I do have spiritual authority from the Word of God to do so. The truth of the matter is that every day should be a day of praise. Sing to the Lord. Sing about the Lord. The reason I declare this to be a Day of Praise is because I have discovered that just one day of true, authentic, genuine praise automatically leads to many more to follow.

While we are living, let's sing to the Lord. After all, this is one of the main things we will spend eternity engaged in. He has given us our being, and we should bless Him with consistent praise while we tabernacle here on earth in these vessels of clay. Now get your praise song ready, and sing to Him while you ride, walk, fly, or are rolled to your responsibilities of this day. Here is a great song to start off with: "How Great Thy Art."

July 13th
Psalm 104:34

My meditation of Him shall be sweet: I will be glad in the Lord.

Take your mind off your responsibilities for today. Empty your thoughts of the problems and issues before you. Purge your outlook of the challenges you expect will confront you sometime during the course of the day. This is God's time! Let's meditate on Him. Let's allow what enters into our minds to be pleasing to Him. I know this may be difficult because when we try to think about Him, the devil floods our minds with so many distractions. Let's overpower the adversary. In the midst of the devil's desire to fill our minds with negativity, we are going to press our way and allow the Lord to know He is the real center of our joy.

Find your contentment and peace in Him. This will not be a perfect day, but it will be a purpose-filled day. Meditate on Him; find consolation in Him; and watch Him fill your heart with His presence.

July 14th
Romans 10:11

For the scripture says, "Whoever believes in Him will not be put to shame."

We believe in the life, ministry, death, burial, and resurrection of Jesus Christ, and have absolutely no reason to be apologetic or ashamed of it. Our shame was connected to our sins. Jesus took both our sins and our shame and allowed them to be nailed to a cross at Calvary. We should share our belief and our testimony about Jesus Christ at every opportunity. He was not ashamed to die for us; we should not be ashamed to live and talk about Him.

We should be bold and have confidence in our relationship with the Lord. Hold your head high. Walk in spiritual freedom and assurance. Let the world know you are proud to own Him because He is holy. He owned us when we were sinful and unworthy. Remove any shame you may have, and replace it instead with spiritual strength.

July 15th

2 Chronicles 20:15

And he said, "Listen, all you of Judah and you inhabitants of Jerusalem, and you, King Jehoshaphat! Thus says the Lord to you: 'Do not be afraid nor dismayed because of this great multitude, for the battle is not yours but God's.'"

Allow me to sum up today's inspirational verse with one simple, true statement: If we have the *faith*, God will do the *fighting*! Have you noticed how quick we are to fight and retaliate when things do not turn out the way we think they should or when we feel as though we have been mistreated? During the times we are quick to fight, we are also slow to exercise our faith. The Lord wants us to know there will be some challenges before us today that we cannot conquer without Him. He wants us to listen and give heed to His Word. We need to be reminded of the fact that He is able to handle all of Judah's, Jerusalem's, King Jehoshaphat's, and our enemies. The multitude of opposition may seem great, but we need not fear because our God is even greater.

Whatever you are confronted with today that seems too hard for you to handle alone, take a moment to remind yourself, "This is not my battle; this belongs to the Lord." Now, you do what He tells you to, and watch Him bring about victory in your life—not just today, but every day that follows.

July 16th
Romans 10:17

So then faith comes by hearing, and hearing by the Word of God.

I am sure we have all said or heard spoken at some point in our lives the following: "I know I need more faith, but how do I go about acquiring it?" Today's inspirational verse provides us with a direct and practical answer. Faith comes by hearing. I will not take time here to give a lesson in verb tense and grammar, but I will point out that the word "comes" is used in the present tense. This means the action is ongoing–it continues and must be repeated for the action to be completed. This helps us understand that if we want our faith to grow, that growth comes about by repeated *hearing*. "Hearing what?" you may be asking. Good question. Hearing of the Word of God. Our faith grows when we feed it continuously on God's Word. Many claim they want their faith to grow, but then only feed it a snack once a week during Sunday worship. Faith keeps coming when we keep hearing from God's Word.

His Word challenges us to move from our comfort zone and walk with Him. Make a commitment to place yourself in an environment on a regular basis where you can be exposed to sound teaching and preaching from the Word of God. If you want your faith to grow, you must feed it more than it has been receiving in the past.

July 17th

Psalm 23:4

Yea, though I walk through the valley of the shadow of death, I will fear no evil; For You are with me; Your rod and Your staff, they comfort me.

Because we are forced to travel through the valley of the shadow of death on more occasions than we would like, let's visit it one more time in our discussion of today's verse. We need a refreshing word from this verse during the hot summer days of our existence. Life has a way of causing us to occasionally walk down dark, dismal, and dreadful paths. If we had our way, we would avoid these corridors at all cost, no? The truth of the matter is they cannot be avoided. Even good behavior does not exempt us from traveling these roads. But the assurance we receive from our inspirational verse for today is that we never have to walk them alone. Even while walking there is no need to be fearful; God is with us. His presence defends us from the devil's attacks. His presence develops us for the assignments God has for us after being strengthened from our walk. His presence delivers us from the assaults of our enemies. Notice the language the psalmist uses: "Yea, though I walk *through* the valley." God has not taken you to a valley to destroy you; rather, He takes you through a valley to develop you. Are you ready for some good news? Here it is: You will never have the strength to climb the mountain God has in your future if He does not allow you to go through the boot camp of training in the valley. Get ready. This is all being used for your promotion.

Does it seem like you are in a valley right now? Be encouraged. You are just passing through on your way to your mountain of victory.

July 18th
John 12:46

I have come as a light into the world, that whoever believes in Me should not abide in darkness.

Jesus gives us some informative and comforting words in today's inspirational verse. He makes us aware that we no longer have to fear the darkness because He has come to light up the world. This also includes His lighting of every nook and cranny of our personal lives. Many times we choose to live in darkness for unnecessary periods of time. Those are not the areas where the Lord wants us to reside. The darkness represents any area of our lives we have not totally released and surrendered to Jesus Christ. He wants us to know that when we open our hearts to Him not just in salvation, but also for His daily abiding, He will demolish our darkness. He offers this to anyone who is willing to trust and believe in Him.

If you are already a believer, the Lord may now be leading you to share this message of hope with someone else who does not have the light of Jesus Christ in their life. There is no need for us to abide in darkness when we can live abundantly in the light of His love.

July 19th

1 Corinthians 16:14

Let all that you do be done with love.

Wouldn't life, relationships, marriages, friendships, and churches be so much better if we just applied the inspirational verse for today? Take a moment to read it again. "Let all that you do be done with love." Much of what we do is done out of selfishness, pride, and in an apparent effort to improve our own lives. Paul commands and admonishes us to remove those divisive, negative things from our hearts and replace them with a disposition of Godly love.

Make this day a day of loving service. Even if others don't appreciate you, the Lord will reward you. Make this a day of loving sacrifice. Put aside what you want for yourself to help another, and don't worry about whether they deserve it or not. Make this a day of loving speech. Choose your words carefully. Build people up, and avoid the temptation to allow anything negative to flow from your lips. Do what you do with love–after all, it was love that brought us into a relationship with our Savior.

July 20th
Exodus 33:14

And He said, "My presence will go with you, and I will give you rest."

As often happens when we feel burnt out and exhausted, we make the mistake of taking a break from everything, including our walk, witness, and worship of the Lord. When we do this, we leave ourselves open and susceptible to all kinds of attacks and temptations from the devil. It is especially during seasons of physical fatigue that we need the Lord's presence more than ever. We need to seek His presence, surrender to His presence, and make ourselves constantly available to serve while basking in His presence. Walking with Him and living for Him add a greater level of renewal and refreshing to our lives than anything we have ever experienced before.

His presence goes with us; please don't make the mistake of sub-consciously leaving Him behind. The Lord will not force Himself on us, but He wants us to know He is always available to us. The rest you truly need will never be found without basking in the presence of our Savior, Jesus Christ.

July 21st

Psalm 40:9

I have proclaimed the good news of righteousness in the great assembly; Indeed, I do not restrain my lips, O Lord, You Yourself know.

This entire 40th Psalm is both testimony and praise from David about the Lord's help during one of his greatest times of danger and distress. I often used to wonder why the Bible has so much more to say to us about how to handle our troubles, difficulties, and burdens than it does about how we should live in prosperity, opulence, and splendor. Then the Holy Spirit spoke to my heart and reminded me of the fact that trouble and difficulties are the things we all have in common. It does not matter what our economic, educational, or ethnic background may be—we will all experience times of sorrow, and we need to learn how to handle those times more than we do the days of splendor. David speaks to us in our inspirational verse for today and informs us of at least three basic things: Trouble has a way of causing us to see God's *majesty*, to see His *mercy*, and to be constantly informed that He is *mindful* of everything we go through.

Share a testimony about God's work in your life while you are in the house of the Lord. It does not have to be a public testimony; simply share with at least one person what the Lord is doing for you, with you, and through you. It may be just the source of encouragement they will need as strength for the balance of their week.

July 22nd
Psalm 40:9

I have proclaimed the good news of righteousness in the great assembly; Indeed, I do not restrain my lips, O Lord, You Yourself know.

If we read today's inspirational verse too fast we will miss one of the main points of emphasis. David says, "I have proclaimed the good news of righteousness in the *great assembly...*" This suggests that he had a regular pattern of being present in the house of the Lord and he never allowed an opportunity to speak favorably about the Lord to pass him by. Did you not know that consistent attendance in the house of the Lord and with the people of the Lord will give us a more positive perspective on our troubles? It will also help us embrace the fact that we should never allow what the devil sends in our direction to stop us from doing what God has called us to do, as that is when we become guilty of allowing him to win by default.

When I played Little League baseball back in Houston, we won a couple of games simply because the other team did not show up. If they had only come, my team, in fact, would have been the one to lose because we had only eight eligible players, when we needed nine. How many times have we allowed the devil to defeat us simply because we failed to show up? David refused to restrain his lips from talking about the goodness of the Lord. Other people were encouraged because of David's testimony, and the Lord wants to do the same through you.

July 23rd
1 Peter 2:11

Beloved, I beg you as sojourners and pilgrims, abstain from fleshly lusts which war against the soul.

For those of us who are saved and washed in the blood of Jesus Christ, we have eternal security. The devil already knows there is absolutely nothing he can do to separate us from Jesus Christ. So he launches his attack on the part of ourselves that we often leave unattended and exposed: our flesh. In today's inspirational verse we are encouraged to guard our thoughts and actions both today and from this day forward. Peter begs us to remember that we are sojourners and pilgrims in this world. This simply means the world is not our permanent home and we should not make the mistake of trying to have all our desires satisfied by only what this world has to offer.

We are told to abstain from fleshly lusts because they rage war against our soul. When we satisfy the flesh we automatically cause weakness to come into our souls and cause a breakdown in our ability to live for Jesus Christ. Say no to those things you know are contrary to God's Word so that you can say yes to Him and add strength to your soul.

July 24th

Isaiah 40:29

He gives power to the weak, and to those who have no might He increases strength.

Have you ever had one of those days when you had trouble just getting started? Your heart was in the right place, but physically it just seemed as though you did not have what you needed. Well, we have all faced those times at one point or another. I have discovered that those feelings often occur just as the Lord is getting ready to do something remarkable and outstanding in our lives. The devil causes these feelings because he wants us to give up, quit, and throw in the towel. The good news of today's inspirational verse is that God, too, knows when we are going through those feelings of exhaustion. He knows we are weak, and He promises to give us power. He knows our might is depleted and He promises to give us strength.

Want something to really shout about? Well, here it is. The power He gives gets us started and the strength He gives keeps us going. Wow, I feel better already. Take a moment to reflect on how, in the past, He brought you through those seasons of exhaustion and feelings of giving up. Now prepare yourself, because He is about to do it again.

July 25th
Isaiah 40:30

Even the youths shall faint and be weary, and the young men shall utterly fall.

We are human and we will, undoubtedly, experience occasional seasons of weariness. The challenge for us from today's inspirational verse is to not allow these periods of human weakness to cause our faith in God to grow cold. He knows where we are and what we face, and He already has plans for our deliverance. Don't trust in your biological strength. Stop depending on your limited number of birthdays. "Even the youths shall faint and be weary, and the young men shall utterly fall." Are you having trouble finding comfort in that one verse? At first, I did, too, until I remembered how our God encourages the weary and how He lifts the fallen.

You may be down right now, but hold on—His lifting is on the way. Just in case you are wondering what God has in store for you, well, you've just got to wait. (No pun intended.) And, if He delays His coming, He will speak to us afresh tomorrow.

July 26th

Isaiah 40:31

But those who wait on the Lord shall renew their strength; They shall mount up with wings like eagles, They shall run and not be weary, They shall walk and not faint.

Does it seem the Lord moves too slowly in answering your prayer request or in granting the things you feel you desperately need? If so, what do you think a good alternative would be? If we are not willing to wait on the Lord, who or what else can we turn to that will offer us a more favorable solution? The answer is absolutely no one or nothing. Waiting is not easy; it is not fun; and it is not something we look forward to. But the wait is always better when we know who and what we are waiting on. In our inspirational verse for today, "Who" we wait on is God Himself. "What" we await is His power to renew our depleted strength. He also promises to mount us up with wings like eagles, and protect us while we run so we don't become weary and while we walk so there is no fear of fainting.

Everything you feel you need is not automatically and immediately placed at your disposal. But we do have a promise from God: His promise is to carry us beyond any and everything we could ever imagine. We must, however, learn and then practice waiting on Him. Trust Him to guide you through this day, and then wait on Him to lead you where He desires for you to be.

July 27th

John 16:33

These things I have spoken to you, that in Me you may have peace. In the world you will have tribulation; but be of good cheer, I have overcome the world.

Trouble and tribulation will come, but the words of Jesus make all the difference in how we deal with them. The arrangement of this verse brings comfort to my heart, even in the midst of the trouble I face on a daily basis. I believe it will do the same for you. Jesus says, "These things I have spoken to you, that in Me you may have peace." The remainder of this verse deals with the problems we face in life. But He begins by speaking words of peace to us. This peace He offers helps us deal with our problems with a much brighter outlook. We shall have tribulations. But don't give up, don't lose heart, and don't throw in the towel. Be of good cheer because He has already overcome the world.

When we are connected to Jesus, we are overcomers. We can look at our problems with a much brighter perspective. They have not come to keep us from reaching our spiritual goals, but rather to help us in our practicing our worry wall-climbing skills. You will face some pressures today, but He is right with you to lift you above every one of them. If it were not for our problems, we would be forced to remain in a stationary position. Be of good cheer–the Lord has already worked those issues out for your good.

July 28th
Psalm 105:4

Seek the Lord and His strength; Seek His face evermore!

When our passions and life's pursuits are centered and focused on the Lord, life has a way of flowing so much more smoothly. It does not mean that our troubles vanish, but we are, indeed, able to focus more on His goodness than on His grief. During those seasons of personal challenge and struggle, we feel drained and expended. In today's inspirational verse the psalmist gives us some wonderful advice. "Seek the Lord and His strength..." We are admonished to pursue Him, and when we do, we will also discover more of His strength. His face, or His purpose for our lives, should be our quest on a daily basis. Is it possible that life seems difficult because you are seeking to accomplish your will, as opposed to surrendering to His?

Seek Him throughout this entire day. You will find His strength and make this a practice each day for the rest of your life.

July 29th
John 14:27

Peace I leave with you, My peace I give to you; not as the world gives do I give to you. Let not your heart be troubled, neither let it be afraid.

I drive one of those cars that do not require a key in the ignition. As long as you have the key on your person, the car will start and operate. One day my son in ministry drove me to the airport to catch a flight. We were in my car, which he was going to keep until I returned from my trip. When I got out of the car at the airport I forgot to leave the key with him. He ran into the airport trying to catch me before I boarded the plane. By the grace of God, he caught me and all was well. If I had left without giving him the key, he would have had a car he would not have been able to start or use. In our inspirational verse for today, Jesus makes us aware of the fact that He did not take His peace with Him when He ascended back to Heaven. If He had done this, we would not have been able to get our lives started or properly operate them.

He left His peace and He has given us His peace. Now all we need to do is receive it and remove the troubles from our hearts and the fears from our minds. This day was intended by God to be a peaceful day for you. Free yourself from any unnecessary stress and worry, and put a genuine smile on that wonderful face the Lord gave you.

July 30th

Hebrews 2:1

Therefore we must give the more earnest heed to the things we have heard, lest we drift away.

The one and only thing that keeps us from drifting away from the Lord in our relationship and responsibilities is His Word. We have no other means of getting to know the Lord or of discovering His plan and purpose for our lives apart from His Word. In our inspirational verse for today we are told we must give the more earnest heed to the things we have heard from the Lord's Word. If we fail to heed this command, the end result will be a drifting away. The devil wants to flood our minds with so many other things that distract and divert us away from our Lord.

His Word gives us a greater dependence on Him; it deepens our level of intimacy with Him, and it helps us focus on the things that are really important in life. Make sure to listen closely when the Word is being preached and taught. It is not designed to just hold your attention for thirty minutes to an hour, but to give you principles to live by for the rest of your life. Carry your Bible with you and read a few verses throughout the day and watch what a difference it will make in your life.

July 31st

Genesis 6:8

But Noah found grace in the eyes of the Lord.

Feeling a little guilty, grief-stricken, or grounded? I have some great news: God's Grace will cure every one of those symptoms. I have read today's inspirational verse more times than I can count, but its profundity did not impact me the way it did until I was preparing this inspirational word. Noah was not a perfect man. He was not a specially gifted man. He was not an extremely educated man. But he was a man who was showered with the grace of God. This verse informs us of how Noah "found grace in the eyes of the Lord." The word *found* has at least two meanings. One definition is "to come into contact with." The other is "to pursue and be favored and blessed by what you have been pursuing and chasing after." Many of us pursue and chase after people and things that add only heartache and shame to our lives. In Noah's time, when everybody else was moving away from God, Noah found grace because He pursued and chased after God.

No matter what you feel about your past, God's grace is still available. If you will make up your mind on this final day of July to seek the face of God and allow His eyes to gaze upon you, you, too, will find His grace. Just knowing that God is willing to look at us, see our faults, and still shower us with His grace should be plenty to brighten our day. What better way to end the month than to look forward to seeking His face for the remainder of our lives. There is grace in the eyes of the Lord.

PRAYER

Lord, We thank You for Your amazing grace and Your undeserved mercy. You held us when we trembled and protected us when we were vulnerable. We have felt the calm coolness of Your assuring love even in the midst of these hot summer days.

We ask forgiveness for our sins and that You perfectly position us so that You may receive the greatest level of glory from our lives.

In Jesus' name, and how we love to call His name,
Amen.

Apples of Anointing in August

August 1st
Isaiah 40:8

The grass withers, the flower fades, But the word of our God stands forever.

Instability always leads to insecurity. Whenever we lack a level of confidence in what we are connected to our hearts and minds fill with anxiety and uncertainty. Many of us have known the pain of being in unstable relationships and unstable places of employment; we have experienced instability in our finances and even in our health. But today's inspirational verse lets us start this new month off with the greatest foundation of stability the world, and especially the Church, have ever known. That foundation is the Word of God. Grass withers because it is dependent on someone else to water it. Flowers fade because they are dependent on someone else to care for them. But the Word of God needs no watering; it provides all the spiritual irrigation we will ever need. God's Word needs no one to care for it; it gives us the care we need to nurture and strengthen our souls.

God's Word does not simply stand; it stands forever. Jesus once said, "Heaven and Earth will pass away before one jot or tittle of My Word shall fail." Take time to read some familiar passages from the Word of God—it stands forever and will help you stand against whatever confrontations you may face. It will also help you to be victorious in every opportunity the Lord sends your way.

August 2nd
Psalm 63:6

When I remember You on my bed, I meditate on You in the night watches.

Peaceful sleep and rest at night can do great things to make the day that follows productive. Likewise, a lack of sleep can hinder our productivity. Many times we have trouble attaining a good night's rest because our mind wanders and is filled with so much, some of which is positive and some negative. The psalmist gives us some helpful information in today's inspirational verse. He shares with us the fact that he not only thinks about the Lord while on his bed, he remembers the Lord. This is important, because while we think about and remember the things the Lord has done for us and brought us through, it serves to remove the stress from our minds.

Whenever your mind wanders to the point that it hinders your ability to rest and sleep peacefully, just remember God's goodness, His grace, and His glory. Meditate on Him, and watch Him dispatch His angels to rock you peacefully to sleep.

August 3rd
Psalm 63:7

Because You have been my help, Therefore in the shadow of Your wings I will rejoice.

Today's inspirational verse is filled with praise and rejoicing. Let's take a moment to focus on how many times the Lord has been there just when we needed Him most. If you are like me and trying to count, the calculator at your disposal does not have enough figures to tally the number. Many times we make the mistake of trying to go through life acting and pretending as though we have it all together and we need assistance from no one. The Lord wants us to recognize our desperate need for Him. We will never discover God's power until we come face to face with our helplessness. Maybe you are feeling helpless right now. Well, things are about to change. Not only is help on the way, it is here in the Person of the Holy Spirit.

He hides and protects us during our seasons of helplessness under the shadow of His wings. Until He brings you out to resume the norm of your daily routine, rejoice and give Him the praise He deserves for protecting you. The only reason your trouble has not scorched you beyond recognition is because His wings have protected you. Now that is worth rejoicing about.

August 4th

Psalm 63:8

My soul follows close behind You; Your right hand upholds me.

My wife Pam is my grace gift, my prayer partner, and my best friend. On those occasions we happen to be driving in two automobiles and she is following me, I do not feel she follows closely enough. She allows too much space to come between us, and other cars prevent her from seeing me when I change lanes, turn, or exit. The psalmist in today's inspirational verse did not have that problem with the Lord. He acknowledges the fact that he follows the Lord with not only his body, but even more importantly, his soul as well. He says, "My soul follows close behind You..." He neither attempts to run ahead of God nor allow anything or anyone to come between him and the Lord.

The final part of the verse really puts the icing on the cake: "...Your right hand upholds me." This is his way of informing us that the Lord feels us as His children at all times. We need to make sure we feel His presence, too, by following Him closely. If you feel as though something or someone has come between you and Him, then do what my wife does. She calls me and says, "Sweetie, slow down and pull over. I can't see where you are." Call Him in prayer and say, "Savior, manifest Your presence to me. I can't see where You are." I'm a living witness that this is one prayer request He answers every time.

August 5th

Genesis 1:26

Then God said, "Let Us make man in Our image, according to Our likeness; let them have dominion over the fish of the sea, over the birds of the air, and over the cattle, over all the earth and over every creeping thing that creeps on the earth."

We have so much to be thankful for. Whatever we have is a gift to us from God. Whatever we face is a developing process from God. We have been made in His image. We are reflections of His Person. We have been made according to His likeness. We are representatives of His Passion. We have been given dominion. We have been trusted with a portion of His Power. Whatever you do throughout this day, make an effort to allow someone to see a reflection of God in your life. However you interact with people, allow them to feel God's passion flowing through you. Whatever challenges you face, overcome them with the power of God that resides within you.

When you apply these simple principles it cannot help but be an absolutely wonderful day.

August 6th
Psalm 118:24

This is the day the Lord has made; We will rejoice and be glad in it.

Whenever people greet me, I respond the same way as I have for the past several years. They say to me, "Good morning. How are you?" I respond back, "Absolutely wonderful and getting better." This is not to suggest that every day of my life is filled with perfection. Nothing could be further from the truth. I have struggles with ministry, struggles with finances, struggles with health, and struggles with depression. But in spite of it all, I know that "I am wonderful and getting better" not because of what I face, but because of who walks with me through it. That statement is just my way of reminding myself multiple times throughout the day that God is in complete control. Perhaps you, too, need to be reminded of the fact that the Lord made the day and He made you to be able to handle whatever you face during the day, regardless of what it is.

God has never made a day that was not designed for His glory and our growth. So rejoice and be glad. Don't reject the challenges. Don't resign your responsibilities. Don't refuse His development. Just rejoice and be glad in this day. A glad heart will give you such a brighter outlook on life. Oh, by the way, please don't make me rejoice alone. Hear me shout: "*We* will rejoice and be glad in it." I'm now waiting for you.

August 7th

Mark 1:12

Immediately the Spirit drove Him into the wilderness.

The Lord has a way of leading us to some strange places, and he seems to do so at strange points in our lives. If you agree with this, you are not alone. He led His own Son Jesus into wilderness right after His baptism. The Lord uses wilderness in our lives for three reasons. First, He uses wilderness as a place to *test.* While Jesus passed His test, many of us fail ours. Have you considered this? Had we not been in the wilderness and away from the crowds when we stumbled and fell, our failures would have become public. Second, He uses the wilderness as a place to *toughen.* He allows us to stay there for a season; and when He releases us, those things that previously would have destroyed us are now being used to mature us. Third, the Lord uses the wilderness as a place of *thankfulness.* While there, we should thank Him for His sustaining grace and protecting power.

Don't run from your wilderness. God used it positively and productively in the life of His Son Jesus and He will do the same for every one of us. Remember the Spirit drove Him to the wilderness. God's Spirit will never lead us where His grace cannot keep us.

August 8th

Genesis 12:1

Now the Lord had said to Abram: "Get out of your country, from your family And from your father's house, To a land that I will show you."

Many songs have been written and sung about God's people receiving the favor of the man named Abram (or Abraham, as his name was subsequently changed by God). I believe the level of favor God showered upon Abraham is available to us only when we are willing to exhibit the same level of faith Abraham demonstrated. The Lord spoke to him and told him to leave his country, his family, and his father's house; and to go to a place where he had no idea what his final destination would be—and Abraham did all the Lord asked him to. Many people are not willing to obey the Lord in things that don't require nearly as many sacrifices as those Abraham made, yet we want the same amount of favor. Today's inspirational verse helps us understand there will be times when the Lord requires us to obey Him even when we cannot completely understand Him.

This is what makes the faith-walk and journey so exciting. Abraham reached his destination by following God's voice and directions one step at a time. It worked for him and it will work for us. Do you feel as though you need an abundance of God's favor? Well, exhibit your faith and watch Him meet every need in your life, even those times you arrive at places and have no idea how you got there.

August 9th
Jeremiah 18:4

And the vessel that he made of clay was marred in the hand of the potter; so he made it again into another vessel, as it seemed good to the potter to make.

Our God specializes in repairing our lives when we have fractured them beyond repair. We have all had accidents and purposeful incidents from which we had no idea how we were going to recover. The good news from our inspirational verse for today is in realizing that, as long as we stay on the wheel, we can be repaired by the master potter, by Jesus Christ Himself. We may become marred, but we are in His hand. We may become infected with foreign ingredients, but we can be cleansed as long as we are in His hand.

Whatever you are right now is not the final product God is shaping and molding you into becoming. He is allowing you to go through His refining process. You are on the wheel of His grace, and you are being shaped into a vessel for His glory. You may get a little dizzy while you go round and round. Don't worry, you are in His hand and He is in complete control.

August 10th

Luke 6:46

"But why do you call Me 'Lord, Lord,' and not do the things which I say?"

Any person who is a parent or who has parents knows how important obedience is. When we sacrifice for our children, provide for our children, and give protection to our children, we automatically expect obedience from them. In our inspirational verse for today Jesus asks the question, "Why call Me Lord, Lord, and not do the things which I say?" It is important for us to know that Jesus never gives us any commands that are designed to make our lives bitter or burdensome. Rather, His commands are designed to make our live blessed and bountiful. Ask yourself about the last time you obeyed the Lord and it led to a situation from which you could not be delivered. Now consider this: When have you disobeyed the Lord and it led to heartache and pain that was more than you could bear? Get the picture?

If He is truly your Lord, express your trust in Him with your unquestioned obedience. Whenever He gives a command, it is designed to bring you closer to Him so that you may abide in His constant reassuring presence. Whatever He tells us to do, don't wait to understand it; just surrender and leave the details to Him.

August 11th
Genesis 2:7

And the Lord God formed man of the dust of the ground, and breathed into his nostrils the breath of life; and man became a living being.

Perhaps you are having one of those days when you feel inadequate or incomplete. Remove those thoughts from your mind right now. You have been formed from nothing—dust—into the wonderful human being you are right now. The devil is aware of not only your potential, but also of your composition. He knows that you were wonderfully and meticulously made and formed by God Himself. Your life has value, purpose, and spiritual significance written all over it. As you read this, you might be saying to yourself, "The person who wrote this has no idea what I'm facing at this point in my life, so how can he possibly assign value to my life?" The reason I can say with confident assurance that your life has significance is because of what we read in today's inspirational verse. After the Lord God formed man, He then breathed the breath of life into him, and man became a living soul. The most valuable part of your being is not what is attached to you, but the breath of God that supports, sustains, and abides within you.

You are not just a living person of existence—you are a living soul with eternal value to your creator, God.

August 12th
1 Samuel 2:2

No one is holy like the Lord, For there is none besides You, Nor is there any rock like our God.

We are connected to a God who is in a class all by Himself. There is no one like Him. This should motivate us to give Him a greater level of service, praise, and loyalty than others give to the false gods they serve. Our inspirational verse for today makes this fact clear beyond a shadow of a doubt. There is none besides our God. In other words, everything and everyone else pales in comparison to Him. No one can stand shoulder to shoulder with our God. When I felt led by the Lord to write this daily devotional, I did not want to limit the information to only encouragement and motivations for us, important and needful as that may be. But what should motivate us the most is the added knowledge of the awesomeness of our God. *The awesomeness of our God*—that just sounds great to me.

He is a *rock of salvation*, a *rock of security*, and a *rock of stability*. When life seems to do nothing more than blow you from side to side, don't worry. You are being held firmly in place by our holy, awesome, rock-strong God. There is no one like Him, and He has allowed us to be connected to Him. Now, go out and make this a great day!

August 13th
1 Samuel 2:8

He raises the poor from the dust And lifts the beggar from the heap, To set them among princes And make them inherit the throne of glory. For the pillars of the earth are the Lord's, And He has set the world upon them.

He's got the whole world in His hands. He's got the whole world in His hands. He's got the whole world in His hands. After hearing this, what more do we need to be assured of? Hannah, the previously barren woman who later gave birth to the prophet Samuel, wrote those words. After years of feeling forgotten, forsaken, and ridiculed, she now rises from her pain and utters these words of magnificent praise. God moved her from the position of beggar on the heap on life to a princess who inherited His throne of glory. When God does great things in our lives, it should lead to a great testimony from our mouths. Her confidence was firmly fixed on God's power. She knew God held the world in place and He would continue to hold her life in place. This is what we, as children of God, need to know.

As God is able to hold the world in place beneath our feet, He can surely hold our lives in place. He's got the whole world and all His children in His hands.

August 14th
Numbers 13:30

Then Caleb quieted the people before Moses, and said, "Let us go up at once and take possession, for we are well able to overcome it."

Is there a great challenge before you? Does it seem too hard for you to handle all by yourself? If yes, you are exactly where the Lord wants you to be. Whenever we face challenges and opportunities beyond our ability, the Lord does not want us to focus on our power, but instead on His promises! If He has given you the assignment, then move your life out of neutral gear and get on the road to spiritual progress. In our inspirational verse for today, a man by the name of Caleb had at least three things working against him: He was eighty years old; he was outnumbered; and he was speaking to people whose hearts were filled with doubt and disbelief. None of this, however, caused Caleb's faith to waver because he knew he had received a promise and a command from the Lord. The promise was: The land would be theirs. The command was: Go up and take possession of it.

God has some spiritual and life blessings for you, but you will never receive them as long as you allow your lack of power and the faithlessness of other people to rule your life. You are well able to handle whatever is before you. The Lord does not send you to it; He accompanies you through it.

August 15th
Proverbs 1:33

But whoever listens to wisdom will dwell safely, and will be secure, without fear of evil.

One of the most disconcerting things in life is making a major decision and then later wondering if you did the right thing. Many times we second-guess our decisions because we know we made them without first seeking wise counsel from Godly people. Before we take and apply the advice or counsel of anyone, we must first stop and analyze the effectiveness of the wisdom in that person's own life. In other words, we must examine the life of the person advising us to see if there are signs of Godly wisdom based on choices they made in the past.

In today's inspirational verse, Solomon tells us, "But whoever listens to wisdom will dwell safely..." This helps us understand that the wisdom of God is available to any person who is in any circumstance. Even if we have made some poor choices in the past, the wisdom of God can lead us through it and out of it. It will bring a level of security to our lives unlike anything we have ever known before. Seek Godly wisdom, and then watch fear slowly dissipate from your life.

August 16th

John 14:20

At that day you will know that I am in My Father, and you in Me, and I in you.

Our inspirational verse for today reveals three truly comforting and reassuring principles about our relationship with our Savior. One, we have *earthly security* in Jesus Christ. Two, we have *effective security* in Jesus Christ. Three, we have *eternal security* in Jesus Christ. Here, Jesus speaks to His disciples about His death, and tells them that when He is crucified these principles will be revealed to them.

We are now more than 2,000 years after His death, burial, and resurrection. And the assurance He made to His disciples at that time is available to us right now. We have earthly security: He lives in us while we are here on earth. We have effective security: His position in His Father gives us power to fulfill our spiritual responsibilities. We have eternal security: We live in Him, and shall do so throughout everlasting ages. That is enough good news to make this not just a good day, but a great day.

August 17th

Mark 6:31

And He said to them, "Come aside by yourselves to a deserted place and rest a while." For there were many coming and going, and they did not even have time to eat.

I do not consider or label myself a workaholic, but I will be honest and admit that I find it difficult to rest and remove myself from the work of the Kingdom of God that I love so much. Jesus knows that we will never be able to be consistently productive in His work if our bodies are worn and physically extended. We often make the mistake of trying to do too much just to prove our sincerity to other people and the Lord. Here is a word of sound advice. We will never be able to totally satisfy and meet the needs and demands of every person who crosses our path. We also need to know that we do not have to attempt to impress the Lord; He already knows the genuineness of our hearts. In our inspirational verse for today, Jesus tells His disciples to come away from the demands of the daily grind and rest a while. When we take the time to rest from our daily labors, at least three things can make it more enjoyable and relaxing. One: Make sure we spend extra time in His *presence*. Don't allow other people and other stuff to crowd your rest time. Two: Make sure you spend extra time with His *precepts*. Allow His Word to calm and soothe your heart and soul. And three: Spend extra time in His *praise*.

Enjoy your life. Worship and praise Him in the privacy of your deserted place, and then return to your responsibilities refreshed and renewed. Take some chill time.

August 18th
Exodus 3:7

And the Lord said: "I have surely seen the oppression of My people who are in Egypt, and have heard their cry because of their taskmasters, for I know their sorrows.

I know it may seem difficult right now, but I have a praise report. God knows exactly where you are, what you are going through, and how long you have been there. He also has your date of deliverance already planned. In our inspirational verse for today, we are informed of some very encouraging truths. The Lord sees where we are. The Lord claims us as His people. The Lord hears our cries. He knows the cause of our pain, and He is aware of all our sorrows. I cannot explain why God allows pain to come upon us from people who seek to cause us harm and destroy our lives. But I do know that He is in total control of every evil person and every injurious predicament.

Don't quit; don't surrender. That is exactly what the devil is counting on you to do. God has a set time to bring you out. And when He does, it will make more sense looking back on it than it did staring that trouble in the face. He knows what you face. That is all you need to know—that, and to leave the rest in His hands.

August 19th

Acts 23:11

But the following night the Lord stood by him and said, "Be of good cheer, Paul; for as you have testified for Me in Jerusalem, so you must also bear witness at Rome."

God is not yet finished with you! Take a moment right now to rejoice and praise God for the truth of this statement. He has some additional places of ministry He is about to take you to. Do you wonder why you have been facing so much adversity lately? Well, it just may be because the Lord wants to freshen and expand your testimony. People have heard about the things He brought you through and the doors He opened a few weeks, months, or years ago. The Lord entrusts you with some trials to expand your testimony. In our inspirational verse for today, Jesus stands by Paul and speaks comforting words to his heart. He does the same for you right now. Paul had gone to Jerusalem to preach, but the Lord was not finished with him because He was about to take him to Rome.

Our troubles provide for us an opportunity to go places where others never have a chance to travel to. The Lord was going to meet Caesar in Rome. He has new places for you to go, and new people for you to meet. This will take place after He has delivered you from those new trials you face. So, hold your head high—God is not finished with you just yet.

August 20th
1 Corinthians 15:10

But by the grace of God I am what I am, and His grace toward me was not in vain; but I labored more abundantly than they all, yet not I, but the grace of God which was with me.

When we think about the grace of God, we usually envision Him giving us some undeserved blessing that will make our lives more comfortable and enjoyable. But in today's inspirational verse, Paul shows us another dimension of God's grace. He enlightens us on this matter of God's ministry-working grace. Paul acknowledges that it was the grace of God that gave him the ability to labor for the Lord more effectively than anyone else around him could do. This is so inspiring. It helps us realize that instead of always looking to use God's grace for our advantage, we should take the time to use it to the advantage of the One who gave it to us.

If you are feeling a bit fatigued in your labor and ministry for the Lord, today's verse will give you just the spiritual uplift you need. God's grace gives identity to us. His grace gives us a new level of responsibility. And finally, His grace helps us take our focus off ourselves and place it on the Giver of grace; "...yet not I, but the grace of God which was with me." Go out and make it a grace-filled day. Need I say any more than this?

August 21st
Genesis 15:1

After these things the word of the Lord came to Abram in a vision, saying, "Do not be afraid, Abram. I am your shield, your exceedingly great reward."

Pastor William Timothy Glynn, a good friend of mine, says, "When God is all you have, that is when God is all you need." I could not agree more. When the Lord transitions us either physically or spiritually, those times can truly test our faith. In our inspirational verse for today, the Lord speaks to Abraham after he has been commanded to leave family, friends, and his familiar surroundings. The first thing the Lord seeks to dismiss from Abraham's mind is the same thing He wants to dismiss from ours: "Do not be afraid." This is God's way of reminding us that it does not matter where we are; He is already there and He was there before we made our arrival.

God is your shield. He protects you, so just keep walking. He's got you covered. I love the final part of this verse. It does not say He *has* an exceedingly great reward for us, but that He *is* our exceedingly great reward. When we have God as our reward, what more could we possibly need? When God is all you have, He is all you need. Allow Him to capture your fear, and He will give you Himself as the reward.

August 22nd
2 Corinthians7:4

Great is my boldness of speech toward you, great is my boasting on your behalf. I am filled with comfort. I am exceedingly joyful in all our tribulation.

When I first read this verse I wondered, "How can we be joyful in the midst of tribulations?" The answer I received from the Holy Spirit was: "When you know that I am right there with you." That was enough to convince me, and it has made all the difference in the world. Allow me to be transparent for a moment. Earlier in my life, when I read books, I often thought the authors were only writing from a theoretical, experimental perspective. I later discovered these authors were writing out of the pain they had gone through and the traumatic experiences God had delivered them from or during which He held their hands while they remained in them. As I write today's inspirational message to encourage you, my own life contains unresolved emotional pains and problems. But I can honestly say that I am exceedingly joyful in all my tribulations because God has proven Himself to be faithful in holding my hand and assuring me of His presence every step of the way. I may not know your name just as Paul did not know the names of everyone he wrote to. But I want to be able say about you what he said about the Christians in Corinth: "Great is my boldness of speech toward you, great is my boasting on your behalf."

Whatever you may face from this day forward, please be assured that, just as the Lord brought Paul (who wrote this book of 2nd Corinthians) through some unimaginable difficulties, He will do the same for you.

August 23rd
2 Corinthians 7:6

Nevertheless God, who comforts the downcast, comforted us by the coming of Titus.

The Lord has an amazing way of allowing us to feel His comfort through other people during some of the most difficult times in our lives. But I must also hasten to remind and inform that this is a two-way street. Many of us love to receive comfort from people when our hearts are heavy, but seldom, if ever, offer comfort to others. Most of us know Titus as one of the preaching sons in the ministry of the Apostle Paul. But here he shares with us another side of his personality: Titus did not allow a pulpit position to rob him of his passion for people. Don't allow your title or prestige to hinder you from reaching out to the downcast.

Keep your eyes and ears open today. There will be people all around whose hearts are hurting and their spirits are wounded. Place your personal issues to the side for a while and express compassion toward these people, just as Titus did for Paul. God sends you to those who need to feel His love for them through you. Don't let them down, and don't let Him down.

August 24th
Mark 8:29

He said to them, "But who do you say that I am?" Peter answered and said to Him, "You are the Christ."

Don't allow any person or circumstance to change your confidence in what the Word of God says about Jesus Christ. When things become challenging and difficult in our lives we have a tendency to give the devil more listening time than he deserves. The Lord wants our faith in Him and our knowledge of Him to remain fixed and firm at all times.

Peter knew Jesus was the Christ of God and the Son of God. Having that assurance in our hearts will carry us a long way not just in life, but all the way to eternal life. No matter what others may say about Jesus in either jest or doubt, proclaim to them as Peter did, "He is the Christ, the Son of God." Now walk in that peace throughout the entire day.

August 25th

Joshua 24:24

And the people said to Joshua, "The Lord our God we will serve, and His voice we will obey!"

It's amazing how we are willing to say we will obey the Lord and follow the commandments from His Word when things are well in our lives. But when difficulties come and His discipline is revealed, we seem to forget all that we have promised. In our inspirational verse for today, Joshua, just a few days from his physical death, has led the people of God into the Promised Land. He takes time to remind them how important it is to obey the Lord because, if not, their blessings could lead to bruises.

I want to challenge you today. Don't say you will serve the Lord when it is convenient and then fail to make good on that commitment. Don't just say you will obey His voice and then live contrary to His Word. If you make those promises, keep them. Then watch Him bless your life in ways you never dreamed possible.

August 26th
Romans 5:10

For if when we were enemies we were reconciled to God through the death of His Son, much more, having been reconciled, we shall be saved by His life.

The Lord never completes anything just halfway. His work in our lives may not be complete in our eyes, but you can rest assured that He will see us through until the day of completion. In our inspirational verse for today, we are informed and reminded of the fact that, prior to our belief in the life, death, burial, and resurrection of Jesus Christ, we were enemies of God and doomed for eternal death. Our sins had placed us in that condition. But now that we have entrusted Him with our hearts, souls, and minds, in addition to having our death sentence removed, we have also been granted eternal life.

Jesus has not only removed the penalty we deserved, He has also given us the eternal reconciliation we do not deserve. No matter what this day holds, walk through it confident that you are being completed daily, because you have already been completed in eternity.

August 27th
Genesis 21:1

And the Lord visited Sarah as He had said, and the Lord did for Sarah as He had spoken.

There are times when I must purposefully ensure that I separate my preaching material from my daily devotional preparation. I have more time to preach from a text than I do to give brief inspiration from a verse of scripture. If I were preaching from today's inspirational verse, however, my subject would be "God will do just what He said." You need to be reminded of that truth right now. I don't know what you face, but I do know that it is bigger than you, and God has promised to see you through it. This verse makes us aware of three things the Lord did for Sarah, and will also do for us. The Lord visited Sarah. He *came* to where she was–God knows your location; he will come to you. The Lord *communicated* with Sarah–He still speaks, and tells you, "Fear not, everything you need I have, and every foe before you, I can conquer." Lastly, the Lord *comforted* Sarah–He gave her just what He promised: a son named Isaac.

God still keeps His Word and honors His promises. All we have to do is trust Him and wait on Him. If He said it, He will bring it to pass.

August 28th
Galatians 5:13

For you, brethren, have been called to liberty; only do not use liberty as an opportunity for the flesh, but through love serve one another.

I hope you will agree with me when I say we now live in a time when people love to push the envelope to the edge. Not only is this true with worldly, ungodly people, but this mindset has also invaded the Church. People love to see just how much border-line "worldliness" they can get away with and still hide behind their so called "Christian liberty." In our inspirational verse for today we are warned to not use our liberty to satisfy our flesh and ourselves, but as a tool to serve one another with the love of Jesus Christ.

Don't ever allow the liberty you have as a mature believer to cause someone to misunderstand what walking with, and for, the Lord is truly all about. Take your eyes off yourself and then ask yourself, "Is what I'm about to do, wear, say, engage in, or condone, really helpful to other people whose faith may not be as strong as mine?"

It's not about us, but it is all about glorifying Him.

August 29th
Mark 10:27

But Jesus looked at them and said, "With men it is impossible, but not with God; for with God all things are possible."

Every child of God who has been walking with the Lord for a significant period of time has faced seemingly impossible situations in their life. I will be the first to be honest and admit that I have had more of those experiences than I can count. But, as I write this daily devotional, I can also say the Lord has never failed to show forth His miracle-working intervening power. You may be feeling as though you face more than one situation you cannot possibly see your way out of. Well, cheer up. I have good news. You are right where the Lord wants you to be. We often think things are impossible because our only point of reference is what other people either cannot or will not do for us. This is why Jesus said, "With men it is impossible, but not with God..."

I have discovered there are times when the Lord purposefully allows others to either deny or ignore us just to force us back into a relationship of total dependence on Him. Whatever you face, turn away from it for a while and turn to the only one who is able to either fix it for you or fix *you* to handle it. Now, walk by faith and leave the results in His hands. With God, all things are possible, even the situation you face.

August 30th

Psalm 119:37

Turn away my eyes from looking at worthless things, And revive me in Your way.

The Lord is trying to get our attention! I cannot even begin to imagine how difficult this must be for Him. When we consider all the troublesome things we focus on that we want Him to move from our lives, and then consider all the so-called positive, materialistic things we want Him to add to our lives, so little time remains for us to focus solely on Him and Him alone. In our inspirational verse for today, the psalmist's prayer was for the Lord to turn his eyes and attention away from worthless things. Perhaps you wonder what those worthless things were. The answer is relatively simple: Anything that blinds us or takes our attention away from the Lord and His Word is a worthless thing.

If you are feeling low of spirit, more stuff added to your life is not the answer. If our spirits are to be revived, it must be done through the reading, teaching, and preaching of, and from, His Word. Focus on that, and watch everything else fall into place.

August 31st

Proverbs 16:3

Commit your works to the Lord, and your thoughts will be established.

If we are going to be successful in any venture or project in life, focus and concentration are extremely important. It is hard to work on one thing when your mind is on something entirely different. In our inspirational verse for today, the wise man Solomon gives us all some excellent advice. He tells us to commit our works to the Lord, and the Lord will establish our thoughts. This simply means we must learn the importance of surrendering everything we do to the total guiding care and direction of our Heavenly Father—not just those things we do in church or for the Kingdom of God, but every aspect of our daily lives should be committed to Him. This is our way of expressing our trust in Him for His *direction*, His *discipline*, and His *deliverance*.

When we surrender these things to Him, He then clears our minds and establishes our thoughts. The end result leads to our lives becoming more productive and fruitful—all because we have placed every facet of our lives in the hands of someone whose expertise is so much greater than ours will ever be.

PRAYER

Most gracious God, we bless and praise Your wonderful and holy name. Thank You for leading us to this point in the year, and by faith we are trusting in You for the great things You still have in store for our lives. Remove any fear, and replace it with faith. Remove any doubt, and replace it with dependence on You. Prepare us to be used by You, and we offer ourselves to be instruments of Your glory.

In Jesus' name,
Amen.

Strawberries of Strength in September

September 1st
Exodus 12:35

Now the children of Israel had done according to the word of Moses, and they had asked from the Egyptians articles of silver, articles of gold, and clothing.

There are times in life when the Lord chooses to bless His people through some unexpected avenues. Those we thought were only part of our lives to bring us harm can actually become some of the same people the Lord uses to add hope for our future. This is exactly what we see in our inspirational verse for today. The Lord is getting ready to deliver His people out of evil Egyptian bondage and tells Moses to tell them to ask their captors for articles of silver and gold. Before we focus too much on what they asked for, I want to focus on the importance of obeying the Lord even when the request does not seem logical or reasonable. No one in their right mind would believe that your greatest enemy would willingly give up their silver and gold to you. But the Lord has a way of completely changing our circumstances when we learn how to obey Him, even when it does not make sense to us. Today there will be opportunities for you to trust the Lord and obey Him outside the box of your comfort zone.

My advice to you is to trust Him, obey Him, and then get ready to watch Him reveal some things to you that only He and He alone can reveal. The question is not, "Can God do the impossible?" The question is simply, "Do you believe that He is able to do the impossible?"

September 2nd
Exodus 12:36

And the Lord had given the people favor in the sight of the Egyptians, so that they granted them what they requested. Thus they plundered the Egyptians.

If this is your first day reading this devotional, I want you to do yourself a huge favor. Even if you have been disciplined in reading each day, do yourself the same favor. Go back and read yesterday's devotional once again.

Okay, are you ready? Here is what happened. The children of Israel obeyed, and God did just what He said He would. He told them to do something that did not seem logical, and when they obeyed, He did something inexplicable: He gave them favor from their foes. The Lord not only released them from their slavery in Egypt, He also made sure they did not leave empty-handed. This story helped me understand that all the Lord waits for us to do is obey Him explicitly. Our obedience triggers His miracle-working intervention. Perhaps there are things you feel you need to make your life full and complete. Before you put forth any effort to attain them, first ask yourself, "Are there any areas in my life where I am not totally obedient to the Lord?" If so, then correct those matters now. While you may feel some people around you want to cause harm to your life, the Lord can use them to be a blessing to your life, instead. All He needs is for you to do exactly what He tells you to.

Today's verse tells us the Egyptians "granted them whatever they requested." Did you catch that? They did not have to beg, borrow, or bargain; all they did was request. When we do what the Lord tells us to do, He will take care of the rest. The Lord does not want you to be empty-handed, but He is, after all, waiting for you to respond to His commands.

September 3rd
Acts 26:16

But rise and stand on your feet; for I have appeared to you for this purpose, to make you a minister and a witness both of the things which you have seen and of the things which I will yet reveal to you.

In today's inspirational verse, the Apostle Paul recounts to a group a people his conversion experience on the Damascus road. More than 2,000 years ago, the Lord, by this one verse, comforted Paul's heart and He continues to comfort our hearts with it today. The Lord gives Paul and us the ability to change our *position*: "But rise and stand on your feet..." He gives us a *purpose* for our lives: "...for I have appeared to you for this purpose..." He gives us both *present* and *perpetual projections* for our lives "...to make you a minister and a witness both of the things which you have seen and of the things which I will yet reveal to you."

My encouraging word for you today is this: God has some great things in store for your future. Just walk with Him by faith, and then watch Him unfold new opportunities for you to represent Him and lead people to Him day by day. You have no idea of the great things the Lord is getting ready to reveal to you.

September 4th
1 Timothy 2:8

I desire therefore that the men pray everywhere, lifting up holy hands, without wrath and doubting.

When we worship and pray to God, He wants our prayers to be passionate, pure, and purposeful. We should not limit the time of our prayers to the one place we call the "Church house." In our inspirational verse for today, Paul tells Timothy, his son in the ministry, that it is his desire for men to pray everywhere. How much time do you spend praying at work? What about your prayer time at home? If you are a parent, when was the last time you prayed not just *for* your child(ren) but *with* them? What about prayer time with friends? Prayer is the Godly glue that holds our lives together. The lifting of holy hands is symbolic of surrendering all our cares and concerns to the Lord. We release what is in our hands into His. When we do this, we must purge our hearts from wrath against other people and doubt about God's ability to meet our needs.

Lift your hands, release that wrath–and embrace His righteousness. Release that doubt–and embrace His confidence. I have found that life is so much more meaningful when I learn to release my fears–and embrace His faith.

September 5th
Proverbs 3:27

Do not withhold good from those to whom it is due, When it is in the power of your hand to do so.

Allow me to give you the Roy Elton Brackins paraphrased translation of this verse: Never overlook an opportunity to be a blessing to someone who you know in your heart is deserving of encouragement, especially when you have the power in your hands to brighten their life. The Lord left us here on earth to fulfill at least three basic responsibilities: 1) We should be instruments of *exaltation* as we freely offer our worship and praise to the Lord; 2) We should be instruments of *evangelism* in leading unsaved people to Jesus Christ; 3) We should also be instruments of *edification*, building up and encouraging those who are already a part of the body of Christ. This is an area many of us neglect. If we are not careful we can spend too much time focusing on what we think we need, while failing to lend a helping hand to others.

Share a kind word today. Perform a gesture of love for another believer. It does not have to be anything costly; just make sure it is from your heart. After all, God gave you the power in your hand to do so.

September 6th
Philemon 1:21

Having confidence in your obedience, I write to you, knowing that you will do even more than I say.

When Paul writes this letter that is tucked away here in the New Testament, he writes it to one friend on behalf of another friend. One friend has made some terrible mistakes, but the other can be used as an instrument of healing and reconciliation. These words show forth the confidence Paul had in the friend who was able and in position to help the hurting friend. Paul had confidence in the friend's obedience to God's commandments and his overflow of compassion "...knowing that [he] will do even more than I say."

Don't make the mistake of holding a grudge or doing just enough to get by. Make this the day you commit to going beyond what people expect from you. Even if you have been hurt in the past, don't do it for them; do it for Him. We have hurt Him more times than we can count, and He continues to do more than we expect. Allow Him to use you as an instrument of His reconciling love.

September 7th
Genesis 22:8

And Abraham said, "My son, God will provide for Himself the lamb for a burnt offering." So the two of them went together.

My word of encouragement for you today is: "Whatever you need, if it is in God's will for your life, He will provide." Under the direction of the Lord, Abraham goes to Mount Moriah to sacrifice his son Isaac. Isaac goes with him willingly without being completely aware of what is about to take place. Isaac sees the fire and the wood, but he does not see the sacrifice. When he asks his father about the sacrifice, Abraham speaks the words of our inspirational verse for today.

There will be times when we will not be able to see everything that God is getting ready to do in our lives. But my advice to you is to keep climbing the mountain. And while you are climbing, just remind yourself of this truth: The Lord will provide. I don't know what your needs are for today, but I do know you have no need the Lord is unable to provide for. So keep climbing. Don't stop. The Lord will provide.

September 8th
Psalm 119:2

Blessed are those who keep His testimonies, Who seek Him with the whole heart!

Our inspirational verse for today gives us a simple recipe for living a blessed life. Those of us who keep the testimonies (that is, the words), commandments, and statutes of the Lord are blessed people. This verse also helps us understand that keeping God's Word gives us reason to have a greater pursuit of Him. Whenever we get closer to Him we cannot help but to experience His bountiful blessings flowing through every phase of our lives. I have discovered the importance of concentrating more on what God wants to place in my heart from His Word than I do on what He wants to place in my hand from this world. This world is temporary, but His Word is eternal. As you seek the Lord throughout this day, don't do so with a callous, uncaring, nonchalant disposition; rather, seek Him with your whole heart.

When we give our whole heart to Him, the reciprocal blessings that flow in our direction are literally too numerous to mention.

September 9th
Zephaniah 3:17

The Lord your God in your midst, The Mighty One, will save; He will rejoice over you with gladness, He will quiet you with His love, He will rejoice over you with singing.

This is one of the most intimate, heart-warming, and reassuring verses in the entire Bible. The image evoked is one of a loving parent keeping watch over a child, calming him or her with His presence and singing lullabies. When I read this, I cannot help but wonder what key God sings in. Is He a tenor or a bass? Then the Holy Spirit helped me realize that God always sings in the key of *love*. He soothes and refreshes us with His presence, and He comforts us with His melodies. Whatever you face today, remind yourself of the truths found in this one verse. God is in our midst. The Lord is mighty and He has saved us. The Lord desires to rejoice over us with gladness, so we must live the kind of life that will give Him something to rejoice about. And should we become frantic, He is right beside us to quiet us with His love.

The Lord waits to rejoice over you with singing. This is His way of letting all creation know that you are His child. Now go out and live this day like He is your heavenly Father.

September 10th
Psalm 118:18

The Lord has chastened me severely, But He has not given me over to death.

It is one thing to go through a difficult period in life with no real idea why such negative things confront us. It is a totally different thing altogether when the Lord disciplines us and we know exactly why, and our only question is, "How long will this punishment last?" In our inspirational verse for today, the psalmist shares both his trouble and his testimony with us. His trouble is found in the severe chastening he received from the Lord. His testimony is found in the fact that the Lord has not given him over to death. Although this verse of scripture seems to be a very somber one on the surface, if you allow me a moment, I would like to encourage your heart. Whenever the Lord punishes, disciplines, and chastises us, He does not design that punishment to kill us, but to keep us from doing things that can lead to an early or untimely death. The Lord often uses our sins and His resulting discipline to slow us down and redirect our focus back on Him.

The discipline may be painful, but it all leads to His allowing you to live a more productive life. He is not trying to destroy you, but to develop you for His glory, and discipline is part of that process. Take it from someone who knows firsthand about the Lord's discipline.

September 11th
Psalm 119:11

Your Word I have hidden in my heart, That I might not sin against You.

I will be honest and admit that this is one of those Bible verses I learned as a child, but had no idea at the time the incredible spiritual profundity it held. Allow me to share with you what the Lord shared with me. Whenever sin is conceived, it takes place in our hearts. Whenever we go against the Word and the will of God it is always because we have left our hearts unguarded and allowed someone or something to temporarily occupy the place where God alone should reside. The psalmist was also aware of this problem, which is why the words in the verse are configured grammatically the way they are. He says, "Your Word I have hidden in my heart..." In other words, he positioned God's Word where he knew the devil would attack even before the attack happened. He was not reactive but proactive.

Temptation and illicit inducements will confront you. But don't leave yourself unguarded. Don't try to run and find God's Word when sinful suggestions come. Instead, hide God's Word in your heart right now, so when they do come, His Word will be your shield of protection.

September 12th
Jeremiah 31:25

For I have satiated the weary soul, and I have replenished every sorrowful soul.

Are you feeling drained, depleted, or despondent? Even if not today, a day like that may await you in the near future. Today's inspirational verse prepares us for both our present exhausted condition as well as for those difficult days yet to occur. The Lord speaks to His people through His prophet Jeremiah and provides him and the people of Jerusalem some comforting information. Notice, God speaks to them in the past tense. "For I *have satiated* the weary soul, and I *have replenished* every sorrowful soul." He does not say that he *will* do it, but that it is already done. This helped me realize that our seasons of exhaustion may be a surprise to us, but they are no surprise to the Lord. He has already prepared us to handle them before we are confronted with them. He does not promise here to give your body energy. He very well may, but this refueling is promised for the soul.

You have no need to look for outside resources to refresh and refuel you, for the Lord has satiated your weary soul and replenished your sorrowful soul. Tap into the power and the presence of the Holy Spirit who lives within you. Yield to Him and He will manifest His energy just when you need Him the most. I am a witness that He does just what He says.

September 13th
Psalm 32:7

You are my hiding place; You shall preserve me from trouble; You shall surround me with songs of deliverance.

Today's inspirational verse tells us that God is a hiding place, and in Him we are preserved from trouble. Perhaps you wonder what this really means. I did, too, at first, but have come to know that it means we find inner peace with our eternal God. Even though we cannot see Him, we run to Him in both prayer and praise and leave all our worries and concerns in His hands. When hiding, we are often alone; but in His hiding place, we are never lonely. Some of us may fear being alone, but that is when we may feel the Lord's presence and hear His voice more clearly than ever before. The psalmist also informs us that His source of spiritual strength came through the kind of music he listened to. He chose to keep his radio on songs that spoke of God's delivering power and His CD case filled with music about the protecting and preserving power of our God.

Whatever we allow to enter our mind has a great impact on our disposition the rest of the day. Find your hiding place in *prayer* to God, *personal connection* with God, and *praise* to God. Your day will be so much brighter when you apply these simple principles.

September 14th
1 Peter 1:18

Knowing that you were not redeemed with corruptible things, like silver or gold, from your aimless conduct received by tradition from your fathers.

The way to get a good idea of what something is worth to someone is to simply ask them how much they are willing to pay for it. Our inspirational Bible verse for today is one that clarifies completely how much God truly values His relationship with us. We are not worth silver or gold, yet the Lord paid so much more on our behalf. Isaiah said that, even at our best, we are but filthy rags. Paul said, "All have sinned and come short of the glory of God." Yet, in spite of our worthlessness, Jesus paid the highest price for us known not just to mankind, but to all creation. The price the Lord paid was the blood of His only Son, Jesus Christ. This should motivate us to serve Him and commit ourselves to Him at a level beyond where any of us are right now. It matters not how much we feel we are doing for the Lord; there is always room for improvement.

Make today the day you start that process. He paid a lot more than we are worth. Let's at least strive to serve Him at the level that reflects just how much He truly deserves.

September 15th

1 Peter 1:19

But with the precious blood of Christ, as of a lamb without blemish and without spot.

Some people who find themselves in a predicament feel they need to call on someone else to bail them out. And, because whoever comes to their aid and gives relief has their own guilty past, they have to be careful about judging the guilty person. But, when Jesus paid the ransom for our sins, He did so with a spotless record, and He had absolutely nothing to gain by doing it. How do we express our gratitude for a Savior who has loved us at this phenomenal level? We cannot pay Him. But we can give Him a greater level of *service*. We can offer Him a greater level of *sacrifice*. We can offer Him complete and total *submission*. I have often wondered why we are afraid to totally surrender to the Lord. Do we really think Jesus would pay what He did for us and then give us commands and directions that would harm and complicate our lives?

He is the spotless Lamb of God, and He has redeemed us with His blood. Let's strive to live at the value level where the Lord has placed us, and not make the mistake of cheapening His amazing grace.

September 16th
Mark 13:32

But of that day and hour no one knows, not even the angels in heaven, nor the Son, but only the Father.

There is no need to consume ourselves with the details of when Jesus will return. We just need to be assured and inform others—especially those who do not know Him—that He is coming back again. There are some who make the mistake of trying to predict the date of the Lord's return. According to our inspirational verse for today, we see what a futile exercise that is. Jesus says the angels do not know when He will return, and the Father has not even told Him when that day will be. Instead, we should be spending our time preparing ourselves for Heaven, as the Lord wants. Beyond that, He also wants us to be working to lead as many people as we possibly can to spend eternity with Him there.

Let's redirect our focus away from those things we cannot change or predict and ensure we zoom in on the responsibility the Lord has left to us—to go and share the message of His life, death, burial, and resurrection—and leave the results and His return in the hands of our Heavenly Father.

September 17th

1 Corinthians 13:11

When I was a child, I spoke as a child, I understood as a child, I thought as a child; but when I became a man, I put away childish things.

Christian maturity is an important element in our relationship with the Lord. He does not want us to remain in our stage of spiritual infancy as we were when we first surrendered our lives to Him. In our inspirational verse for today, Paul speaks to us from what has been called by many the "Love chapter" of the Bible. Many of us fail to realize that in order to have strong, loving relationships, we also need mature people to comprise them. Paul mentions at least three things that were part of his former "childish" life that his relationship with the Lord allowed him to change. We, too, must change these same things. Paul mentions his speech, a reference to his *communication.* He mentions his understanding, a reference to his *comprehension.* And lastly, he mentions his thoughts, a reference to his *conception.* Once he became mature in Christ, he put all those things away.

Take inventory of your spiritual life today. Put away whatever causes you to display childish behavior and allow the world to see the mature, strong person God designed you to be.

September 18th
Revelation 22:12

And behold, I am coming quickly, and My reward is with Me, to give to everyone according to his work.

For those not familiar with Biblical doctrine, today's inspirational verse can be a bit misleading. We do not work to be saved; we work for the Lord because we have already been saved. When Jesus says He is going to reward every one of His children for their work, His meaning behind this statement is much broader. Our good deeds earn neither His grace nor His favor. The Lord's reward is based on the work we will have done for Him based solely on our love for Him and our willingness to follow His plan for our lives. Whatever you do for the Lord, at all times ensure it is a labor of love and not forced participation. He has a reward for all of us, and it will be far greater than all the work and service we give to Him combined.

The reason I know this is true is because the Lord never allows us to give more to Him than He gives back to us. I also know it to be true because this reward will never be replaced or repaired, or need upgrading. It will last throughout all eternity. Whatever you offer the Lord in service, make sure it is your very best, as His very best is waiting just for you.

September 19th
2 Chronicles 7:14

If My people who are called by My name will humble themselves, and pray and seek My face, and turn from their wicked ways, then I will hear from heaven, and will forgive their sin and heal their land.

I do not believe it possible for legislators or the government to take prayer out of school or any public place. You may not agree with me at first, but I hope your position will change before we conclude today's devotional reading. The only way to take prayer out of school and public places is to remove all the "praying people" from those schools and public places. We do not have to pray aloud and we do not have to pray collectively at a certain time for the Lord to hear us. If we would learn the importance of pausing during the day to pray at our desk, prayer can be reinstated at your place of employment. If we would teach our children the importance of prayer before taking a test in school, engaging in extracurricular activities, or before becoming connected to other unbelieving students, we can reinstate prayer in school. It is our job as believers to make sure we take time during the day to pray for our world, country, state, city, neighborhood, and all of our elected officials. In our inspirational verse for today, the Lord promises that, for those of us who humble ourselves, pray, seek His face, and repent of our wickedness, He will hear, He will forgive, and He will heal.

Let's remove from our minds the fact that the government has taken prayer out of school; let's return, instead, to teaching our children how to pray while they are in school. Have I changed your mind? Hopefully I have. Let's pray and watch God heal.

September 20th
Proverbs 4:7

Wisdom is the principle thing; Therefore get wisdom. And in all your getting, get understanding.

Don't jump to a conclusion until you have all the details. The Lord does not want us living our lives with constant frustration over things that are non-consequential. Our goal should be to gain a greater level of Godly wisdom. While we may not need more knowledge, we do need the ability to use the mental intellect and insight we have to the glory of God and for our own spiritual growth. When we gain a greater level of wisdom it gives us the ability to understand things better and place them in their proper perspective. When I use the word *understand* I am not speaking in terms of the ability to figure out or rationalize all that God is doing and all that He allows in our lives. We will never reach that point. I am speaking in terms of having sufficient wisdom and understanding, as well as the knowledge of knowing when to release those things which are beyond our control into the all-competent hands of God.

When we do this, we remove stress, worry, and doubt from our lives. Seek wisdom throughout this day, ensuring it comes from a Godly source.

September 21st
1 Thessalonians 4:14

For if we believe that Jesus died and rose again, even so God will bring with Him those who sleep in Jesus.

Death is one of the great certainties in life. I realize that may sound paradoxical and ironic, but it is the truth. So often, in matters relating to death, we call it anything other than what it is, as if our euphemisms change the situation. We say, "She *passed away* this morning." Or, "He *transitioned* in his sleep." And, I know you have heard this one before: "I *lost* a dear friend last week." But the Bible does not call the end of our earthly lives passing away, transitioning, or being lost. The Bible calls it death. We do not believe Jesus passed away, transitioned, or was lost was Friday; we believe He died. We will never begin to deal with the temporary pain of death until we first call it what it is. Then we must also realize that death is not the end of the story in the life of any person: unbelievers will be eternally separated from the Lord in hell, while we believers will be eternally connected to the Lord in Heaven.

Jesus died and rose again, and when He returns, we do not have to worry about ourselves or our loved ones who trusted in Him. Those who have died before us will be with Him, and those of us who are still alive will be caught up to meet Him. Don't live in fear of death—live in expectation of the *real* life He has for us in eternity.

September 22nd
Exodus 20:3

You shall have no other gods before Me.

Most, and hopefully all, of us would never admit to being guilty of serving idol gods. The truth of the matter is that the devil has a way of distracting us with things that seem more important to us than the Lord. And before we know anything, we have allowed those things to occupy a predominant amount of our time, talents, and treasure. The Lord was aware of this problem over four thousand years ago. As a result, He instructed Moses to tell His people to not commit the horrendous and ungodly act of placing anything or any other person ahead of Him. And just imagine: At the time this commandment came down, cell phones, cable TV, fax machines, texting, Twitter, Facebook, and Instagram did not exist. Today, these things distract us to the point we are more concerned with what others say about us, and are completely blinded and unable to hear what the Lord is saying.

Our challenge for today and the days to follow is to turn our attention away from the world's lure, and focus, instead, exclusively on the Lord. He sent a text message to you today and is waiting for your response:

"You shall have no other gods before Me."
Sent from My eternal phone.

A proper response would be:

"Yes, Lord, I received Your message and I commit to being obedient to Your commands. You have my wholehearted and undivided attention."

September 23rd
Leviticus 8:24

Then he brought Aaron's sons. And Moses put some of the blood on the tips of their right ears, on the thumbs of their right hands, and on the big toes of their right feet. And Moses sprinkled the blood all around on the altar.

This is one of those verses in the Bible that may be confusing on the surface but is filled with profound spiritual simplicity. The Lord instructed Moses to consecrate Aaron and his sons to serve Him as priests. And Moses did exactly what the Lord told him to do. Likewise, Jesus was instructed by His Father to consecrate us to serve Him as New Testament priests in sharing His message everywhere we go. Each of these consecrations contains one important element: In the Old Testament it was the blood of a ram; in the New Testament it is the blood of Jesus. Moses strategically placed the blood in three important areas: on the men's right ears to symbolize the purification needed to hear God clearly; on their right hands to symbolize their ability to work effectively for God; and on their right feet to symbolize their ability to walk effectively wherever the Lord would lead them. Lastly, Moses' sprinkling of the blood around the altar served to symbolize their eternal connection to God.

The Lord wants us to know that our ears, hands, and feet have been anointed by the blood of His Son Jesus Christ. He has done this so that we might represent Him with pure hearts and minds. Let's not make the mistake of polluting what God has already purified. Be careful what you allow your ears to hear and your hands to touch, and take care where you use your feet to walk.

September 24th
Proverbs 10:17

He who keeps instruction is in the way of life, But he who refuses correction goes astray.

Most of us love to receive encouragement and compliments, but few of us welcome correction. The Lord shares an important principle that has blessed me tremendously, and I hope it will do the same for you. People usually give encouragement based on our current events or circumstances. They give compliments based on what we have done in the past. Correction, on the other hand, is designed to guard us against the mistakes we have the potential of repeating in our future. We look around; we look back; and we look forward. The wise man Solomon tells us to "keep instruction." Don't just politely receive it, but apply it constructively to every phase of your life.

When we refuse to do this, we can stray from the path the Lord wants us on. The Lord has purposefully placed Godly people in our lives. Don't turn them off when they offer helpful words of instruction. Embrace them and their Godly, Biblical instructions. Then trust the Lord to promptly grant you the opportunity to share with others what God shared with you from another saint. Godly instructions will keep us on the way of life.

September 25th
Romans 10:3

For they being ignorant of God's righteousness, and seeking to establish their own righteousness, have not submitted to the righteousness of God.

In Proverbs 16:25 we read these words: "There is a way that seems right to a man. But its end is the way of death." Both Paul in today's inspirational verse and Solomon in this Old Testament verse give us a strong warning. They warn us of the danger in overlooking what God says is right and seeking instead to establish our own standards of righteousness. If we are to live a life that is pleasing to our Heavenly Father, we must begin with submission to His Word and surrender to His will.

The world wants to distract you today from what God has said, and fill your mind with the ideologies and situational ethics of others. Don't be taken in by it! Stand for righteousness. Walk in holiness, and allow God's Word to govern, guide, and guard your life. We are saved because we believe the truth from His Word. We can also be preserved by the truth from that same Word.

September 26th

Luke 1:68

Blessed is the Lord God of Israel, For He has visited and redeemed His people.

At first glance, our inspirational verse for today may not seem as important as it really is. There are two key words found in this verse: *visited* and *redeemed.* They contrast each other and yet show the amazing interaction of our God with His people. Most of the time, when people visit our home, they consume and take away more than what they brought into our home. But the way in which the Lord interacts with us is just the opposite. He visited us, but His visit was not to take anything away from us, but rather to add redemption to our lives. I am absolutely amazed by this. The Lord did not make us stand in line, take a number, and fill out a form in order to be saved; He came from Heaven wrapped in human flesh and brought redemption directly to us.

The knowledge of this should immediately raise your self-esteem. The Lord came into your life, perhaps when others had walked out of it. When others took from you, the Lord gave you the most precious possession you could ever own: Himself and His salvation. Now, allow that to simmer on your mind, and make today one of the best of the year.

September 27th
2 Corinthians 10:4

For the weapons of our warfare are not carnal but mighty in God for pulling down strongholds.

It just may be that the reason many of God's people seem to lose their battles against the devil is because they fight with the wrong weapons. Even when we use our intellect, trickery, schemes, and even physical force, the devil can match and overcome them all. Consider the truth: Our battle is not against flesh and blood, or even against other people, but against the power that causes both us and others to act in ungodly ways. Are you expecting to encounter any opposition today? If so, what are you planning to fight with? Allow me to suggest at least three very powerful deterrents with which to arm yourself: *prayer, patience*, and *praise.* Use your weapon of prayer when things come against you that you are unable to handle; pray before you act or react. Use your weapon of patience; don't be in a hurry, as patience is a virtue and part of the fruit of the Spirit. Use your weapon of praise; take your focus off your problem and zoom in on your problem-solver instead–and don't wait for the situation to be resolved; praise Him in advance.

The Lord has given us both an arsenal of mighty weapons and the "spiritual permit" to carry them, so we may as well use them.

September 28th
Joshua 6:27

So the Lord was with Joshua, and his fame spread throughout all the country.

Many people, among them believers, have made the mistake of pursuing worldly fame, and it has caused them a tremendous amount of heartache in the process. In our inspirational verse for today, Joshua does not pursue fame, but the Lord gives it to him. Joshua was not famous for his wealth, number of children, or even his military might. According to this verse, Joshua was famous for his relationship with the Lord. The verse informs us that the "Lord was with Joshua..." I encourage you to make that your pursuit and goal in life. Strive to live in such a way that people will consider you famous because of your *compassion* for the Lord, your *commitment* to the Lord, and your *confidence* in the Lord.

Wouldn't it be great if someone at your place of employment walked up to you and said, "I want you to know that everyone in the company has been admiring your daily walk with the Lord"? Nothing would bring Him more glory or you the fame He has sanctioned and ordained.

September 29th
Mark 9:23

Jesus said to him, "If you can believe, all things are possible to him who believes."

In Romans 10:9 we are told that "if we confess with our mouths and believe in our hearts that God raised Jesus from the dead, we shall be saved." This helped me understand that our eternal relationship with the Lord started as a result of our belief in Him. Since we have trusted Him for our eternal well-being and provision, He also wants us to trust Him to meet our daily needs. When we face things in life that are larger than we are capable of fixing, the question is not if God can handle the matter so much as if we *believe* He can handle the problem. The issue is never His power—but our faith in that power.

God may not resolve our issue when we think it needs resolving. He may not fix it the way we think it should be fixed. If, however, we just trust Him and place it in His hands, when He is done it will work out for our good and His glory. I am witness to that. "All things are possible to him who believes." Do you believe? If so, your situation is not impossible. Case closed!

September 30th
Colossians 2:8

Beware lest anyone cheat you through philosophy and empty deceit, according to the tradition of men, according to the basic principles of the world, and not according to Christ.

Okay, let's get one thing straight: God has done so many things for us, with us, through us, and even in spite of us, that we will never be able to explain it all. The Lord has not saved us to be explainers, but to be evangelists and witnesses. In our inspirational verse for today, Paul gives us a strong warning: Don't allow anyone to cheat you of your joy or rob you of your God-given time by engaging in disputes where you try to explain the ways and the power of God. We are saved based on what we believe, and not on what we thoroughly understand.

The tradition of men tells us we must understand it before we embrace it. But our faith in God says we embrace it, even though we may never completely understand it in this life. Guard your time and your words wisely, and don't allow anyone to weaken your faith or cloud your vision of God with empty words and meaningless ramblings. Place everything on the shoulders of Christ, and allow Him to handle the rest.

PRAYER

Most gracious God, we thank You for bringing us through not only the hot months of summer, but also the heated situations we have faced in our lives. Your grace has been nothing short of amazing. Many of us did not know if we would even make it to the end of this month, but Your hand of protection kept us safe. For this and so much more, we thank You. Prepare us for the blessings and the responsibilities before us.

In Jesus' name,
Amen.

Oranges of Opportunity in October

October 1st
Numbers 6:24

The Lord bless you and keep you.

There are times in our lives when we expect one thing and receive something completely different. There are also times we feel we require a whole lot when, in actuality, all we truly need is a whole lot less. I believe this is what today's inspirational verse provides for us as we begin a new month. Maybe you feel you need something to help you become fortified against the devil's attacks. Maybe you need something to help you properly handle the pain you may be feeling in your body. Or, maybe you feel as though you need a word of strength for the challenges you experience in your family. Whatever you need, today's verse cuts right to the chase: "The Lord bless you and keep you." In case you did not receive the full impact of this verse, I will take the liberty of asking a question and adding a brief commentary. "What situation do you face that God's blessing and keeping power of you cannot resolve?" I hope you get the picture.

As we begin this month, don't focus on the problems that exist or lie ahead. Just walk in full assurance of the facts that the Lord blesses you and keeps you.

October 2nd

Numbers 6:25

The Lord make His face shine upon you, And be gracious to you.

Over and over, the Bible informs us that we are never out of the visual range of our God. Even when we sin and go contrary to His Word, He still has His eyes on us. In today's inspirational verse we are told of another component God adds to our lives when His looks at us. He makes His face shine upon us. His face gives radiance to what the devil thought was going to be a dark and gloomy day. Not only does he shine His face on us, He also treats us with graciousness. The Lord specializes in adding righteous refulgence to a previously grim, dismal, demonic day. And He showers us with His generous grace that flows in our individual direction.

You may be wondering what to do to receive His light and grace. The answer is relatively simple: Just look in the direction of where the light and grace originate. Keep your eyes on the Lord, and He will allow His face to protect you and His grace to provide for you.

October 3rd

Numbers 6:26

The Lord lift up His countenance upon you, And give you peace.

When we take the time to juxtapose our treatment of the Lord with how He continues to provide for us, we see a contrast that is nothing less than amazing. We live in a time when it seems many Christians are always looking for ways to do less and less for the Lord. This goes on even as He simultaneously continues to do more and more for us. In today's inspirational verse, we are informed of another aspect of God's generous offering to His people: He lifts up His countenance upon us. This simply means that the Lord overshadows us entirely with His presence and His divine approval. When we are left exposed, our hearts become gripped with fear about our failures being revealed to the people around us. In His loving and forgiving ways, He overshadows us, and then, while we hide beneath His wings of protection, He gives us His peace.

Walk in His covering, release your anxiety, and embrace His peace. We don't deserve the peace, yet He gives us peace. Take a moment right now to thank Him for giving you everything you did not deserve, and for keeping back much of what you do. Now go out and have an absolutely wonderful day.

October 4th
2 Corinthians 10:3

For though we walk in the flesh, we do not war according to the flesh.

In challenging times, we need to embrace one important truth, and our inspirational verse for today makes that truth clear. Our walk occurs in the world, but we do not use the weapons of the world. Our walk is designed to glorify the Lord and to bring attention to Him. If we are going to do this successfully, we must use the fighting equipment He gave us. He armed us with the war weapon of *faith.* The devil cannot see our faith, but only the results of our faith. It is impossible for the enemy to defeat an opponent he cannot see, so we must learn the importance of using our weapon of faith. The Lord has also given us the weapon of *fellowship.* If you feel yourself growing weak in your walk with the Lord, make sure you closely attach yourself to other stronger believers in Jesus Christ. Lastly, we have the weapon of God's *favor.* The attack the devil launches against you pales in comparison to the favor God has for you.

October 5th

Romans 8:6

For to be carnally minded is death, but to be spiritually minded is life and peace.

When in a situation with limited or nonexistent options, it is normal for us to feel backed into a corner. But this is not the case in today's inspirational verse. We can choose to use our carnal minds, which lead to death, or our spiritual minds, which lead to life and peace. The choice seems overwhelmingly obvious, yet many people consistently make the wrong decision. The use of the carnal mind equates to doing things our way according to the standards of this world and common logic. But our spiritual mind is directed by the Word of God and the spirit of God, while we simultaneously walk in the protection of God Himself. The Lord may challenge you with things that seem beyond your control. Don't, however, reject them based on your carnal mind, as that will lead to death and separation from the Lord. Instead, allow His spirit to control your mind.

Did you pay close attention to the end result at the close of the verse? He promises *life* and *peace*. What more could we ask for than eternal life with Him and peace from Him until our earthly journey is ended?

October 6th

Hebrews 10:23

Let us hold fast the confession of our hope without wavering, for He who promised is faithful.

There is nothing that brings more satisfaction to the devil than discouraging a child of God. If such discouragement is not immediately addressed, it can easily lead to disconnection and defeat. We are admonished in today's inspirational verse to hold fast the confession of our hope and not waver. Now, read this next sentence slowly and carefully: *Never allow your circumstances to corrupt your confidence in God!* You may want to go back and read that sentence again. Let me help: *Never allow your circumstances to corrupt your confidence in God!* Our circumstances are temporary, but our God is permanent and all powerful.

The final part of today's verse says, "...for He who promised is faithful." If we were at the Grace Tabernacle Church, I would ask you to lean in real close and listen to the following: "When trouble comes into our lives, we have a choice of what to hold onto. We can grip our problems real tight, or we can clench the promises of God. Don't waver; stand tall—the promises of God will hold you in place every time."

October 7th

Hebrews 10:35

Therefore do not cast away your confidence, which has great reward.

When I first started reading this verse, it reminded me of the old cowboy and Western movies I used to watch as a boy growing up in Houston. For every bad guy in the movie, there was always a "Wanted" poster hung around town for his capture. The poster usually read something like this: Wanted Dead or Alive - Reward $500. People placed their lives in jeopardy, not just to eliminate the criminal from their community, but also to receive the reward. In our inspirational verse for today we discover there is no need to place ourselves in danger or in harm's way, even given the sizeable reward. To receive the reward referenced in today's inspirational verse, all we need to do is hold onto what the Lord has given us. As long as we don't cast away our confidence in Him or allow our faith in God to grow weak, our reward will be much greater than $500.

The reason we don't have to go looking for the bad guy and defeat him is because Jesus already took care of that for us at Calvary. Keep a firm grip on your confidence and get ready for your reward.

October 8th

Psalm 68:19

Blessed be the Lord, Who daily loads us with benefits, The God of our salvation!

Without question, today's verse is filled with inspiration. It includes the praise we should give the Lord, the possessions we receive from the Lord, the pardon the Lord showers us with. The way this psalm begins is so refreshing. The writer of this psalm does not focus first on what God has done, but on what God deserves. He deserves to be blessed! When I first read this verse in reference to what we should do for the Lord, I wondered how on earth I would be able to render blessing to the Lord. It was then that the Holy Spirit revealed to me my limited understanding of the word "blessed." I was thinking in terms of cars, clothes, cash, and other commodities. I have since learned that God is blessed when His people give Him the praise, glory, and honor He deserves, and we do so with no ulterior motives in mind.

He has loaded us with daily benefits. Don't limit your thinking of the word *benefits* to the amount of material things you have received from God. Expand your thinking and know He has loaded us with more oxygen than we can breathe, more water than we can drink, more beauty than we can consider, and more grace than we can expend. If that isn't enough, He is the God of our salvation; we are saved, sealed, and secure because of Him. Take a moment to bless the Lord who has loaded you with all these benefits and more. He is blessed when we show Him how much we appreciate His many blessings.

October 9th

Jeremiah 33:3

Call to Me, and I will answer you, and show you great and mighty things, which you do not know.

The Lord has much more in store for our lives than we have any notion of. He has not revealed all He intends to do for us, with us, or through us—not to mention all He is going to accomplish in spite of us. Our God is an amazing God. And beyond tolerating us, He also forgives us and stores blessings in Heaven with our names on them. The key to discovering God's plan and purpose for our lives lies in maintaining constant communication with Him. This word *call* at the beginning of the verse is used as an imperative, and means literally to *keep calling*. He tells us to keep calling because God loves to hear from His children. A parent's heart fills with pain when their children stop contacting them with any regularity. And when they do call, it is typically to ask for something. The Lord gives us permission to call Him regularly, and His promise to us is that He will always answer.

He waits to show us great and mighty things—things we have no idea He has in store for our lives. Don't wait to pray until you feel you desperately need the Lord. Pray and communicate with Him on a regular basis, and He just may prevent those times of desperation from ever occurring.

October 10th

Mark 10:16

And He took them up in His arms, laid His hands on them, and blessed them.

In today's inspirational verse we see the connection and the compassion of Jesus toward some children that had been brought to Him, children His disciples wanted to rebuke and turn away. Why? Perhaps they thought Jesus was too busy to spend time with them. Have you ever had a problem you needed help with, but thought it too small and trivial to bring to the attention of Jesus? If so, pay close attention to this verse. What Jesus did for these children is what He is waiting to do in the lives of all of His children. He *lifted* them by taking them up in His arms. He expressed His *love* for them by laying His loving hands on them. He *lavished* them by taking the time to bless them.

Perhaps you feel a little down today. Well, Jesus is waiting to lift you. If you are feeling unloved, the Master is extending His arms toward you so that he may lay His hands on you. Receive His touch and bask in His embrace. Now get ready, for He is about to bless you. There you go! It just happened! He kept you alive another moment. Don't miss the small things in your search for the big things. And remember, you won't be traveling alone or on your own power today. Jesus has reached down to you and taken you in His lifting, loving, lavishing arms.

October 11th
Colossians 2:7

Rooted and built up in Him and established in the faith, as you have been taught, abounding in it with thanksgiving.

In today's inspirational verse Paul tells us to be "rooted and built up in Him and established in the faith." The lives of many Christians are crumbling because they are trying to build on the possessions of God without being grounded by the principles of God. Being rooted in Him means we are wrapped around Him and held firmly in place. Being built up in Him means he supports our growth, the level of which is determined by how closely connected we remain attached to Him. God will not allow us to grow beyond our root-handling ability. A building without a firm foundation will be destroyed in a storm. Just as a building's foundation must be established, so must our faith. God does this by giving us opportunities to utilize what we have been taught. God pours His Word out to you even today because He wants you to develop.

When our roots are firm in Jesus Christ, a natural progression occurs. When we are *grounded*, we *grow. Growth* leads to being *guarded* by what we have been taught. The end result is that we learn how to be more *grateful*, which is why Paul says, "abounding in it with thanksgiving." Our lives in Christ should be examples of abundant thanksgiving.

October 12th
2 Corinthians 1:3

Blessed be the God and Father of our Lord Jesus Christ, the Father of mercies and God of all comfort.

When trouble confronts us, we need to ensure we view it from the proper perspective. Trouble does not come to destroy us, but to develop us. When Paul wrote this letter, he had been through more trouble than most us of collectively will ever face in a lifetime. In spite of all his past and present difficulties, notice how Paul begins our inspirational verse for today: "Blessed be the God and Father of our Lord Jesus Christ..." This should help you realize that the manner in which you approach your troubles determines how well you handle them. Paul shares three important factors that help him take the right approach: God's *control,* God's *consecration,* God's *compassion.*

God is our Father. What He did in and for Jesus, He can also do for us. He is the Father of mercies, holding back the punishment we really deserve. He is the God of all comfort. When we approach our troubles with these truths on our minds the pain will not seem so difficult.

October 13th
2 Corinthians 1:4

Who comforts us in all our tribulation, that we may be able to comfort those who are in any trouble, with the comfort with which we ourselves are comforted by God.

Today's inspirational verse highlights many prominent truths. One such truth is that we have a responsibility to appropriate to others around us the comfort the Lord gives us. God's comfort should never become stagnant in our lives, but rather flow through them. Paul helps us realize that trouble is real; Christians will face trouble. Then he also informs us that the only way Christians will learn to handle trouble is to be taught by those who have already been through that trouble. God comforts us during all our tribulations. God comes to us in our times of trouble. And if you were not aware, God even allows trouble to occur so that He might get closer to us. Now, it is not that He is unwilling to be close to us during peaceful seasons, but at those times, we have a great tendency to take Him for granted and not recognize his presence.

When we go through extreme difficulties, God holds us close and never lets anything escape His control. He allows the difficulty to occur so that we may then comfort others in trouble, as indicated by the final statement of this verse "...with the comfort with which we ourselves are comforted by God." This means our job is to render to others the comfort that has been given to us by God. We all have His comfort whether we realize it or not–without it, we would not survive a single moment.

October 14th
2 Corinthians 1:5

For as the sufferings of Christ abound in us, so our consolation also abounds through Christ.

All we have to do is hold on and keep the faith. The Lord has renewed abundance waiting for us through His Son Jesus Christ. Our inspirational verse for today informs us of a very reassuring principle: Just as we seem to have more than our share of suffering *for* Christ, so also *through* Him we have more than our share of comfort. Christ knows what we can handle and He develops us according to our maturity levels. The verse tells us that, the more we suffer for Him, the more abundant comfort we receive for our faithfulness to Him. I have discovered that much of our suffering is not for the sake of Christ, but a result of poor choices we have made in life. In spite of it all, He is still there to see us through every stormy season.

I want to share just a final word of encouragement for today. The suffering we can handle as humans is limited. But the consolation Jesus offers is immeasurable. His consolation abounds in us right now, helping us make it from one moment to the next.

October 15th
Ezekiel 34:15

"I will feed My flock, and I will make them lie down," says the Lord God.

Being part of the family of God includes not only a spiritual change by the Lord, but also steadfast connection to the Lord and His people. In our inspirational verse for today, the Lord promises to feed His flock, a grouping representative of more than one sheep. Don't ever allow anything or anyone to disconnect you from fellowship with the Lord or His people. This promise of feeding is made to those of us who are part of the fold. When I hear people say they are not connected to a church family because some they observe in church don't live up to their standards, my response to them is: "We need you to come and show us how to do it the right way." In other words, stay connected and be an encourager. God has a relationship with us; we are part of His flock. He has rest for us; He will make us lie down from the labor of our difficulties and find respite in Him and the reward He has for us. The Lord spoke these words Himself.

Are you hungry for compassion? God is waiting to feed you with His love. Are you weary from your journey? God is waiting to lay you down and refresh you. Don't make the mistake of isolating yourself when He appears with His hands filled with blessings for His flock.

October 16th

Proverbs 29:25

The fear of man brings a snare, But whoever trusts in the Lord shall be safe.

There is perhaps no greater level of mental assurance than that of feeling safe and secure in the midst of an unstable, stormy situation. We may not realize it, but this is exactly how the Lord wants His children to feel at all times. As often occurs, feelings of security leave us or are lacking altogether because we fear the people around us. When this happens, it prevents us from trusting in our God who reigns and rules our lives above us. In our inspirational verse for today, the wise man Solomon gives us some additional great advice: Fearing people will only lead to filling our lives with snares. The word *snare* as it is used here means a *hook* or a *noose*. Out of fear, we allow others to lead us by force, as opposed to walking with the Lord out of faith. Remove that hook; you have the power to do it. Take that noose of human dependence from around your neck. Now you are ready to totally and completely trust in the Lord.

Other people can offer you only shackles; the Lord offers you safety. Now go out and make it a great day.

October 17th
Psalm 46:1

God is our refuge and strength, A very present help in trouble.

Today's inspirational verse is one I have heard and learned to quote since childhood. Over time, it had become so commonplace and rote I failed to ever realize its full profundity. I thought it focused only on the power and might of God. In reality, however, I realized it focused on God's strength in helping His children in our time of need. No one likes or welcomes trouble, but God promises to be right there with us when trouble comes. I have had to remind myself more times than I can count of God's constant presence in my life. According to today's verse, God provides a place for us to run to as our *refuge*. He provides a place for us to be *refreshed,* as He is our strength. He also provides *resistance* for us, as He is an ever-present source of help in our times of trouble. Imagine! We don't have to search for Him during times of trouble, because He is ever present whenever and wherever our trouble may be.

There will be times when God allows trouble to manifest another display of His strength in our lives. Be encouraged. Whatever you face, you are not in it alone. The Lord is there as a refuge and refresher, and as resistance against your difficulties.

October 18th
Romans 12:12

Rejoicing in hope, patient in tribulation, continuing steadfastly in prayer.

Today I have three brief, yet direct and helpful, admonishments for you. You will not need a Bible commentary or Greek lexicon to understand them. They are simple, yet filled with spiritual strength and profundity. Here they are. One, always be joyful about the hopeful expectations you have in Jesus Christ. Two, when trouble comes, don't try to rush through it or run away from it; press on until you discover what the Lord is trying to teach you, remove from you, or display through you. Finally, don't ever allow anything or anyone to stop you from maintaining a consistent, passionate prayer life. If you will just learn to daily apply these principles to every aspect of your life, your heart will be filled with peace that passes all understanding.

Our troubles and problems may not flee immediately, but our mental approach to them will advance to a higher level. Rejoice, be patient, and continue praying. And leave the rest in the hands of the Lord.

October 19th
Psalm 13:5

But I have trusted in your mercy; My heart shall rejoice in Your salvation.

More times than I care to admit, I have been overwhelmed with worry about things the Lord had already resolved. I could have saved myself countless hours of anxiety if only I had learned earlier the joy of trusting in God's unfailing love. So often we doubt His love for us based on how we have been treated by other people. We interact with them more than we interact with the Lord and, based on that, reach the wrong conclusions about God's unfailing love for us. Our Father wants us to trust Him at all times and in all situations. When we learn the discipline of doing this, doubt will flee and be replaced by Godly confidence.

As Christians, we believe He has saved us. Now let's rejoice in our salvation. Put a smile on your face—not just a mask or a façade, but a true expression from your heart.

October 20th
Colossians 3:23

And whatever you do, do it heartily, as to the Lord and not to men.

Whatever we do for the Lord He deserves our very best—not just some of the time, but all the time. It never ceases to baffle me how some people say they are working for the Lord, yet they allow others to discourage them from fulfilling their spiritual responsibilities. Although our work in the Kingdom of God is directed at people, it is, in actuality, for the Lord. We must never lose sight of this paramount truth. God never should be offered half-hearted service by His people. Our hearts should be passionately aligned with His will. We should never feel coerced or forced to do what we do; it should be a labor of love. No mother enjoys the pain of child birth, but she endures it because she knows the joy of having a child is about to take place. Our work for the Lord will become difficult at times. But this is no reason for us to quit, slow down, or become inactive. It's true: Not all people show appreciation, but God does on a daily basis. Need some proof? Those are His eyes with which you are reading. Those are His hands you used to open this book. Those clothes you are wearing? His. The body you used to get out of bed? His, too. I think you get the picture. He loves you. He has a plan for you. And He has work for you.

Now do what you do for Him with a positive and joyful disposition.

October 21st
Psalm 89:15

Blessed are the people who know the joyful sound! They walk, O Lord, in the light of Your countenance.

I remember an incident between a young man and an older gentleman that occurred when I was younger. The older man was listening to a particular genre of music, and the young man, while sitting next to him, was snapping his fingers to the beat. The older man asked the younger man, "Do you know what it is you are listening to?" The young man said no, he just liked the beat. The older man said, "Well, that is what you call real music." I think the inspirational verse for today gives us all the opportunity to realize just what "real music" truly is. We are blessed just knowing and familiarizing ourselves with the joyful sound of the praise our God is worthy of. The music that encompasses praise to our God allows our daily walk to be filled with the lighted countenance of God Himself.

Take some time today to turn off the R & B. Give the jazz a brake. Put the country and western to the side. Even classical music needs to have an opportunity to rest. Today is about gospel, Christian sounds. I have discovered that when we allow His praise to really penetrate our hearts, one day leads to many more. He wants to light up your pathway. He is just waiting for you to establish a praise atmosphere so He can do it.

October 22nd
Psalm 89:16

In Your name they rejoice all day long, And in Your righteousness they are exalted.

I cannot even begin to imagine what it will be like in Heaven to have the opportunity to praise the Lord all day every day. Our inspirational verse for today does, however, give us an earthly glimpse of the spiritual serendipity that takes place in Heaven. Life is not only more manageable, but also more joyous when we fill our days with the praise of our God. We can do so easily if we just hum songs about His grace throughout the day; read scriptures about His love throughout the day; and offer prayers for His blessings throughout the day.

When we rejoice in Him, the end result is that we are lifted by His righteousness. Praise raises our spiritual position and moves us into closer proximity to the Lord. What on earth could be better than getting closer to the One who lives in heaven? Now go out and make it a great day.

October 23rd
2 Peter 1:2

Grace and peace be multiplied to you in the knowledge of God and of Jesus Christ our Lord.

Today's inspirational verse helped me realize a tremendous truth: One of the reasons many of us suffer from a lack of peace may be the result of a lack of knowledge about God and Jesus Christ. When Peter wrote this verse he wanted his reading audience to understand an important fact: God's grace and peace can be multiplied in our lives when we have a greater level of knowledge about Him. It is difficult to serve, trust, obey, and commit to someone you do not know very well. For this reason, Bible study and being attached to a ministry in your local church are so important. We learn so much more about the Lord through these spiritual entities.

Something amazing happens when we get to know the Lord better through His Word. Grace and peace don't just come to us in singular fashion; they come in a multiplied format. He is ready to teach you as much about Himself as you need to know. The only question is, "Are you ready to learn?" If so, there is multiplied grace and peace just waiting for you to retrieve at Heaven's distribution center.

October 24th

Psalm 34:19

Many are the afflictions of the righteous, But the Lord delivers him out of them all.

An old James Cleveland song entitled "I Don't Feel No Ways Tired" contains a line that says, "Nobody told me that the road would be easy, I don't believe He brought me this far to leave me." Whoever said that gave some good, honest advice. The Lord has not promised that life will be easy for us. The easy living awaits us in the uninterrupted bliss of Heaven. While here on earth we will always have challenges and struggles. But today's inspirational verse tells us how we can be assured of the Lord's deliverance. The psalmist says, "Many are the afflictions of the righteous..." When trouble comes into our lives, the first thing we must examine is our level of righteous living before the Lord. While we cannot attain righteousness, we have been made righteous by the sacrificial work of Jesus Christ at Calvary. The real question then becomes, "How are we living up to the standards God has designed for our lives?"

He is able to deliver, but we must make sure we are in a position to be delivered. Trouble occasionally comes to do nothing more than call our attention to making sure we are living the kind of life that pleases the Lord. Our discipline to righteousness will ensure His divine deliverance. Hold on–help is on the way!

October 25th
Micah 7:7

Therefore I will look to the Lord; I will wait for the God of my salvation; My God will hear me.

My inspirational word for you today is simple and sweet. It is direct and developing. It is powerful and productive. Listen to me when I say to always be looking and expecting God to do the unexpected. I know that sounds like an oxymoron or a paradox, but that is simply how our God works in the lives of His people. The prophet Micah shares his testimony with us and it speaks the same sentiments. He was watching with hopeful expectations; he was waiting faithfully; and he knew God would hear him, which speaks to his constant communication with the Lord.

Keep your spiritual eyes open. He is going to reveal some things to you that are totally unexpected. Don't grow weary or become impatient; He will do it in His own time. God hears you. He knows what you need. He will either deliver you from it, or remove it from you. Either way, you will know it was His mighty hand that did the work.

October 26th

Hebrews 7:25

Therefore He is also able to save to the uttermost those who come to God through Him, since He always lives to make intercession for them.

Today's inspirational verse contains at least three important principles for us to understand: 1) We should have *confidence* in our Savior—"He is able to save..."; 2) We have *cleansing* because of our Savior—We have been brought to God through Him; and 3) We have *constant communication* with the Father on our behalf because of our Savior—"...He always lives to make intercession for us." This is not just good news, but in the words of some of my childhood friends, it is "super-duper good news!"

Whatever you face in terms of difficulties or opportunities that seem beyond your ability to manage, have the confidence in God to handle them. When you fall and find yourself out of the will of God, immediately readjust and realign yourself. You have been cleansed by the blood of Jesus. When you feel weak and don't have the strength to pray, look up. Jesus prays to His Father on your behalf. Now go out and face your day with a revived mind and a recharged spirit.

October 27th
1 John 5:2

By this we know that we love the children of God, when we love God and keep His commandments.

Three persons comprise the Godhead: God the Father, God the Son, and God the Holy Spirit. We call them the Trinity. There are also three important components of love that should exist in the life of every child of God: love for our Savior, Jesus Christ; love for the statutes of God, His Word; and then we should also have love for other saints, our brothers and sisters in Christ Jesus. In our inspirational verse for today we are both motivated and enlightened. Our motivation comes in knowing we can be confidently assured of the fact that we are God's children. We don't have to go through life hoping we will be saved; we can have assurance of eternal salvation. Our enlightenment comes through realizing that our salvation is connected to our love for other believers and our discipline to God's commandments.

Make this a day you express your love for God by showing your affection for other believers. Don't follow your feelings when you are faced with decisions in life. Instead, show the Lord how much you love Him by keeping His commandments. They are not designed to keep good things from us, but to keep everything bad away from us.

October 28th
Exodus 23:30

Little by little I will drive them out from before you, until you have increased, and you inherit the land.

In today's inspirational verse we are introduced to another aspect of God's interaction with His people. This verse makes us aware that the Lord does not move all our troubles, difficulties, or even our enemies at one time. He moves things little by little, while also motivating us in our level of trust in Him. The children of Israel had been promised this land of Canaan, but enemies of theirs were there before they made their arrival. The Lord sent the Canaanites there even though challenges awaited them. Don't walk away from God's promises to you simply because there are problems attached to the promise. He wants you to trust Him step by step. He will give you the power to drive out what needs to be removed, and all the while you will be growing in your relationship with Him.

Little by little, those debts get paid. Little by little, sickness will be healed. Little by little, depression fades away—some of it just left a moment ago. Don't become discouraged because your problems don't all vanish immediately. Don't feel God has abandoned you when you know He has sent you to a place where difficulties await your arrival. He will take care of you and handle your problems "little by little."

October 29th

Deuteronomy 8:7

For the Lord your God is bringing you into a good land, a land of brooks of water, of fountains and springs, that flow out of valleys and hills.

My inspirational word for you today is, "God has so much more in store for you." He brings you out of some *dark* places. He brings you through some *difficult* places. He takes you to some *delightful* places. Just keep walking and trusting. It's too soon to quit. This verse contains some very comforting words, but if we read it too fast we will miss its full significance. Consider the word *bringing*. He does not just lead you; He brings you. He knows you get weary along the journey, so He carries you when you are too tired to walk on your own. Then, once your strength is renewed, He places you on your feet again.

The references of water here denote God's constant refreshing of our lives. Many times He does that with His presence alone. Don't ever take your quiet time with the Lord for granted. He brings you to a land where you can be refreshed to fulfill His assignments and walk in His anointing.

October 30th
Job 42:2

I know that You can do everything, And that no purpose of Yours can be withheld from You.

We will all experience seasons when life simply does not make sense to us. We cry out to God and hear nothing but silence. During those seasons, don't rebel, don't throw in the towel; just surrender to His will. This is what Job does in our inspirational verse for today. God has just finished speaking to Job after he complained to the Lord throughout the more than thirty-five chapters of the book that bear his name. I am by no means making light of Job's suffering. He went through what most of us will never be able to even imagine. The heartache and pain he faced must have shaken his faith in God to the core. Yet, in spite of it all, he held on. I also do not make light of the difficulty you may be facing at this very moment. But I can tell you from experience that the pain becomes more bearable when we stop sulking and start surrendering.

God can do everything. He can move the trouble. He can give us strength to handle the trouble. And He can even delay the trouble. Whatever His purpose, it will not be withheld from Him. Ask the Lord to give you the strength to leave every situation beyond your ability in His hands while also becoming more attentive to the assignments He equipped you to handle.

October 31st
Matthew 6:27

Which of you by worrying can add one cubit to his stature?

There is really nothing comical about worry. But Jesus seems to be using His sense of humor in our inspirational verse for today. He helps us realize that worry offers no emotional or physical benefit. It does not help us grow, and it may even cause us to shrink. Surrender your cares to the Lord. Your anxiety may not all leave at once. But during the day, reflect on those things the Lord has already done that had you wondering how He was going to work them out. He handled those, and He will handle whatever you are faced with on this 31st day of October.

Get ready. We are now approaching the season set aside for thanksgiving. Of course we know that, for a child of God, every day is a day of thanksgiving. But this season we want to be free from worry and allow a positive attitude to carry over for the rest of our lives. Don't shrink because of worry–instead, grow in your faith in God.

PRAYER

Lord, We thank You for Your loving kindness and tender mercies. We are at this point in our lives because You have brought us and led us every step of the way. We ask for Your forgiveness of our sins, and we thank You for not dealing with us according to our iniquities. Continue to use us to Your glory and cover us with Your grace.

In Jesus' name,
Amen.

Nectarines of Nourishment in November

November 1st
Psalm 107:1

Oh, give thanks to the Lord, for He is good! For His mercy endures forever.

For the first ten months of this year we have received information from the Word of God to help us, encourage us, and direct us. This entire month's focus will be centered exclusively on *thanksgiving!* Our focus will be on a multitude of things for which we should be thankful. We begin today with thanksgiving for God's *goodness.* He is good! There is no past tense or future tense about God's goodness. He *is* good. Even when things don't seem to us to be good, we can rest assured that they are. His goodness coupled with His Mercy should always lead His people to adopt an attitude of thankfulness. In the midst of our waywardness, sinfulness, and ungodly rebellion, He is still good. Take a moment to recall the times you know you did not deserve God's goodness. He still gave it, though, in spite of our unworthiness. What a positive and encouraging way to start these final two months of the year.

When I was a child and someone would give me something, my parents would always say, "Roy, don't forget to say 'thank you.'" I give the same advice to you. Don't forget to tell the Lord "Thank You." Let's not beg Him for anything, but instead thank Him for all He has done. He is good!

November 2nd
Psalm 100:4

Enter into His gates with thanksgiving, And into His courts with praise. Be thankful to Him, and bless His name.

Can you even begin to imagine what every corporate worship experience would be like if every participant had arrived with a spirit of divine gratitude? No one would complain or focus solely on what they feel they need. All attention would be on God and the appreciation He is worthy of. Most of us make the mistake of waiting until we get inside the place of worship before preparing for worship. This psalm informs us that we should arrive at the place of worship *ready* for worship. This does not usually happen because our mind is on everyone and everything else but the Lord. Then, once we arrive, we feel we need a *praise team* or *worship leader* to get us ready. This is the month to change that pattern. Each time you leave home to worship the Lord at His house, focus your mind on Him and Him alone all along the way.

Once you arrive on the church campus, get out of your car with a song of praise on your lips. Then enter His gates with thanksgiving, and come into His courts with praise. Just tell God "Thank You!" and you will feel so much better.

November 3rd
Psalm 97:12

Rejoice in the Lord, you righteous, And give thanks at the remembrance of His holy name.

The name *Jesus* is an *anointed* name. It is an *awakening* name. It is also an *amazing* name. Just the mention of His name should cause our hearts to flood with joy. I can understand how people who do not know the Lord are not excited about His name. But those of us who have been born again should spend time thanking God for the power that is housed in the name of His Son, Jesus Christ. Today's inspirational verse admonishes the righteous to rejoice in the Lord. We should give thanks to Him at the mere remembrance of His name. When you look around and see how He has kept you, healed you, protected you, and provided for you, you should remember that it was no one but the Lord who did all that.

This leads to what I want to call "all day, every day thanksgiving." We have so much to thank God for. If you're stuck trying to think of something, start by using your memory. While typing these words, I just thought of something else and I thanked Him. Did you remember anything while you were reading? If you did, tell Him thank You.

November 4th
Luke 17:15-16

And one of them, when he saw that he was healed, returned, and with a loud voice glorified God, and fell down on his face at His feet, giving Him thanks. And he was a Samaritan.

In the verses leading up to today's inspirational reading, Jesus had healed ten lepers. But only one of them returned to thank the Lord. At times it will seem as though you are the only person in your circle of friends with a thankful heart. If so, don't allow their ingratitude to diminish your level of thankfulness to the Lord. Life may not be perfect, but we still have so much for which to thank God. The man in these verses fell on his face and, with a loud voice, thanked the Lord once he saw that he was healed. He did not simply say, "Thank you, Jesus." He exclaimed, "*Thank you, Jesus!*" and repeated his thanks over and over. The other nine men were Jews, but he was a Samaritan. This distinction serves to help us understand an important truth: The people who should be thanking the Lord the most are often the ones who fail to do it.

Why don't you stand out from the crowd this month? No matter what you are faced with, whenever someone asks you how you are doing or how your day was, respond with something that shows your thankfulness to the Lord. The more you thank Him, the more you will find to thank Him for.

November 5th
2 Corinthians 9:15

Thanks be to God for His indescribable gift!

The Lord sometimes does things in our lives that are literally beyond description. It is evident that Paul, who wrote this verse, was having that same thought. Many of the things we jump up and down and shout for joy about are temporary and fleeting. We get excited about them because we can see them and think they will make our lives happier. The real truth of the matter, however, is just the opposite. The real gifts in life are things we cannot see and the things God does for us about which we are totally unaware—the sickness He kept at bay; the car accident we were not involved in; the break-in that took place at someone else's home; the child strung out on drugs who did not live in our home. And even if you have experienced one or more of these events, you should thank God doubly. While He may not have kept them from you entirely, He kept them from destroying you, which gives you an even stronger testimony.

Spend time thanking the Lord for the indescribable things He has done in your life. One in particular comes to mind: He saved us with the precious blood of His Son, Jesus Christ. He truly is an *indescribable gift*!

November 6th
Philippians 4:6

Be anxious for nothing, but in everything by prayer and supplication, with thanksgiving, let your requests be made known to God.

Every year on Christmas Day we have dinner at the home of my oldest sister, Eleanor. She and my baby sister Jerri give leadership by assigning what every family member is to bring to contribute to the dinner. There is one dish in particular that most of the family always looks forward to eating. One year, however, it did not taste the same as it had in previous years. When the person who made the dish was asked about it, she said she had run out of a certain ingredient and didn't think anyone would notice. (She was wrong.) Well, when it comes to prayer, I have also discovered that many Christians leave out an important ingredient: the component of *thanksgiving*. In our inspirational verse for today, Paul tells us to remove anxiety from our lives and replace the void with prayers about everything that includes this very important component. Before you place your grocery list of requests at the altar, take time to thank Him for everything He has done.

I have discovered that while thanking Him, He starts to meet our needs even before we ask Him for anything. The next time you pray, don't forget to add the main ingredient of thanksgiving. If you leave it out, it will be noticed.

November 7th

2 Samuel 22:50

Therefore I will give thanks to You, O Lord, among the Gentiles, and sing praises to Your name.

When David wrote and spoke these words, I believe he had one main goal in mind: to make sure that the people who did not know the Lord would at least know how much he loved Him and how thankful he was to Him. To give thanks simply means to purposefully make up your mind to live with a grateful heart. We must place our personal issues to the side and focus on blessing Him not only for what He has done, but also for who He is. Why not allow this to be a period in your life when your thankfulness goes a little beyond the norm? This is the season to let the people around you know how much you thank the Lord for all He has done for you. Many times the heathen (Gentiles) and the unsaved are not interested in our God because we are occasionally displeased with Him.

Give Him the thanks He is worthy of. Then allow those spoken words to become a melody of pleasant praise to Him. Wow, a song that fits perfectly right here just came to mind. "Thank You, Lord; thank You, Lord; thank You, Lord; I just want to thank You, Lord." I believe a smile just appeared on the face of our God as we expressed our genuine gratitude to Him.

November 8th

1 Chronicles 16:8

Oh, give thanks to the Lord! Call upon His name; Make known His deeds among the peoples!

In this inspirational verse David admonishes us to "Give thanks to the Lord!" This is not a suggestion, but a command. I guess the best way I can explain this is by referring to an incident from my childhood. One year, I received a very nice birthday gift from my godparents. I was so excited about the gift that I forgot to tell them thank you. My mother told me to stop playing with the toy and go back into the room where my godparents were sitting to express my appreciation by saying thank you. I said to her, "I will in just a minute, as soon as I finish putting this game together." Well, I didn't complete the game. And I don't think I ever got to play with it, either. She gave me a whipping I will never forget. (C.P.S., no disrespect intended, but I needed it, deserved it, and now thank God for having received it.) My mother telling me to say thank you was not a suggestion; it was a command.

David commands us to give thanks unto the Lord, to call on His name, and to let everybody know what He has done in our lives. Don't wait for discipline to come. Just obey the command. As we make His deeds known among other people, we let them know how much we truly love and thank God for all He has done.

November 9th
Psalm 119:62

At midnight I will rise to give thanks to You, Because of Your righteous judgments.

Today's inspirational verse is especially encouraging. If you have ever had difficulty sleeping, I'm sure you can relate to the feelings of the psalmist. Instead of complaining about being deprived of sleep, he chooses to use it as an opportunity to give the Lord some *midnight thanksgiving*. He does not just lie in the bed, toss and turn, or complain. He gets up from his bed, goes to his place of prayer, and offers thanksgiving. This verse has helped me tremendously. When I have difficulty sleeping, I spend most of that time praying to God to give me the sleep I feel I need. In this case, however, the psalmist does not ask the Lord for a thing, and what he thanks God for is just as noteworthy. He offers prayers of thanksgiving for the righteous judgments and the instructions that are housed in the Word of God.

He knew what we all need to realize: God's Word kept him in the past, and the power of that Word would continue to do the same in the future. So, instead of complaining, he thanks the Lord for the consistency of His Word. I want to use my sanctified imagination right here, and say that after the psalmist finished thanking the Lord for His Word, God rocked him back to sleep. He will do the very same for every one of His children. Thank Him, and He will provide the rest and sleep we need.

November 10th
Psalm 140:13

Surely the righteous shall give thanks to Your name; The upright shall dwell in Your presence.

Our inspirational verse for today helps us realize there is a direct connection between our righteousness and our level of thankfulness. The psalmist says, "Surely the righteous shall give thanks to Your name." The Roy Elton Brackins translation of this verse would read something like this: If no one else sees the value of thanksgiving to the name of God, those of us who are righteous are the first to lead out by example. Thanksgiving alters our *perspective*; it helps us see how valuable God truly is. Thanksgiving alters our *praise*; we publically offer our gratitude to the Lord. Thanksgiving alters our *position*; it moves us into the very presence of God. The verse tells us that "The upright shall dwell in Your presence."

If you are feeling a bit melancholy and down in the dumps, thanksgiving can adjust your mental location. His righteousness has been bestowed and given to us. Let's reveal it by elevating our gratitude. After all, we should desire to be in His presence, no? And in His presence there is fullness of joy.

November 11th
Mark 14:23

Then He took the cup, and when He had given thanks He gave it to them, and they all drank from it.

Prior to submitting to the pain and agony at Calvary, Jesus takes the time to thank His Father for the cup that would represent His suffering. The disciples of Jesus were able to drink from a cup that had been sealed and consecrated in a prayer of thanksgiving. Jesus does not curse the cup. He does not avoid the cup. He does not walk away from the cup. Instead, He does something positive: He thanks God for the cup. I believe this is designed to teach us a valuable lesson. We must learn to thank God for even unpleasant things that occur or appear in our lives. When we do, it is an act of faith. By giving thanks to the Lord in the midst of adverse circumstances, we say to Him, "We know You have our deliverance already mapped out."

After Jesus gave thanks for the cup, the disciples were able to drink from it. Take a moment to thank the Lord for everything He has blessed so that we might endure. He will never place anything before us which has not already been blessed by Him. Now, that is a whole lot to thank God for.

November 12th
Colossians 3:15

And let the peace of God rule in your hearts, to which also you were called in one body; and be thankful.

God wants His peace to be the dominant occupant in our hearts. There are times when we directly or indirectly allow unauthorized tenants to come in. Even during those times when we are invaded with unwelcome visitors such as doubt, distress, and depression, His peace still rules. Negative thoughts may enter, but we don't have to submit or surrender to them. God's peace with us was manifested at Calvary. The blood of His Son Jesus Christ saved us and brought us into the family of God.

There is one simple thing we can do to express our appreciation to the Lord. Are you ready? It's found at the end of the verse: "...and be thankful." He has done so much for us. Now, just be thankful. Peace rules in our hearts. We are called into the body of Christ. We are members of the eternal family of God. Just be thankful.

November 13th
Nehemiah 12:31

So I brought the leaders of Judah up on the wall, and appointed two large thanksgiving choirs. One went to the right hand on the wall toward the Refuse Gate.

If only we read the Bible more carefully, we would be more selective in naming our church choirs and singing groups. Some may disagree with me, but I state this based on the information provided for us here in today's inspirational verse. I have heard of Inspirational Choirs, Contemporary Choirs, Traditional Choirs, Young Adult Choirs, Children's Choirs, and Male Choruses. But in this verse, Nehemiah appoints two large singing groups after the rebuilding of the wall of Jerusalem. He names them *thanksgiving choirs.* I have seen how difficult it is to get the people who populate the pews to sing God's praises, usually because our minds are on everything else but giving thanks to God. But think about this. Imagine the harmony that would exist in the music ministries of all Christian churches if every member of the ministry focused on thanksgiving.

When it comes to musical praise you may not be a soprano, alto, contralto, tenor, or bass. But if you have a thankful heart, you can be a member of the thanksgiving choir. There's no need to audition and you don't have to wear a robe. Just sing God's praises, allowing melodies of thanksgiving to flow from your mouth; and know He has a long, white robe waiting for you in Heaven. Stand on the wall, and let the world know you have a God worth singing about.

November 14th
Jeremiah 30:19

Then out of them shall proceed thanksgiving And the voice of those who make merry; I will multiply them, and they shall not diminish; I will also glorify them, and they shall not be small.

The Lord speaks this word to His prophet Jeremiah while His people of Israel were going through some of the most difficult periods in their history. It was not anything they did not deserve. Yet, in spite of it all, the Lord helps them by giving them a word of hope and teaching them the importance of being thankful even in adverse circumstances. By this, He helps us understand some important principles. When thanksgiving flows from our mouths and our very being, it can lead to some dramatically positive change in our lives. He promises to multiply those things for which we will have to thank Him. He promises to keep our reasons for offering Him thanks from diminishing and, in fact, to make them even more glorious. Then He promises they will not be reduced in size or number. As we thank Him, His glorious presence manifests itself in our lives.

It all begins with a thankful heart. While you are probably not in a captive situation, it may feel like you are being held hostage by one or more situations beyond your control. This is the time to allow thanksgiving to proceed from your life. And in the course of thanking Him, just watch as He keeps every promise He has made.

November 15th
Romans 1:8

First, I thank my God through Jesus Christ for you all, that your faith is spoken of throughout the whole world.

Many of us have learned how to thank the Lord for our family members and friends. But Paul, in our inspirational verse for today, adds a new group to the list of people for whom we should give thanks: those with whom we worship and who are part of the body of Christ. Take time to thank the Lord for your pastor. Thank God for the worship and praise leaders at your local church. Thank God for the ushers who seat you with a smile. (And if they did not express a smile, thank God they at least pointed you to where you could find a seat.) Those ministry leaders at your church should cause you to have a thankful heart. They may not be perfect, flawless people, but they are willing to work for the Lord. Paul was grateful because the faith of these people at Rome was being talked about all over the then-known world.

Take a few moments to think about the positive qualities in some of the Christians you know. Now thank God for the positive impact their lives and ministries have had on you.

November 16th
Romans 5:8

But God demonstrates His own love toward us, in that while we were still sinners, Christ died for us.

Thank God for Jesus. Thank God for salvation. Thank God for His precious sacrifice. Thank God for forgiveness of sins. Thank God for showing us publically how much He loves us. Do I need to go on? This verse houses these sentiments and so many more. Take some time today, not just a moment, but some real, significant time to thank the Lord for His demonstration of love toward you and for you. He did not wait for us to "get ourselves right" before saving us. He demonstrated His love while we were still wallowing and basking in our demented sinfulness.

He died for us. He paid the extreme price for us. He made the ultimate sacrifice for us. Now surely He deserves some thanksgiving from us. Allow me to close today's inspirational word where I started. Thank God for Jesus!

November 17th
Psalm 40:3

He has put a new song in my mouth—Praise to our God; Many will see it and fear, And will trust in the Lord.

Thank God for the melody in your mouth and for using you as His demonstration of divinity. Thank the Lord for choosing to showcase you as an example of what can take place in a person's life when they totally surrender to Him. Some people would not even consider using you as a spokesperson; in their minds you don't have what it takes. But the God of Heaven and Earth has chosen to allow people to see Him manifested through your life. Don't let Him down! Thank Him with your songs of praise. Don't be ashamed of doing both publically and consistently that which you do for Him. According to our inspirational verse for today, when we display God's goodness, something amazing will happen. "Many will see it and fear, and will trust in the Lord."

Did you catch that? Well, if not, let me bring it to your attention. The *thanks you give to God* can lead *someone else to trust in God.* Need I say anymore?

November 18th
Psalm 37:25

I have been young, and now am old; Yet I have not seen the righteous forsaken, Nor his descendants begging bread.

Thank God for His provisions. You may not have all you want, but you do, in fact, have everything you need. I don't need to know who you are; I don't need to know your background. All I need to know is that you are a righteous child of God. And if you are, He has met—and will continue to meet—all your needs. Thank Him for keeping you during those periods you felt all hope was lost. Perhaps you are experiencing one of those seasons now. Don't try to pout your way out of it. Don't try to cry your way out of it. Don't try to complain your way out of it. *Thank* your way out of it. Instead of focusing on what you don't have and what you think you need, thank Him for all He has blessed you with. *Shelter*, *salvation*, and *security* are just three of the multitude of things for which we should be thankful.

In the yesterdays of our lives, when we were younger, He kept us. He is not about to forsake us at this point in our lives. In an earlier devotional I said those of us who are righteous will never have to beg. We may have to borrow, but don't worry; He will help us repay the debt. Thank Him, for He is just that kind of God.

November 19th

1 Timothy 4:4

For every creature of God is good, and nothing is to be refused if it is received with thanksgiving.

There are times when the devil uses his craftiness to distract us from the positive qualities in the blessings of God. When this happens, we must remember that everything God made is good in and of itself. The problems come when we take what the Lord has intended for a holy and wholesome purpose, and use it for an ungodly and unwholesome purpose. Our mindset needs to be focused on thanking the Lord for all He has done for us and all He has given us. And, as we thank Him, we should seek to please Him with the manner in which we use all that He has blessed our lives with. If anything comes into our lives for which we cannot truly thank God with a clear conscience, it did not come from God. We need to release it or remove it. The Lord will never bless us with anything intended to separate us from Him—He blesses us only with things that bring us closer to Him.

Thank Him for what He has added to your life, and remove those things that hinder your work and witness for Him. Then you will be ready to receive all that He has in store for you.

November 20th
Colossians 2:7

Rooted and built up in Him and established in the faith, as you have been taught, abounding in it with thanksgiving.

Have you ever had one of those days, weeks, or seasons when it seemed as though your life were literally falling apart? If so, today's inspirational verse shows us why we are still standing and why we owe the Lord a great deal of gratitude. The only reason we did not come apart at the seams is because we have been "rooted and built up in Him, and established in the faith..." He has been our foundation, and our faith in Him has held our lives together. Take just a moment to lift your hands and thank the Lord for holding your life in place when all hope seemed to have been lost. I have had those same times in my life, and they have served to strengthen my confidence in God and my ability to celebrate Him. The second half of this verse also provides a great deal of insight. We are able to hold on because we have been rooted, built up, established, and "taught." Please don't forget to thank God for teaching you some valuable lessons during life's most difficult and unraveling times.

God's holding power should result in an abundance of thanksgiving pouring forth from us. Not just a minimal, mandatory "Thank You, Lord," but He should hear us say, "*Thank You, Lord!*" with gusto and glory. Let your thanksgiving abound. No complaining. No moping, no sadness. This is our time to let Him know how much we really appreciate all that He has done.

November 21st
Colossians 4:2

Continue earnestly in prayer, being vigilant in it with thanksgiving.

Don't stop praying. I repeat: Don't stop praying. Be persistent in your prayer life. You may, however, want to consider changing the method of your prayers. If you spend a great deal of time asking God for things, yet none of them materializes, it may be because God is waiting to first hear you say "Thank You." Our inspirational verse for today informs us of the importance of being committed in our prayer lives, and to "continue earnestly in prayer." While we do so, it must be inclusive of a vigilant disposition, and we must never forget to include the important element of thanksgiving. Take a moment to think about this. No one looks forward to giving someone more of what they are asking for if they have not demonstrated thanks for what they already have.

Today, before you ask God to grant you a better day, thank Him for seeing you safely through yesterday. Before you ask God for help with this month's expenses, thank Him for providing everything you needed last month. If you did not get it, and you survived without it, then you did not really need it. So, thank Him for teaching you how to live without it.

November 22nd

Ephesians 5:20

Giving thanks always for all things to God the Father in the name of our Lord Jesus Christ.

This is one of those verses in the Bible that really puts our thanksgiving and gratitude to God to the test: "Giving thanks always *for all things...*" I'm sure we would all agree that this is so much easier said than done. Many of the things we are forced to deal with in life make it nearly impossible to thank God for, yet they are part of the "all things" referenced in today's verse. The key to understanding this passage is found in the latter part of the verse. We thank God for all things and we do it in the name of our Lord Jesus Christ. This simply means we surrender to God everything that is too difficult for us, and we ask Him to give us the strength to handle it through His Son Jesus Christ. Because He is in control of all things, we can be thankful even in the midst of physical painful and emotionally excruciating seasons.

Release that worry with a word of appreciation to God. He will comfort you with the presence of His Son. When we thank Him, He strengthens us to hold on just a little longer. There is power in the name of Jesus, and He works on your behalf to bring peace in your time of crisis. Just give Him thanks, even when you face hardship and difficulty. Did you do it? Now, don't you feel better?

November 23rd
Matthew 11:25

At that time Jesus answered and said, "I thank You, Father, Lord of heaven and earth, that You have hidden these things from the wise and prudent and have revealed them to babes."

The Lord not only commands us to give Him thanks, but also shows us how to do it through His Son Jesus Christ. In our inspirational verse for today, Jesus thanks His Father in Heaven. His gratitude centers on how His Father has hidden some spiritual things from people we might call *know-it-alls.* He is also grateful that His Father has revealed these spiritual truths to common, everyday people like you and me. We should follow His lead and use today to thank Him for the following: for allowing you to *receive* the message of the Gospel, without which we would all be headed for hell; for allowing you to *respond* to the Gospel—He loved you enough to allow your heart to be softened so that you would say yes to Him; for allowing you to be *rewarded* by the Gospel. God is your Father. Jesus is your Savior. The Holy Spirit is your comforter and guide. Life is now so much sweeter, and Heaven is your eternal home.

Even as a babe in Christ, He has revealed to you everything you needed to know about Him—enough to keep us busy with thanksgiving for a lifetime.

November 24th
Psalm 26:7

That I may proclaim with the voice of thanksgiving, And tell of all Your wondrous works.

Today's inspirational verse shares with us another element of thanksgiving. When we start thinking about how good God has been, it should lead to testimonies about His goodness. We often make the mistake of neither *talking* about Him nor *thanking* Him because we fail to *think* about Him until something bad happens to us. People should hear about God's goodness from His people. Did you not know that it is a privilege to be able to talk about our Heavenly Father? He chooses to reveal His goodness to the world through creatures like me and you. We cannot afford to fail Him in this area. The word "proclaim" simply means to report publicly. As you go through the day, don't report on your struggles but on your Savior, instead. Don't complain about your difficulties, but publish the news of your deliverance. Tell of His wonderful works. He rocked you to sleep last night. Even if you didn't sleep well, He provided a comfortable bed for you to toss and turn in. Life may not be perfect, but we serve a Savior who is.

Make it your business to tell someone of the great things the Lord has done for you, and then watch Him start turning your life around.

November 25th
Psalm 50:14

Offer to God thanksgiving, And pay your vows to the Most High.

Thank Him, then sacrifice and give to Him. Whatever you have vowed to honor the Lord with, make sure you keep that commitment. I often hear people say, "I don't like making commitments to the Lord or to the Church because I never know what my financial situation will be." Isn't it strange that those same people are never hesitant to make a five-year commitment to an automobile loan or a thirty-year commitment to a mortgage? Yet they hesitate to make a one-to-three-year commitment to help their church build a new edifice that will last for more than fifty years. When we honor the Lord with our financial resources, we are giving thanks to Him. When we give back to Him, we show Him that we recognize that all we have has come from Him.

As you give and spend throughout this season, don't forget to honor your vows to the Most High. After all, everything that is in our hands has come from His hands.

November 26th
Romans 1:21

Because, although they knew God, they did not glorify Him as God, nor were thankful, but became futile in their thoughts, and their foolish hearts were darkened.

What a terrible thing it is to know God yet fail to glorify Him after all He has done for us. Failure to glorify God automatically leads to an ungrateful heart toward Him. This is exactly what we discover in our inspirational verse for today. The people Paul references had an opportunity to become acquainted with the Lord. But they did not want to take the time the Lord required to serve Him, live for Him, turn away from sin to Him, and give glory to Him. The end result was that they were not thankful, they became futile in their thoughts, and their foolish hearts were made dark—all things that happen to so many people today. What a sad commentary. People with tremendous potential, yet they missed out on God's best for their lives, all because they had ungrateful hearts.

It's time to break this vicious cycle. If your heart is filled with gratitude toward our God, you are right where He desires for you to be. His challenge to us now is to help turn the hearts of others in the right direction. Gratefulness places us in the light; ingratitude keeps us in the dark. Use your thankful disposition to transition someone into the same joyous relationship you have with the Lord. Turn on the light in their heart.

November 27th
Leviticus 22:29

And when you offer a sacrifice of thanksgiving to the Lord, offer it of your own free will.

No one should have to force us to do anything for the Lord! Don't you agree? But wait—there's more! Why do some people even feel forced in the first place? Could it be because they know they are not fulfilling their basic Christian responsibilities? When we offer our thanksgiving to the Lord, we should do so with a sacrificial attitude. We should sacrifice our wants in order to give Him the gratitude He deserves. Has it not dawned on you that we don't deserve anything He has done for us? And yet, we have never given Him all the gratitude He deserves. It seems we always desire more from Him while offering less to Him. Make this a week when no one has to remind you to offer thanks to the Lord. It's such a small word. It's such a simple word. Yet it soothes the heart of God and allows Him to know He has birthed grateful children into His family.

I can remember one of the elders at the church where I grew up in Houston making this statement: "Nobody likes an ungrateful child." Offer the Lord your service. Offer the Lord your sacrifice. Offer the Lord your stewardship. Offer the Lord your skills. After all, He offered us His Son. Need I say anything more?

November 28th
Nehemiah 12:8

Moreover the Levites were Jeshua, Binnui, Kadmiel, Sherebiah, Judah, and Mattaniah who led the thanksgiving psalms, he and his brethren.

I know it might be a bit difficult to pronounce the names of the men here in our inspirational verse for today. Let me be honest and admit it was difficult for me. But I want us to focus on the content of what these men did, not on their names. They came together and led the people in singing songs and psalms of thanksgiving. They did not have a collective pity party. They led a consecrated praise party! The Levites were the priestly tribe of Israel. It was their responsibility to lead the people in praise. But we are *all* part of the *royal priesthood* of God. We have been saved and sealed by the precious blood of Jesus Christ. Make it your business to partner with some praise-minded people. Tell the grumblers, fault-finders, and complainers that you are moving up to a new level. Once you arrive there, don't even consider going back down into that pit of self-pity.

Today, too, we encounter people who have hard-to-spell, hard-to-pronounce names just like the people in this verse. They may be just the ones you need to partner with in choruses of thanksgiving praise.

November 29th
Psalm 69:30

I will praise the name of God with a song, And will magnify Him with thanksgiving.

Today's inspirational verse is actually self-explanatory. It helps us understand the importance of praising the name of our God with a song, which automatically leads us into the realm of magnifying the Lord. My baby sister Jerri helped me understand the importance of the word *magnify* from a spiritual perspective. She said, "It simply means to blow God up, and make Him larger, because the image we have of Him is always too small. We need to magnify Him so we can at least get a better idea of how great and grand He truly is." When we magnify Him with thanksgiving, in our minds His image grows even larger. Praise His name. Offer Him a melody from your heart. There are times when I call my wife or one of our daughters and sing a simple love song to them. I can hear them sniffling and know their eyes fill with tears of joy. They do not, however, cry tears of joy because I sing well, but because I thought enough of them to sing a song of love just for them.

God wants to hear you sing to Him today. May I suggest a hymn? "Jesus Paid It All and All to Him I Owe." Before you end your selection, don't forget to thank Him for the price He paid for your soul. That is how you magnify the Lord with thanksgiving.

November 30th
Revelation 7:12

Amen! Blessing and glory and wisdom, Thanksgiving and honor and power and might, Be to our God forever and ever. Amen.

In our inspirational verse for today, we are informed of another tremendous truth. Even in Heaven we will still be offering praises of thanksgiving to our God. This helped me understand that giving thanks to God never gets old and will never go out of style. In this verse, the angels lead the thanksgiving praises to God. They were thanking the Lord. Angels, who have never been healed of sickness, protected from enemies, or forgiven of sins, were thanking God. Angels who have not received one infinitesimal amount of the favor that we have received were engaged in continuous praise and thanksgiving to the Lord.

This helps us understand how important this matter of thanksgiving truly is. As we end the month, I challenge you to not end your disposition of thankfulness to the Lord. Whatever He allows, thank Him. He knows you will handle it, or He will either change it or change you to handle it. Thank You, Jesus!

PRAYER

Lord, we thank You for all of Your many blessings. We thank You for the difficulties that strengthen our relationship with You. We thank You for every good and perfect gift that comes from You and You alone. All we ask is that You accept our gratitude.

In Jesus' name,
We thank You, Lord!

Dates of Development in December

December 1st
Genesis 1:3

Then God said, "Let there be light" and there was light.

This month, every day's inspirational verse is going to be about Jesus Christ, God's Son and our Savior. Most of us think we have to wait until we reach the New Testament before we read anything about Him. Nothing could be further from the truth. He is present here in the very first book of the Bible. When God said, "Let there be light" and there was light, Jesus is that light of the world. The light was already in existence; in creation He was revealed as the second person in the God-head. He was present in creation and He manifested His presence as a baby in Bethlehem. The life of Jesus was in existence even before what we know as the physical birth of Jesus occurred. He is the only baby in history to have an amazing distinction. Usually, when babies are born, they resemble their mother. But when He was born, it was the other way around: His mother looked like Him. He was older than His mother and as old as His Father.

Jesus is the light of the world, and His is the light that has brought each of us out of eternal darkness. God said it, and Jesus made it a reality.

December 2nd
John 1:2

He was in the beginning with God.

Jesus was with God when this world was created. The beginning spoken of here was not the beginning of our God, but the beginning of His revelation to mankind. He chose to make Himself known to us. He loved us even before we knew we would need His love. When He created this world He made sure everything we would need was already here before He created us. This helped me understand that the Lord can be depended upon to provide for us now that we are here on earth. The main reason I know this to be true is because He put everything in place even before we made our arrival.

No matter what issue you may face today, be encouraged. He was here before that issue arrived and He already has the solution to it worked out. Focus on Him and leave the rest in His hands.

December 3rd

Exodus 14:13

And Moses said to the people, "Do not be afraid. Stand still, and see the salvation of the Lord, which He will accomplish for you today. For the Egyptians whom you see today, you shall see again no more forever."

When we take the time to carefully study the Word of God, we make an amazing discovery: Every book in the Bible–both the Old and New Testaments–references Jesus Christ. In our inspirational verse for today we see another vivid presentation of Him. Moses represents the modern day spokesperson for God. The dilemma people face represents the devil's attempts to destroy all of our lives. The fear gripping at our hearts represents the panic we encounter whenever the Lord leads us out of something negative and into the unknown of something positive. The Egyptians represent those who have been deputized by the devil to try to stop us from reaching God's best for our lives. Moses the spokesman says, "Do not be afraid. Stand still and see the salvation of the Lord..." Now, I don't need to tell you who the Lord is, do I? This is a pre-incarnate representation of God's Son, Jesus Christ. He has come to allow us to see Him reveal His salvation right before our very eyes.

Whatever difficulties you may face today, they are not as severe as those presented by the Red Sea. Even if they may seem so, don't worry, and don't be afraid. The Son of God, Jesus Christ, has already saved you from your sins, and I know He can save you from your present situation. After all, salvation is His area of expertise. He has washed away all your sins. He also has the power to wash away all your fears.

December 4th

1 John 2:15

Do not love the world or the things in the world. If anyone loves the world, the love of the Father is not in him.

For this and the next two days I want to deviate just a bit to share my personal testimony. It is my hope that the inspirational workings of the Lord in my life will also be a source of inspiration to you. December is a very special month for me for three reasons: It is the month we celebrate the birth of our Savior Jesus Christ; it is the month of my physical birthday (December 21); it is also the month I accepted Jesus Christ as my Savior and Lord (December 6). My journey with Jesus began on a Tuesday night in 1973. After a night of doing drugs and playing Rock and Roll, I returned home spent and exhausted. I noticed the Living Bible on top of the coffee table in our living room, and was led by the Lord to open it to the passage which is our inspirational verse for today. I am so thankful that my salvation was inextricably connected to the Word of God. This has given me a tremendous desire to learn more about God's Word and to study it on a daily basis. This one verse helped me realize that everything I pursued as an aspiring Rock and Roll star was the complete opposite of God's plan and purpose for my life.

That night was the beginning of a three-day journey in my desire to purge myself of what the Lord wanted me to remove and to add what would be pleasing to Him. Take time to thank the Lord for the positive changes His Word has also made in your life. Don't become attached to the world–instead, attach yourself to the Word made flesh, Jesus Christ!

December 5th
1 John 2:16

For all that is in the world—the lust of the flesh, the lust of the eyes, and the pride of life—is not of the Father but is of the world.

After I read the verse immediately preceding our verse for today (see December 4), the Holy Spirit would not allow me to close the Bible until I read the next two verses—verses that spoke words of confrontation directly to me. My conversion experience (fully detailed in my first book, *A Marvelous Model of Ministry*) helped me understand a very important lesson: God's Word speaks not only in calm, compassionate tones, but also with words and tenor of pending condemnation intending to lead to change. Before my conversion, I wanted people to know my name; I wanted to be a famous star—without realizing it was the Lord who had given me my musical gifts in the first place. These verses helped me come to several important realizations: I could not go through life trying to straddle the fence; my ungodly desires needed to be defeated; my pride needed to be purged; and my goals needed the right guidance.

What goes on in your life that you know is not pleasing to the Lord? Why not give Him an early Christmas gift like I did and surrender them all to Him? Our Heavenly Father has everything we need. The people and things of this world will only fail us, frustrate us, and ultimately forsake us. Box up all of your sins and place them in the hands of Jesus. He will ensure you never have to deal with or answer for them again.

December 6th
1 John 2:17

And the world is passing away, and the lust of it; but he who does the will of God abides forever.

For lack of a better phrase, the verse in our inspirational reading for today sealed the deal for me. It was about 4:30 that Thursday afternoon in 1973, and I could not get this verse out of my mind. I finally said *yes* to Jesus Christ. At the same time, I also said *no* to nearly three years of drug use and ungodly living. This verse helped me understand that the things I was pursuing were all passing away. I was raised in a Christian home and I knew the reality of Heaven and hell. After a concert that afternoon, I decided I could not run any longer and my arms were too short to box with the Lord. While your struggle may not be the same as mine, we all struggle in one way or another. The good news is the struggles may be different, but the Savior who fixes them is not–His name is Jesus.

He stands with open arms to either receive you into His family or to purge from your life those things that hinder your relationship with Him. I have not regretted one day the decision I made to live for Him. I now use my music for His glory. I preach to lead people to Him and I write to help people discover more about Him. He can make whatever changes you need. I am a living witness. I no longer have to worry about where I will spend eternity, as I know I am going to live with Him throughout it all. What about you?

December 7th

Isaiah 7:14

Therefore the Lord Himself will give you a sign: Behold, the virgin shall conceive and bear a Son, and shall call His name Immanuel.

The physical birth of Jesus may have been a surprise to the people of Bethlehem, mainly because they failed to take seriously what the Old Testament said about His arrival. This sign Isaiah refers to was not limited to Him changing their geographical location or economic status; it was the sign of God redeeming His people from their sins, and was related to their sins being forgiven and their souls being saved. This verse also speaks to the virgin birth of Jesus Christ. Jesus was not conceived by a man, but by the Spirit of God Himself, and His name was to be called Immanuel, which means *God with us.* Don't be confused, however, by the name we best know Him by which is Jesus Christ. The name Immanuel is what He *does*—He is constantly with us. Jesus is who He *is*—our Savior and Redeemer. I'm sure we all have our special names for Him. We call Him Healer, Deliverer, Provider, Protector, Comforter, and Guide, to name a few.

Thank God He was born among us; thank God He died for us; and thank God He now lives within us. Celebrate these truths throughout this season and every day of your life.

December 8th

Matthew 1:21

And she will bring forth a Son, and you shall call His name Jesus, for He will save His people from their sins.

The lengths God has gone to in order to express His love for us is nothing short of absolutely amazing. He chose a virgin to give birth to His Son, and she was totally surprised at being selected. This helps us realize that God can use any person who is willing to make him- or herself available to Him. Our pedigree or level of success does not matter; all He needs is a positive response from us. Jesus' primary assignment from God in coming to earth was to save us from our sins. It seems we have deviated considerably from that truth. We want to focus on how much stuff He can give us or pursue the titles and accolades we think He should help us attain. Then all the while we miss out on His real purpose for coming in the first place. Why not allow this to be a day you spend some serious time thanking God for nothing more than saving you from your sins?

You may not be living in the home of your dreams or driving the automobile of your choice. But if you are saved, you have a tremendous amount for which to thank the Lord. He came to save us, and we can now say, "Mission accomplished!"

December 9th

Matthew 2:2

Saying, "Where is He who has been born King of the Jews? For we have seen His star in the East and have come to worship Him."

Wise men came from the East looking for Jesus. They were not interested in what He could offer them. They did not come looking for healing or any other miracle. They left their homes and came to the place where Jesus was for one main purpose: They wanted to worship Him. They had seen His star, which simply means they had received insight concerning where He could be found. I cannot help but wonder how many of us would have taken advantage of an opportunity to follow a star to find Jesus. The truth of the matter is that most of us already know where He can be found, yet we fail to make a fifteen- to twenty-minute drive once or twice a week to spend some time with Him in His house.

We know He was born. We know He now lives. The only thing left is for us to make a new commitment to worship Him on a regular basis. Make this the month you commit to attending worship on a more frequent basis. I guarantee that each time you leave your house headed to His house it will be a worthwhile trip.

December 10th

Matthew 2:11

And when they had come into the house, they saw the young Child with Mary His mother, and fell down and worshiped Him. And when they had opened their treasures, they presented gifts to Him: gold, frankincense, and myrrh.

Once the wise men located where Jesus was, they wasted not another minute, but went right into the house. Upon their arrival, they did not find *what* they were looking for, but *Who*: They saw Jesus with His mother Mary and immediately fell down and worshipped Him. Of course, they did not come to this worship opportunity empty-handed. The wise men presented to Him gifts of gold, frankincense, and myrrh. It is evident these men had made a collective decision concerning the value of Jesus before arriving at His house. When you leave home and head to the house of Jesus, what thoughts are on your mind? What concerns you more? – What you need Him to do *for* you or what He truly deserves *from* you?

These men worshipped and gave in abundance, yet they had never seen Jesus work a single miracle. Surely after all He has done for us we can strive to honor Him at the level He is worthy of. If you don't have a bag or chest filled with treasure to offer, don't worry. Simply open up your heart and your mouth and give Him your best praise. He is always pleased whenever His children give Him our best.

December 11th

Matthew 2:12

Then, being divinely warned in a dream that they should not return to Herod, they departed for their own country another way.

After the three wise men finished worshipping Jesus, they did something important—so important, in fact, it should take place in each of our lives after every worship experience. First, they did not return to the negative environment of Herod. Second, they returned home another way, which refers to more than the geographic route they traveled. This other way also includes the manner or condition of their hearts, their hopes, and their holiness. These men discovered what I hope we all have: It is impossible to have an encounter with Jesus and then return home the same way. Although you may travel to the same physical location, you should have a new spiritual destination. Many of us don't allow worship experiences to minister to us properly because we make the mistake of returning to our own Herod, which represents negative surroundings where people doubt Jesus and try to discourage you from serving Him.

Since this is the month we celebrate His birth, let's make sure that after each encounter with Him, we go home with a new level of *commitment* to Him, *confidence* in Him, and *celebration* of Him.

December 12th
Luke 2:7

And she brought forth her firstborn Son, and wrapped Him in swaddling cloths, and laid Him in a manger, because there was no room for them in the inn.

My inspirational word for you today is: Don't worry about what you don't have, and use what you do have for the glory of Jesus Christ. This is exactly what Mary the mother of Jesus did. She did not have sheets of silk or satin; she did not have a mahogany crib; she did not have Waterford crystal bottles—but she did have swaddling cloths, and that was what she wrapped the Baby Jesus in. Anytime the Lord gives you a blessing, make sure you use it to honor Him. We often make the mistake of feeling we don't measure up because we don't own what others have. Take a moment to consider the following: We can safely say that many other women gave birth to sons at the same time Jesus was born. Perhaps some of these women had comfortable homes to welcome their sons into. Perhaps they had what would have been the equivalent of a baby shower to prepare for the birth of the baby. They may have even had a nice nursery for the baby to sleep in. We don't, however, know the names of any of those mothers or any of those children.

The one name we do know is that of Jesus! (I know you saw that coming.) He did not own much from a human or materialist perspective, but, from a Godly perspective, He owned so much more than all the others, and so do we. Make the best of what the Lord has given you to work with.

December 13th

Luke 2:15

So it was, when the angels had gone away from them into heaven, that the shepherds said to one another, "Let us now go to Bethlehem and see this thing that has come to pass, which the Lord has made known to us."

Day after day, God reveals Himself to us through His only begotten Son Jesus Christ. He allowed Him to come and dwell among us so that we could see His love for us being lived out in the flesh. After the angelic host finished their proclamation and praise both to and about God's Son, some of the shepherds wanted to see Jesus for themselves. One thing we discover about the events surrounding the birth of Jesus is that there was a lot to traveling involved. Mary traveled to Elizabeth's home where she discovered Elizabeth was pregnant with John the Baptist. Mary and Joseph traveled to Bethlehem to pay their taxes, and while there, Jesus was born. Wise men traveled from the east to the home where they worshipped Baby Jesus. And in our inspirational scripture for today, we read about shepherds who wanted to travel to Bethlehem to see this Child who had been born of the Virgin Mary. This just may be the Lord's challenge for you.

Don't get stuck in a holding pattern in your relationship with Jesus. Move out of your comfort zone and go where you know He manifests His presence. Given that a nearly-nine-month-pregnant woman, three wise men with treasures, and a group of shepherds all travel to Jesus, what is it that hinders you from doing the same? Make a commitment to search for Him, and when you find Him, give Him your attention, your affection, and your assets. After all, He has given us His anointing.

December 14th

Luke 1:35

And the angel answered and said to her, "The Holy Spirit will come upon you, and the power of the Highest will overshadow you; therefore, also, that Holy One who is to be born will be called the Son of God."

The angel Gabriel told Mary the good news about the Child to whom she was about to give birth. The Lord continues to use angels today to speak His people. We sometimes find it difficult to accept this because of our inability to differentiate between Heavenly angels and earthly angels. Earthly angels are simply those people the Lord uses as messengers from Him to His people. Our inspirational scripture for today helps us understand just how powerful and important the Holy Spirit's presence is in our lives. Mary was able to conceive Jesus because the Holy Spirit deposited Him into her life. (If you have been saved and born again, you know He has done the same for you.) Mary was not only filled with the Holy Spirit's *presence*, she was also covered with His *protection.* The angel said to her, "...the power of the Highest will overshadow you..."

Go through this day fully confident of the fact you have Jesus living in you. You have Jesus protecting and covering you. And God wants to use you as an angel, or spokesperson, for Him, as He desires to do in the lives of people you come into contact with the same as He did in the life of Mary. In case people ask what God did in the life of Mary, just tell them He used an angel to tell her she was about to be filled with Jesus. And I have come to tell you that He wants to do the same in your life—he wants to fill you with Jesus.

December 15th
Luke 2:32

A light to bring revelation to the Gentiles, And the glory of Your people Israel.

Jesus is the Light of the World. There is no need for us to remain as prisoners, bound by satan's vice-grips of demonic darkness. When Jesus was born, we are told He came as a light for the Gentiles, which includes those of us who were not born as Jews. He is the light which brings revelation to our lives. At times, we are unable to clearly see God's plan for our lives because we examine life's issues without the Light of Jesus Christ. He does not make us search for the light—He brings the light to us.

Once His light is seen, His glory is automatically revealed. The light of Jesus is discovered in His *word*; it is discovered by doing His *work*; and it is discovered as we engage in *worship*. Use your faith to flip the switch and turn on the light. He is just waiting for you to reach out to Him. When you do, you will discover He was there all along.

December 16th
Luke 2:47

And all who heard Him were astonished at His understanding and answers.

The Bible does not provide much insight into the formative years of the life of Jesus. We have only the well-known event of His going to the Feast of the Passover with His parents. The Bible tells us that, while they were there, Jesus became separated from them. His parents left Jerusalem on the supposition that Jesus was part of the larger caravan with which they traveled, although they were later unable to find him. They subsequently searched for three days. Much to their surprise, He was in the temple sitting among the teachers, listening to them and asking and answering questions. We are informed in today's inspirational verse that everyone who heard Him speak was astonished at His level of understanding and the He answers provided. This should bring a great deal of comfort to the hearts of each of us. Jesus is willing to sit with us, listen to our questions, and then provide answers that will give us a greater level of clarity about life and God's purpose for us all.

As you go through your day, be reminded of the fact that we have a Savior who listens to us, answers us, guides us, and most importantly, cares about us.

December 17th

Luke 2:52

And Jesus increased in wisdom and stature, and in favor with God and men.

When I first read this verse I wanted to know how on earth Jesus could possibly have increased in anything. The Holy Spirit then informed me that this *increasing* is not limited to just His growing in size but also in *our ability* to perceive and understand Him better. The more we know about Jesus, the more we will come to understand how sensitive He is to each and every one of our needs. Whenever people have a lack of trust in God, it can always be traced back to a lack of knowledge about the Lord. During His earthly life, people saw Him increase in wisdom and stature. We have a similar opportunity today. The word *stature* speaks to how He experienced growth and development as a human being. He received favor with both God and men.

Jesus waits for an opportunity for you to allow Him to grow in your life. You will discover, as He increases in stature, that you serve a great God who can handle problems of any size. The challenge lies in remaining close to Him. He has favor with God and men. When we walk with Him on a daily basis, He will share that favor with each of His children.

December 18th

John 1:29

The next day John saw Jesus coming toward him, and said, "Behold! The Lamb of God who takes away the sin of the world!"

John the Baptist, who was first cousin to Jesus, was in complete awe upon first seeing Him. And his first testimony was that Jesus is the Lamb of God who takes away the sin of the world. During this season of gift giving and receiving, we often become blinded to the true meaning of the season. God sent His Son to live and die here on earth for one main purpose: to take away the sin of the world. Jesus is the Lamb of God, the perfect sacrifice. He was not murdered or killed by surprise attack. He willingly laid down His life as ransom to pay for our sins. John the Baptist shows us the most important thing we should distinguish in Jesus. It is not about what He can do for us. It is not about what we expect Him to shower our lives with. But it *is* about what He has already done. What you do or do not receive from other people during this season makes no difference at all.

The most valuable gift is the love of God expressed through His Son who removed the debt of sin from our lives.

December 19th

Mark 1:8

I indeed baptized you with water, but He will baptize you with the Holy Spirit.

When Jesus came to earth, He was keenly aware of the fact He would not have a prolonged stay. His tenure here in the flesh did not even reach thirty-four years. But we find comfort in knowing that, after His resurrection and ascension, He did not leave us without the help we would need to live for Him and to represent Him. In our inspirational verse for today, John the Baptist expresses his own limitations. He also reveals Jesus' limitless, indwelling power. John could baptize only with water. But Jesus has baptized us with His presence through the third person of the trinity–the Holy Spirit.

We have His abiding assurance every day of our lives. Even when you do not feel Him, His presence is not obliterated. Jesus did not come to earth to simply bring us into the family of God. Through the Holy Spirit, we discover He also keeps us secure in that family. Our baptism is God's presence overshadowing us. He displays His connection, His commitment, and His compassion by allowing His Comforter to abide in us forever. Yield to Him and allow Him to guide you every step of your journey.

December 20th
Luke 2:26

And it had been revealed to him by the Holy Spirit that he would not see death before he had seen the Lord's Christ.

I can only hope and pray that every person alive would desire this. The man referenced in this verse was Simeon. He was a man of prayer, patience, and persistence. The longing desire in his heart was for the Lord to keep him alive until he had an opportunity to see Jesus. Simeon's first Christmas was life-changing. Not because of the tie he received or the scrumptious meal he ate. It was memorable because he met Jesus. If you should happen to already know Him, this season would be a good time to establish an even closer relationship with Him. Allow your mind to be filled with the wonder of His very presence. We don't need to see Him in the flesh as Simeon did; we can see the results of His life all around us. Celebrate Jesus.

Do you realize Christians don't have to worry about seeing death before seeing Jesus? That is because, when death approaches us, His presence transitions us into eternity.

December 21st

Galatians 4:4

But when the fullness of the time had come, God sent forth His Son, born of a woman, born under the law.

God moves at His own pace, but always with precise timing. Take a moment to consider this. We would be seriously upset with an airline that allowed our flight to take off an hour early. We would be upset to pay our money and arrive at the movie theater only to discover the film started thirty minutes earlier than advertised. We would be especially upset to arrive at our favorite department store to shop for a much-needed item, only to discover the store closed two hours early. We never complain when God shows up and resolves our issues early; we only complain when He seems to be late. When was the last time you were running late to catch a plane and the flight was delayed which meant you were able to make it? Have you ever complained when you thought the cleaners closed at 4 p.m., but when you arrived you discovered they changed their closing time to 5 p.m.? Have you ever heard anyone express sentiments of frustration because the sporting event started late after they arrived late? I think you get the picture. It seems we are patient when we and everyone else, God excluded, are late.

Understand, God sent His Son into this world to be born of a woman "in the fullness of time," or simply put, at the right time. He sent Jesus here to save us at the right time, and He will send Jesus at the right time to resolve your crisis. Just keep waiting, trusting, and believing.

December 22nd
John 1:11

He came to His own, and His own did not receive Him.

In my opinion, this is one of the saddest verses in the Bible. It reveals how a debased and disgraceful humanity turned its back on Divinity. Jesus came to save us, and people turned and walked away from His love. He came to rescue us, redeem us, and restore us back into fellowship with God, but the wretchedness of mankind caused us to refuse Him. Even though I view this as one of the saddest verses of scripture in the Bible, there is still good news to be gleaned: He did not give up His pursuit of us. Praise the Lord! He refused to allow satan to keep us alienated. Jesus came to earth only to encounter rejection by His creation and creators. While our rejection was not a surprise to Him, it was no less painful.

Take a moment to thank Him for not ending His determination to reach us and save us. Thank Him for not accepting the easy way out. Thank Him for loving us even when we did not realize how much we needed to be loved by Him.

December 23rd
John 1:12

But as many as received Him, to them He gave the right to become children of God, to those who believe in His name.

In our inspirational verse for today, we see the immeasurable extent of God's love for fallen mankind. His Son was rejected by some who saw no need to be forgiven of their sins. But His love would not be stopped. As many as were willing to receive Him, He gave the right to become children of God. I am so glad I can attest to the fact that I am part of the "as many as received Him" group. There is no limit to the number of people who can become part of the family of God. While eating at a restaurant a few days ago, I saw a sign posted that said "Occupancy not to exceed 230." No more than 230 people would be able to assemble in that place at one time. Some would have to leave before additional people could come and enjoy the food being served there. In contrast, in our relationship with the Lord, no one has to leave His family before new people can join it.

When we receive Him, and believe in Him, He gives us new heavenly spiritual rights. Those rights include a new identity, a new family, and a new destination. He has given us the best gift we could ever imagine. The least we can do now is live up to the standards of the new name He placed on us. We are now children of God, and Godly children should act like their Father.

December 24th

Luke 2:14

Glory to God in the highest, And on earth peace, goodwill toward men!

When we offer praise and glory to God, it seems to me that 99% of the time it centers on something He has done for us. In today's inspirational verse, shepherds offered this proclamation of praise, and they did so not because of what He had done, but simply because they recognized who He was. I want to take some liberty here and call this the very first "Christmas Eve praise." The shepherds had not yet seen Jesus, but the angel had spoken to them and informed them of His arrival on earth. This should motivate us to elevate our level of service, sacrifice, and surrender to the Lord. He deserves great glory from us. He has come to give us His peace and break down the barrier of separation between God and mankind. His desire is that our lives be filled with His goodwill.

Take a few moments away from your ham and turkey to give Him the glory He deserves on this Christmas Eve. Don't get so caught up in preparing the food that it causes you to neglect and ignore the Provider of that food. Give Him glory; give Him the highest glory. Set time aside today to pray with, and praise, your family. He is worthy, and we are so undeserving.

December 25th
Isaiah 9:6

For unto us a Child is born, Unto us a Son is given; And the government will be upon His shoulder. And His name will be called Wonderful, Counselor, Mighty God, Everlasting Father, Prince of Peace.

Merry Christmas. I often hear people say, "Keep Christ in Christmas." To be honest, we simply cannot have Christmas without Christ. I have proof. When you take *C-H-R-I-S-T* out of *Christ*-mas, all that remains is _-_-_-_-_-_-mas. What is *mas*? It makes no sense. My point exactly. Our inspirational verse for today reveals the real meaning of Christmas. A Child was born. Not just any child, but God's only begotten Son. He was given to us. We did not ask for Him; we could not afford Him; and we surely did not deserve Him. His name is *Wonderful*, which refers to His presence among us. He is also called *Counselor*, which speaks about His patience with us. He is called *Mighty God*, which references His power for us. He is an *Everlasting Father*, which addresses His protection over us. And He is a *Prince of Peace*, which speaks to His passion around us.

We have been given the greatest gift imaginable. Jesus has been born. Jesus has died. Jesus now lives. Jesus is coming back again. When you open this gift, you discover that He is the gift that keeps on giving. Merry Christmas.

December 26th
Matthew 2:13

Now when they had departed, behold, an angel of the Lord appeared to Joseph in a dream, saying, "Arise, take the young Child and His mother, flee to Egypt, and stay there until I bring you word; for Herod will seek the young Child to destroy Him."

The gifts have been opened. The food has been consumed. The carols have been sung. The lights on the tree are now dark. Today is the day after Christmas. What does the Word of God say to us about this day? I'm glad you asked. After the celebration in the house with Jesus, a celebration that included the wise men and gifts of gold, frankincense, and myrrh, they also had a day after Christmas. It is written about in our inspirational verse for today. The angel spoke to Joseph and told him to leave Bethlehem and travel to Egypt because Herod was going to attempt to destroy Jesus. And today, if we are not careful, the devil will seek to do the same thing. Even more than two thousand years after Jesus' physical birth, the devil wants to kill and destroy His influence and impact on our lives by inducing us with so many less important things. The devil knows he cannot destroy the Son of God, so he tries to destroy His importance in our lives with things such as high credit card bills post-Christmas, a sad and depressing mind-set after family and friends have left to return home, and feelings of neglect because we did not receive the gift we felt we deserved.

Let's do what Joseph was told to do. He took Jesus from one location to another. This is our after-Christmas responsibility. He was born in our hearts; now let's take Him to the hearts of others who do not know Him as Lord and Savior. Travel with Jesus—the trip is always so much more pleasant.

December 27th

Matthew 6:6

But you, when you pray, go into your room, and when you have shut your door, pray to your Father who is in the secret place; and your Father who sees in secret will reward you openly.

The only way we are to be fortified for the attacks the devil launches against us is to spend quality time in prayer with the Lord. In our inspirational verse for today, Jesus teaches us three important lessons about prayer. He first teaches us about the importance of having a *special place to pray.* I realize it may be difficult to always use the same physical space, but we should all have a special place where we feel we are able to connect with the Lord. Second, He teaches us about the *privacy of prayer.* Growing up in Houston, some people were viewed as having a truly strong prayer life based on their ability to pray publically. The strength of our prayer life, however, is not based on our ability to string words together in front of other people; rather, it is based on our ability to maintain our commitment to the Lord in the midst of adverse circumstances. Lastly, He teaches us about the *provision that results from prayer.* Our Father, who sees us in secret, will reward us openly.

God loves to hear from His children. Even if you don't believe you speak well in public, don't ever feel you lack the ability to pray. Remember, God wants your conversations to be directed to Him and Him alone. The Holy Spirit interprets what you feel unable to verbalize, and God will reward you openly. Just keep praying.

December 28th
Philippians 3:7

But what things were gain to me, these I have counted loss for Christ.

As we embark on these last few days of this year, let's strive to purge ourselves of selfish ambition. One of the reasons many of us have difficulty serving the Lord with consistency is because is it hard to move ourselves and our desires out of the way. In our inspirational verse for today, Paul helps us tremendously in this area. He learned to count as loss for Christ things that could have brought him gain and benefit. In case you did not know, whenever we give up something for Jesus' sake that we think is important, He always replaces it with something more valuable.

What do you strive to attain that may be causing you to compromise your relationship with the Lord? Whatever it is, let it go. Release any and everything that prevents your spiritual growth. Remove that which leads you to place your responsibilities for the Lord on the back burner. He sacrificed everything for us; the least we can do is surrender to Him whatever it is that hinders us. Now go out and make it a great day.

December 29th
James 1:12

Blessed is the man who endures temptation; for when he has been approved, he will receive the crown of life which the Lord has promised to those who love Him.

It's only a test. Whatever difficulties confront you are only tests. They are designed to prevent you from reaching your God-ordained destiny. In our inspirational verse for today, one key word stands out: *endure*. Don't quit and don't give up. The Lord uses this as your approval process. Allow me to encourage you. The Lord is not like banks, automobile dealerships, or furniture companies that ask us to fill out their credit applications to see if we get approved. The Lord allows us to go through temptation and difficulty because He has already approved us. At the end of the process, a crown of life awaits placement on our head.

Remain faithful and hold on so your crown will not have to remain packed away. You have been approved by God and you can endure, so push your way through. The best is yet to come.

December 30th

Ruth 1:16

But Ruth said: "Entreat me not to leave you, Or to turn back from following after you; For wherever you go, I will go; And wherever you lodge, I will lodge; Your people shall be my people, And your God, my God."

The lives of many of us would be so much better if only we learned the importance of having Godly connections and Christ-like companions. In today's inspirational verse we learn some valuable principles from a young lady by the name of Ruth. Both her husband and father-in-law have died. Her mother-in-law Naomi, who was about to return to her homeland, was the only person with whom Ruth had a close Godly connection. She told Ruth to return to her own people. But Ruth had learned some valuable lessons from Naomi and refused to go back to her old comfort zone. Where do you turn when tragedy strikes? Do you rely on the very people and things God delivered you from?

Do not spend another day of your life without finding and developing a strong relationship with a spiritual mentor. Ruth had confidence in not only her mother-in-law Naomi, but even more importantly, in the God she served. She trusted her God for traveling grace, lodging, and a new set of family and friends, and He provided them. And just as God provided for Ruth and Naomi, He is able to do the same today.

December 31st

Ephesians 4:22

That you put off, concerning your former conduct, the old man which grows corrupt according to the deceitful lusts.

It is time to be honest with ourselves and most especially with the Lord. We all have things in our lives that we have been carrying all year but which need to be released. My challenge to you is to not enter a new year with old baggage. Put off, or as we would say "pull off," all former conduct that is not Christ-like. Say good-bye to the old man and walk in the newness of life. Don't wait until tomorrow, because what you do tonight determines how serious you are about your commitment to Christ. Spend this evening in the company of Godly people, doing Godly things, and giving God the worship and praise He deserves. Don't allow your lust to give you a loser's limp. And don't allow the devil's deceit to defeat you from walking in your deliverance. A new day is dawning, and we want to be free to receive and embrace all that God has for us.

The journey throughout this year has been challenging and exciting. But through it all, God has been faithful!

PRAYER

Lord, We thank You for every door you have opened, every prayer You have answered, and every lesson You have taught us. We thank You for the frustrations which have taught us to trust You. Thank You for the lean times which have taught us about Your provision. Thank You for the lonely times which have taught us about Your comfort. On this final day of the year, we thank You for everything You have done and allowed over these past 365 days. We love You and magnify Your holy name.

In the name of Your Son, Jesus Christ, we pray,
Amen.

It is my hope and prayer that this daily devotional has been a source of strength for you and a source of encouragement to you. My prayer is that you have been blessed in at least three areas of your walk with the Lord:

- Your *relationship* with Him
- Your *representation* of Him
- Your *responsibilities* for Him

Biographical Profile of Dr. Roy Elton Brackins

Reverend Brackins, born December 21st, 1955, is the eldest son of Mr. and Mrs. Leroy and Lucy Brackins. He is a native of Houston, Texas, and a preaching son of the True Light Baptist Church of Houston, Texas. He is married to Mrs. Pamela Doreen Brackins. Together, they are the proud parents of three daughters and one son. He serves as President Emeritus of the Board of Directors for One Church One Child Inc. of the Dallas-Fort Worth area. He also serves as the Assistant Treasurer for B.E.L.A. (Black Ecumenical Leadership Alliance). He is a member of the National Baptist Convention of America International, Inc., where he has served and worked with the Evangelical Board for more than thirty years.

Reverend Brackins accepted Jesus Christ as his personal savior in December 1973, at the tender age of seventeen. He confessed his call to the Gospel ministry on the first Sunday in August 1976, and preached his first sermon on the second Sunday of that same month and year under the pasturage of the late Dr. William Bowie Jr.

Reverend Brackins is the founding Pastor of the Grace Tabernacle Baptist Church which had her genesis in May of 1987. The Church has grown from twenty-seven members with two ministries, to better than 500 active members with more than twenty-five vibrant, need-meeting ministries since her beginning. The Church offers an outreach center called Garments and Groceries from Grace. This outreach center opened in August 2002, and is tailored exclusively to meet the needs of those in the community of the Grace Tabernacle Church who are less fortunate.

Pastor Brackins has led Grace Tabernacle to completing three phases of a $2.8M church campus which rests on nearly seven acres. It includes a 500-seat Worship Center, Fellowship Hall, Children and Youth Activities Area, Family Life Center, and Gymnasium. The entire building project was completed in just six years, while retiring over $1.2M of the debt in the process.

In April 2009, Pastor Brackins published his first book, *A Marvelous Model of Ministry, A Message from the man in the Middle.* His second book, *Making a Difference in the Kingdom of God,* was released in February 2013. In August 2014, Pastor Brackins was recognized for his outstanding service in the Christian community by the St. Thomas Christian University of Jacksonville, Florida, with an Honorary Doctor of Divinity Degree. Pastor Brackins is also a musician; he plays the guitar, bass, piano, and organ. He has preached extensively throughout much of America, and his greatest passion is the preaching of the Gospel to the end that lost souls are won to Jesus Christ.

Contact Dr. Brackins for preaching engagements, book signings, and seminars at Gtabernacl@aol.com or 817.568.0295.

18547854R00214

Made in the USA
San Bernardino, CA
19 January 2015